The Fundamentals of Reasons

The Fundamentals of Reasons

NATHAN ROBERT HOWARD
AND
MARK SCHROEDER

OXFORD
UNIVERSITY PRESS

Great Clarendon Street, Oxford, OX2 6DP,
United Kingdom

Oxford University Press is a department of the University of Oxford.
It furthers the University's objective of excellence in research, scholarship,
and education by publishing worldwide. Oxford is a registered trade mark of
Oxford University Press in the UK and in certain other countries

© Nathan Robert Howard and Mark Schroeder 2024

The moral rights of the authors have been asserted

All rights reserved. No part of this publication may be reproduced, stored in
a retrieval system, or transmitted, in any form or by any means, without the
prior permission in writing of Oxford University Press, or as expressly permitted
by law, by licence or under terms agreed with the appropriate reprographics
rights organization. Enquiries concerning reproduction outside the scope of the
above should be sent to the Rights Department, Oxford University Press, at the
address above

You must not circulate this work in any other form
and you must impose this same condition on any acquirer

Published in the United States of America by Oxford University Press
198 Madison Avenue, New York, NY 10016, United States of America

British Library Cataloguing in Publication Data

Data available

Library of Congress Control Number: 2023946442

ISBN 978–0–19–289627–8 (hbk.)
ISBN 978–0–19–289628–5 (pbk.)

DOI: 10.1093/oso/9780192896278.001.0001

Printed and bound by
CPI Group (UK) Ltd, Croydon, CR0 4YY

Links to third party websites are provided by Oxford in good faith and
for information only. Oxford disclaims any responsibility for the materials
contained in any third party website referenced in this work.

Contents

Preface vii

PART 1 THE *PARTS* OF REASONS

1. Introduction 3
2. What Are Reasons? 21
3. Arguments 44
4. Structure 62

PART 2 THE *PROVINCE* OF REASONS

5. Objective and Subjective Reasons 81
6. Reasons and Evidence 103
7. Reasons and Explanation 119
8. Reasons and Deliberation 133

PART 3 THE *PLACE* OF REASONS

9. What Can Reasons Analyze? 151
10. What Can Analyze Reasons? 172
11. Weights 192
12. The Fundamentality of Reasons 209

Works Cited 225
Index 233

Preface

So you're sick and tired of reasons. You became interested in moral philosophy because you wanted to answer the question, "how ought I to live?", but it seems like every book or article that you read has more to say about reasons than about the good life. You became interested in epistemology because you wanted to know what we know, but some corners of epistemology also seem to have been taken over by talk about reasons to believe. Or you became interested in action theory because you wanted to understand what makes us different from animals, but here, too, you find reasons everywhere you look. Philosophy—or at least, too much of philosophy, it seems—has become overrun with reasons.

And worse, ordinary talk about reasons is an incredible mess, by anyone's admission. We say that the Smithsonian is a reason to visit Washington, D.C., but so is democracy. And another reason to visit is that there is great Ethiopian food. But what do the Smithsonian and democracy have in common that they share with *that there is great Ethiopian food*? We say that the fact that the sidewalk is slippery is a reason for us to be careful, but also that it is a reason for being careful, and that it is the reason for which she was careful. But which is it for? For us, or for being careful—or for which she was careful? And we talk about reasons why, reasons that, and reasons to, as well as reasons for. It's a terrible mess, really.

Worse yet is the way in which philosophers talk about reasons, using expressions like 'her reason' as if the possessive construction were not massively context-dependent and as though it had some kind of privileged meaning. Then they contrast talk of what "there is" a reason to do with what "you have" a reason to do, as if 'has' was not as context-dependent as the possessive construction. Likewise, they talk about what reasons "are for", as if we couldn't clearly observe that while some of them are for us, others are for being careful and yet others are for which we are careful.

And if that weren't bad enough, philosophers who like to talk about reasons—*reasonologists*, if you will—seem preoccupied by the darndest things. They make a slew of distinctions between senses of 'reason' and kinds of reason. They engage in endless debates over whether reasons are facts, propositions, or mental states. They cite each other in complicated networks that make it hard to untangle why people became interested in their questions in the first place. They seem to always be presupposing things about reasons, and seldom to be presupposing the same things as one another. And in keeping with the bewildering array of grammatical uses of the word 'reason', they use the word in very different ways from one another.

If you, like many others, find this situation frustrating or puzzling, this book is for you. We have three overarching goals. First, we try to explain the roles that make reasons so useful in so many areas of philosophy. Second, we try to unpack how the tensions between these roles combine with complications in how we talk about reasons to lead philosophers into very different kinds of picture thinking about how reasons work. And third, we try to unravel the interrelated mess of debates that have come to constitute contemporary reasonology, paying attention both to how these debates bear on one another and to where their answers matter for many of the questions that we began with in other areas of philosophy long before starting to pay attention to reasons themselves.

Our hope is that the book can be used as a resource for working philosophers to find their way into a messy topic that can sometimes feel intimidating for its unwieldiness. But we also hope that it has the right shape to form the backbone of a graduate seminar on the topic of reasons, or even of an upper-level undergraduate course for well-prepared students. As a result, we have paired each chapter with a chapter summary, with a list of recommended readings including advice that we hope will be relevant for choosing primary source readings to assign along with the chapter, and with a set of pedagogical exercises designed both to encourage comprehension and to extend some of the issues in the main text either by pushing them further or by introducing key qualifications or objections that are not considered in the main text.

On the whole, this book is what you might call a *mildly opinionated* introduction. We have tried to cover a wide range of views. We have tried to take all of them seriously, and an important part of our goal is to help you see inside of some of the views that you might doubt. At the same time, we do take some views more seriously than others, and even where we don't officially endorse a view it will be clear to most readers where we remain skeptical. We have definitely exercised our own judgment over which kinds of ideas are worthy of greater consideration than they have received so far, and over which that have received great consideration deserve even more. And in a few places we do reject particular claims outright. In the process of writing this book, some of our own sympathies have changed, and we hope that this happens to you when reading it as well, whether or not it leads you to actually change your mind.

Special thanks are due to everyone either of us has ever discussed any of these issues with and learned from. Listing them all would add too many pages for this book to go to print, but any executive summary would include, at the very minimum, Rima Basu, Matt Bedke, Selim Berker, John Brunero, Nate Charlow, Alex Dietz, Jamie Dreier, Adam Elga, Steve Finlay, Amy Floweree, Rachel Fraser, Alex Gregory, John Hawthorne, Max Hayward, David Heering, Tim Henning, Joe Horton, Jessica Isserow, Stephen Kearns, Benjamin Kiesewetter, Maria Lasonen-Aarnio, Stephanie Leary, Woo Ram Lee, Janet Levin, Clayton Littlejohn, Errol Lord, Susanne Mantel, Sarah McGrath, Tristram McPherson, Christian Miller, Michael Milona, Robert Myers, Kate Nolfi, Jared Oliphint, Hille Paakunainen, Caleb Perl, David Plunkett, Abelard Podgorski, Jim Pryor, Robert Reed, Andrew Reisner, Gideon Rosen, Neil Roughley, Andrew Sepielli, Nate Shardin, Nico Silins, Daniel Star, Sergio Tenenbaum, Claudine Verheggen, Shane Ward, Jonathan Way, Ralph Wedgwood, Daniel Whiting, Alex Worsnip, and Vida Yao.

For help with our work on this manuscript, in particular, and for keen advice along the way we need to thank Daniel Fogal, Chris Howard, Kenny Easwaran, Anne Jeffrey, Nick Laskowski, Shyam Nair, Justin Snedegar, two blind referees for Oxford University Press, and our editor, Peter Momtchiloff. We have also tested draft material from the manuscript in Nathan's graduate seminar at Texas A&M in the fall of 2021, in which we benefited greatly from the audience and feedback of Haley Burke, Nicholas Charles, Victoria Green, Pak-Him Lai, Abouzar Moradian, and Gedalyahu Wittow. Particular thanks are due also to Jonah Dunch, who helped proofread the book.

Nathan: This is a book for teachers, not only in the sense that it is suitable for teaching, but also as a tribute to all teachers, especially mine. I've learned from Katharine Streip, Mark Russell, and Ariela Freedman, from Concordia's Liberal Arts College; from Derek Parfit, Andrew Reisner, and Michael Blome-Tillmann, as an undergraduate in philosophy; and from Jessica Brown, Nate Charlow, Mohan Matthen, Tom Hurka, Andrew Sepielli, Steve Finlay, Ralph Wedgwood, and John Hawthorne, as a graduate student.

Mark Schroeder's dedication to his students is peerless. He is Humean in many ways, not least in terms of mentorship. Humean approaches to normative reasons privilege means-end reasoning. Mark's Humean approach to mentorship means he takes up his student's ends and then helps the student figure out the very best means to those ends. I am incredibly lucky to have benefited from his patience and wisdom, doubly so because I managed to extend my apprenticeship by convincing him to write this book. Thank you. Most of all, for her love and support, this book is for Heidi Craig and for our Pascale, for Lance and Frances Howard, and for Ian and Sue Craig.

Mark: Writing this book together with Nathan Howard has been one of my great professional pleasures. It has been my pride to be able to collaborate deeply and over an extended time with a former student as a colleague, my joy to plumb the surprising depths of the issues on which we agree, and my humbling to come to grips with the new and different ways of thinking about the issues to which he has pushed me. And if not for his eagerness to undertake this project, my most recent book *Reasons First* would have been littered with several unnecessary chapters full of extra setup and distinction-mongering which Nathan helped me to carve off of that project. But as always, my greatest debts are to Maria Nelson, Caroline Maria Schroeder, and William Nelson Schroeder, my reasons for reason.

PART 1
THE *PARTS* OF REASONS

1
Introduction

1.1 Welcome!

This is a book about reasons. It is also a work of philosophy. Over the last fifty years, many philosophy books have been written about reasons. That is in part because there are many prominent, interesting questions to ask about reasons. But, to an even greater extent, it is because reasons have been found, or at least alleged, to be hiding behind even more prominent questions—lying in the interstices between issues in not just normative ethics and metaethics, but social and political philosophy, philosophy of law, aesthetics, philosophy of action, epistemology, moral psychology, and other parts of the philosophy of mind. Answering these other questions has seemed, to many philosophers at least, to require first answering or at least defending answers to related questions about reasons. Hiding behind these other issues has therefore given reasons a kind of derivative prominence in contemporary philosophy. It is the kind of prominence peculiar to philosophers—that is, among thinkers who are particularly interested in getting to the bottom of things and in seeing the spaces in between.

This book is not, for the most part, about the most historically prominent questions about reasons. It is about the hidden questions that themselves lie behind those questions. It is about the things that philosophers most often take for granted when they turn their attention toward reasons, either rightly or wrongly. As reasons themselves have become increasingly prominent over the last twenty years or so, these questions behind the questions have begun to be studied in their own right—some of them much better than others. We are interested in these questions for their own sake, but more importantly, for how they inform many of the most independently prominent questions about reasons. This book is a guide to this terrain. It is intended to introduce anyone to what is known and what is up for grabs about the structure and nature of reasons, and about the words we use to discuss them, as well as to what is at stake over such questions, and some of the chief pieces of evidence that bear on them. But more: its goal is to equip readers to recognize and appreciate where others are taking for granted—either explicitly or even implicitly—assumptions about these background questions. If we are successful, then whether or not you agree with any of our own assessments of the issues that we consider, you will depart a more critical reader of discussions of reasons in any form.

We also have a second, auxiliary aim, in writing this book. As will rapidly become apparent, there are *many* distinct questions lurking in the background of issues about reasons. It is conventional in contemporary analytic philosophy to expect authors to define their terms, explaining what they mean by each key term and what assumptions they are making about it. It will soon be obvious that there are a great many fascinating questions surrounding reasons over which people have actually disagreed. Indeed, even setting aside possible views which have not yet found advocates, there are far too many such questions for it to be reasonable to expect every book focused on reasons to take up them all—let alone every article which draws only incidentally on assumptions or theses about reasons. However, by bringing these questions together, by showing how they relate to one another, and by developing a common vocabulary for doing so, we also hope to create a common point of reference. Our hope is that this common reference point will help philosophers working on and with reasons to articulate even more explicitly which assumptions they are taking for granted and which they are not—as well as to point in directions where further inquiry can be expected to be particularly fruitful.

The book is divided into twelve chapters, which we have endeavored to keep short and direct, the better to serve our purpose as an accessible gateway into the issues and, derivatively, into the literature. The chapters, in turn, are organized *very* loosely into three main parts, which move very roughly—and metaphorically—from the inside out, starting with the internal structure of reasons and claims about reasons (Part 1: *Parts*), proceeding through interrelationships between kinds of reasons and the role of reasons (Part 2: *Province*), outward to the relationship between reasons and other things (Part 3: *Place*).

We have not succeeded at keeping our discussions in each chapter independent from one another—indeed, we take it that one of the virtues of a book-length discussion like this one is that it allows us to explore the threads that connect our topics to one another in illuminating and sometimes surprising ways. Nevertheless, we hope that much can be gained even from reading individual chapters in isolation as introductions to particular topics or as guides to particular portions of the literature.

In Part 1: *Parts*, we focus on the internal structure of reasons and their ascriptions. This title is loose; we don't mean in every instance to be describing the parts of reasons in the literal sense of their mereology, but simply to be looking inward, in some broad sense, at the insides of how reasons and talk about them work.

In Chapter 2 we will begin closest in, with the ontology of reasons. Then in Chapter 3 we will look slightly further out, looking at what clues are provided about the structure of the *reason relation* by the structure of sentences reporting about reasons. Finally, in Chapter 4 we will look yet further outward, considering a number of possible views about what *other relata* may figure in the reason relation, *relata* which may be implicit only in context. But first, we must start at the beginning, setting up some background about what has drawn philosophers' attention toward reasons to make it worth attending to such questions behind the questions, drawing some key distinctions, and setting up some of the vocabulary that we will draw on throughout what follows. We begin with some of what we take to be the key background to the contemporary prominence of reasons.

1.2 Reasons as Right-Makers

Mentions of reasons are common in English stretching back for centuries. But, for a very long time, the word 'reason' occurs most often in philosophical prose as a name for the faculty of reasoning or capacity to reason, as in sentences like 'reason is the slave of the passions' or 'his reason was impaired'. Philosophical attention to reasons, in the contemporary sense, arose largely during the second half of the twentieth century. The increasing prominence of reasons since then can largely be attributed to two different roles that reasons have often been thought to play, imperfectly or otherwise: that they somehow *explain what we ought to do*, and that they play a role *in reasoning*.

The role of reasons in explaining what we ought to do is best brought out by examining one of the main contributions of W.D. Ross's 1930 book, *The Right and the Good*, and the way in which it grew out of and responds to the central argument of Sidgwick's *The Methods of Ethics*.[1] Much of moral philosophy between the seventeenth and nineteenth centuries, insofar as it

---

[1] Ross [1930], Sidgwick [1907].

gave us explanations of what we ought to do, did so by seeking out highly general *rules* for conduct—rules that articulated sufficient conditions for some action to be obligatory. Some theorists, like Kant and Mill, held that a single such principle could encompass all of moral conduct, while others, like Clarke and Price, held that there were many such principles. But everyone who discussed what we ought to do seemed to expect there to be such principles.[2]

In *The Methods of Ethics*, Sidgwick defined 'intuitionism', for his purposes, as the view that there are some such principles that are independent of the consequences of an action. He preferred this definition because it clearly distinguished intuitionism as an *a priori* method for determining what to do, whereas egoism and utilitarianism, since they require knowledge of the long-term consequences of an action, are essentially empirical methods. Yet as Sidgwick argued in part 3 of the *Methods*, it is very difficult to formulate any such principles that could be both plausibly true and plausibly intuitive. Once we start to think about interesting real-life cases, Sidgwick demonstrated at length, it is hard to find any principles at all that are both exceptionless and simple. Sidgwick's diagnosis was that the only exceptionless principles entail utilitarianism, and so generalizations like 'tell the truth' can *seem* perfectly general because in ordinary cases not telling the truth has bad consequences. However, sometimes, as when there is a murderer at the door asking for the location of your friend, telling the truth can have such bad consequences that these effects override the normal bad consequences of lying—and that is why in those cases you ought not to tell the truth.

Ross, writing several decades later than Sidgwick, argued that Sidgwick's diagnosis of the source of his counterexamples to various simple deontic principles did not go deep enough. Sidgwick was right, according to Ross, to note that the counterexamples to principles like 'tell the truth' typically come up in cases in which there will be bad consequences to telling the truth. But just like as are intuitive counterexamples to principles like 'tell the truth', there are *also* intuitive counterexamples to principles like 'maximize the good'. And in fact, there is a general recipe for constructing such counterexamples. What you do is construct cases in which something else is at stake—justice, for example, or honesty, or some benefits that are produced only at the cost of directly harming others. Ross argued, therefore, that the

---

[2] Kant [1993], Mill [1963], Clarke [1706], Price [1748].

counterexamples to both deontic rules and to utilitarianism deserve a unified diagnosis.

Ross's diagnosis, which has since become justly famous, we believe, was that what you ought to do in any situation—which he called your duty proper—is a *product* of the competition between something like moral forces, which may pull in different directions. He called these moral forces *prima facie duties*. Ross's hypothesis offers an elegant explanation of why much of the time, when our *prima facie* moral duties do not come into conflict, we are required to tell the truth; of why, much of the time, we are required not to directly harm others; of why, much of the time, we are required to benefit others, and so on. Yet it also explains why we are not so required *all* of the time, and in fact it tells us precisely when we are not so required—this is when the conflicting *prima facie* duties are more forceful.

Indeed, Ross's diagnosis leads to some quite wonderful and subtle predictions. Take, for example, the case of promissory obligation. Usually, it is morally obligatory to keep your promises. But sometimes, it is justifiable to break a promise. For example, if you promise a friend to meet them for tennis, but on your way across campus you encounter someone who has had a significant accident on their bike and you are the only obvious person who can help them seek medical attention, it may be morally okay to break your promise to your friend and show up late. Similarly, if you promise your fiancé to show up for your wedding on time and there is a mass shooting in the small town where you are the only emergency room physician, it may be morally okay to break your promise to your fiancé and show up late. But while it would be permissible to show up late for your tennis match if you were required for a mass shooting, it would not, we speculate, be permissible to show up late for your own wedding on account of being a bystander to a bicycle crash.

Ross's theory of *prima facie* duties provides an elegant explanation of why this is exactly what we should expect. More serious promises will correspond to stronger duties, and so will be outweighable only by stronger duties to aid. One can imagine a theory of very specific promissory duties that says that you are obligated to keep promises to play tennis unless you are the bystander to a bicycle accident or the emergency room physician in a small town where there has been a mass shooting, and that you are obligated to keep promises to show up for your wedding unless you are the emergency room physician in a small town where there has been a mass shooting. But even if we *could* explain these things separately, it is not at all obvious that we should want to. Ross's theory gives us an attractive explanation that encompasses both—and it is much, much more general, explaining similar disparities in terms of what sort of levels of injustice give rise to counter-examples to utilitarianism when different benefits are at stake, what sorts of harms justify not telling the truth in what sorts of circumstances, and many, many other kinds of cases.

Few contemporary moral theorists frame their work in terms of Ross's terminology of *prima facie* duties. But the terminology of reasons is ubiquitous, and one of the prominent reasons why that is so is that it has come to be widely accepted that Ross was right about something important—what we ought to do *is* or is *often* explained by the competition between moral factors that sometimes pull us in different directions. These competing forces have come to be known as *reasons*, following a plausible identification of the role in Ross's theory with a concept that ordinary speakers plausibly grasp. Similar ideas have been applied by some to explain justification, rationality, appropriateness, correctness, and many other normative properties and relations, including what is good.

We may describe the role of reasons in this Rossian diagnosis by calling it reasons' *explanatory* role. According to this proposal reasons play a role in making something what we ought to do—or similarly, of what is justified, appropriate, rational, correct, or good—through their competition with one another. But it is important, at least for the sake of not ruling out any important possibilities prematurely, not to over-interpret the intuitive idea that *reasons explain*. On one view, when reasons play their explanatory role, facts about what we ought to do are made true by *facts about reasons*. On this view, facts about reasons are in a natural sense more fundamental than facts about what we ought to do.

But on a contrasting view, the explainers of what we ought to do are not, in the first instance, facts about reasons and how they compete against one another, but rather the reasons themselves—the things that are properly said to *be* reasons. It is compatible with this view that though reasons themselves are more fundamental than facts about what we ought to do, *facts about* reasons are not. For example, according to John Broome, what *makes* something a reason is that it plays a certain kind of role in explaining what someone ought to do.[3] On this view, it is correct to characterize the explanatory role of reasons by saying that *reasons explain* what we ought to do, whereas on the former view, this is a slightly sloppy way of talking, and

---

[3] Broome [2004].

what is more careful to say is that *facts about reasons* explain what we ought to do. The contrast between these two competing pictures of the explanatory role of reasons will turn out to be important throughout this book, and throughout philosophical discussions of reasons more generally, although authors are seldom explicit which they have in mind.

Ross's Picture	Broome's Picture
Facts about what you ought to do are explained by facts about what reasons there are.	Reasons are the facts that explain what you ought to do.

1.3 Reasons in Reasoning

The explanatory role of making actions right is only one of the two central roles that have been taken to be played by reasons, and for the sake of which they have come to play such a prominent role in contemporary philosophy. The other such central role is that they figure in *reasoning*—or at least in *good* reasoning. We will call this the *deliberative* role of reasons.[4]

The connection between reasons and reasoning is intuitive and pre-theoretical, and it goes much deeper than their etymological connection in English. When you are deliberating about what to do, you may sometimes find yourself saying something like 'on the one hand...but on the other hand...'. If you were to formalize your deliberative process in the sort of way suggested by Benjamin Franklin, you might put your 'one hand' considerations in the 'pros' column, and your 'other hand' considerations in the 'cons' column.[5] If this process goes well, the thought goes, you are identifying reasons in favor of the action that you are considering, and reasons against it.[6]

---

[4] For a skeptical perspective on whether the same thing plays both the explanatory and deliberative roles of reasons, see Wedgwood [2022].

[5] Franklin [1772, 348-349], as prominently quoted in Horty [2012] and discussed in Titelbaum [2019].

[6] Although this is disputed, it seems to many that there are reasons to feel certain ways—reasons to be afraid, reasons to love, and so on. But what we feel is seldom the product of explicit deliberation. So 'deliberation', in "reasons' deliberative role" must be understood broadly enough to encompass the mental activity that underlies loving or fearing for a reason. Likewise, action from reflex or from habit can be driven by reasons, but neither reflex nor habit involves deliberation in the conventional sense.

Bernard Williams drew on this role when he maintained that there must be a 'sound deliberative route' from any reason toward motivation—some good way of reasoning that could lead someone who learned of this reason to actually act on it.[7] When despite noting that on the 'one hand' it will be delicious, you remind yourself that on the 'other hand' you are on a diet, and as a result decline the dessert menu, it is natural to describe your action not just in terms of what *counts in favor* of it, or what *counts against* it—its pros and cons—but in terms of the reason *for which* you did it. Pros and cons can be described prospectively, before you have acted or even formed an intention to act, and do not depend, in general, on what you actually do or how you actually end up doing it. When the word 'reason' is used in this way, it picks out what philosophers have come to call *normative reasons*. By contrast, talk about the reasons *for which* you do something does not make sense before you have done it. The reasons *for which* you do something depend on what you actually do, and how you actually do it. When the word 'reason' is used in this way, it picks out what philosophers have come to call *motivating reasons* for doing so.

We will follow the standard convention of using the terms 'normative reason' and 'motivating reason' to refer to what is picked out when the word 'reason' is used in each of these two ways. But when we use 'reason' without such a qualification, either explicitly or in the immediate context, we will always be referring to normative reasons, which we take to be the central topic of this book. It is also common to say that the normative and motivating uses of 'reason' correspond to different "senses" of 'reason', and we will often talk that way as well throughout the book, though we intend this talk in the least loaded way possible. The linguistic differences in how 'reason' is used could come from different lexical meanings, or they could come from modulation of some contextual parameter, or they could come from a thin core meaning elaborated with additional information that is clear in context. Which of these, or some alternative, is the case, is just one of the many rich background issues about reasons that it is the purpose of this book to explore, and so it is important not to rule out any answers in advance.

Indeed, even though we can distinguish 'normative' and 'motivating' senses of 'reason', these two kinds of 'reason' talk are not totally unrelated. When you decline the dessert menu upon reminding yourself that 'on the

---

[7] Williams [1979].

other hand' you are on a diet, it is natural to think that the reason *for which* you have declined the dessert menu is that you are on a diet. And strikingly, this fact looks like exactly the right sort of thing to be a normative reason for you to decline the dessert menu, as well. And this looks like no coincidence: you are reasoning *well* if your diet *is* in fact a better normative reason than the deliciousness of the desserts. And you will be reasoning poorly if—perhaps because you ought not to be on a diet at all—this does not count much at all in favor of declining the dessert menu. So normative and motivating reasons are not simply unrelated meanings of a common string of phonemes in English; it is instead quite plausible that they share quite a close relationship. And this observation about reasoning *well* makes it natural to think that this relationship must be somehow connected to the deliberative role for (normative) reasons—their role in reasoning.

In fact, this point is more general. Aristotle importantly distinguished between acting *from* a virtue and acting *in accordance with* a virtue.[8] Similarly, Kant distinguished between doing the right thing and acting with *moral worth*.[9] The difference, for both, lies in not just *what* you do, but *how* you do it. In particular, it depends on your motives—the shopkeeper who gives correct change not because it is the right thing to do or because it is owed but because to do otherwise would affect his Yelp ratings is the paradigmatic example of someone who does the right thing, but does not act well or with moral worth, because he does it for the wrong reasons. By contrast, morally worthy action results from doing the right thing for the *right* reasons—a relationship between normative and motivating reasons.

But the role of reasons in reasoning is not restricted to reasons for action. We don't just do things for reasons. We also, according to many philosophers, believe for reasons, intend for reasons, fear for reasons, and hope for reasons. And when we do, our beliefs, intentions, fears, and hopes are more or less rational, depending on what our reasons are. And more. At least when you believe for reasons (and possibly in general), whether you know seems to depend on the reasons for which you believe. If you truly believe that it is raining outside because the tea leaves say so, you don't know it. This closely parallels our observations about moral worth.

Similarly, the difference between fearing rationally and merely fearing what it is rational to fear—for example, the man chasing you with a knife—plausibly lies in the reason for which you fear. If you fear him for his clown

---

[8] Aristotle [2009].   [9] Kant [1993].

makeup rather than for his knife, you are fearing the right thing but for the wrong reasons. And so the deliberative role of reasons has lent them importance not only in the philosophy of action but also in epistemology, the theory of moral worth and character, and the study of the emotions. But because there is no equivalently simple way of expressing this thought in more general terms, we will continue to say that reasons can be acted on (in some sense), trusting that we can all remember that this includes believing for, intending for, and so on.

In this section we have not attempted to say *what* the deliberative role for reasons is, any more than we attempted to say in the last section *how* reasons explain what we ought to do. What we have been trying to do, instead, is to point toward what has led philosophers to believe that there is *some* deliberative role for reasons—one that has something to do with attention, motivation, and/or the relationship between normative reasons and motivating reasons. There are many ideas here to be explored and many of them have been explored, about the relationship between reasons, reasoning, and motivation. We mean our characterization of the deliberative role of reasons to be neutral among them. But it is clear that this deliberative role has been crucial in establishing reasons' importance over the last fifty years or more.

Reasons' Explanatory Role	Reasons' Deliberative Role
Normative reasons explain what we ought to do in some sense that will be more controversial to work out.	Normative reasons can be acted on in some sense that will be more controversial to work out.

1.4 Normative, Motivating, Explanatory

In the last section we distinguished between normative and motivating reasons. Our tests for whether normative reasons or motivating reasons are being discussed are, as we have said, whether the claim's truth depends on what the agent actually *does*, and whether it depends on *how* they actually do it. Motivating reason claims depend on both of these things, and normative reason claims depend on neither. Philosophers often characterize this distinction instead in terms of the paradigmatic sentences or constructions that are used to ascribe each kind of reason. But this is problematic, because both normative and motivating reason claims can be made using a variety of natural language constructions. This causes different philosophers who are trying to define normative and motivating reasons in this way to appeal to different constructions. They are obviously, we believe, trying to talk about the same thing, and the thing that they are trying to talk about is fruitfully distinguished using our two tests.

Some common ways of expressing motivating reason claims
  Her reason for going
  The reason why she went
  The reason for which she went
  Why she went

The terminology of 'normative' and 'motivating' is not perfect. Attempts to carve out this distinction go back at least to Francis Hutcheson, who distinguished between 'exciting' and 'justificatory' reasons.[10] Grice called motivating reasons 'personal' reasons, an idiosyncratic use that derived from his choice of which kind of natural language construction ascribing motivating reasons to focus on.[11] So there are many pieces of related vocabulary floating around covering similar territory. And the term 'motivating' is especially imperfect, because it is strange to talk about a belief being "motivated" except in cases of wishful thinking[12]—and likewise for fear, hope, and other attitudes. But despite these imperfections, this choice of terminology is the closest to being standard and the least misleading, so we will use it in what follows, with the periodic reminder that the motivating reason for a belief is just the reason for which it is held, and the motivating reason for your feeling is just the reason for which you feel that way.

It is also helpful to distinguish both normative reasons and motivating reasons, at least in principle, from explanatory uses of the word 'reason'. For example, we can say that the reason why the dinosaurs went extinct is that the earth was hit by a major asteroid. That is not a normative reason—it is neither a pro nor a con of the dinosaurs going extinct, and it depends on whether they actually did go extinct. But it is also not a motivating reason. This can be seen intuitively by observing that going extinct was an event, not an action, belief, or other attitude of the dinosaurs, either individually or collectively. But the contrast can also be drawn out by seeing how explanatory reasons for an agent's behavior

---

[10] Hutcheson [1728, 138].   [11] Grice [2001, 40–41].
[12] Indeed, Scanlon [1998: 19] calls motivating reasons for belief *operative reasons* because of this strangeness.

can fall short of being motivating reasons. For example, if in answer to the question 'why did she do that', we tell you that everyone in her family acts that way, we may have explained why she did it, but we haven't rationalized it—we haven't told you the reason *for which* she did it—and more generally, there is a very natural question that you plausibly had in mind that we haven't actually addressed. The question that you had in mind was what her *motivating* reason was for doing it, and all that we have given is an *explanatory* reason why it is the case that she did it.

As with normative and motivating reasons, it is very likely that it is no coincidence at all that the word 'reason' is used for explanatory reasons as well as normative and motivating reasons. According to some, for example, this is because normative and motivating reasons are both special cases of explanatory reasons—explanations of particular sorts of thing. This was Davidson's view about what have come to be known as motivating reasons, for example—that they are explanations of a very specific kind of event—*actions*.[13] Similarly, some views of normative reasons take them to be explanations of a very specific sort of thing—of what you ought to do, according to John Broome, or of what is good in some way, according to many others.[14]

But it is also possible that the connection between explanatory reasons, normative reasons, and motivating reasons is less direct. For example, instead of being explanations of a particular kind of thing, motivating reasons could be things that play a particular *role* in a particular *kind* of explanation. This is another view on which it would be no mystery how we could have ended up with the same word for both. Similarly, perhaps the explanatory role for normative reasons is enough to explain why a word, 'reason' that plays a role in explanation, is naturally adapted to apply to normative reasons, even if claims about normative reasons are not, strictly speaking, simply analyzable as special cases of claims about explanatory reasons.

With only this three-way distinction on the table, we can already see some of the rich ways in which subtle background assumptions about reasons can inform philosophical thinking about them. If we assume, for example, that motivating reasons are just a special case of explanatory reasons, then everything that is true of explanatory reasons must be true of motivating reasons as well. For example, if the 'P is the reason why Q' construction is

---

[13] Davidson [1963].   [14] Broome [2004], Finlay [2014].

factive in both argument places, then it will follow that motivating reasons must be truths—a surprisingly consequential upshot. We will have much more to say about background assumptions like this one in later chapters; here we wish merely to illustrate how questions like whether 'reason' is univocal or not in these contexts can have pervasive philosophical consequences.

1.5 Two More Distinctions

We must make two more distinctions before moving on. The first is between what have come to be called 'objective' and 'subjective' reasons. Here vocabulary is even less fixed and can be even more confusing. But we find it helpful to distinguish 'objective' and 'subjective' reasons by comparison to a familiar distinction often made in ethical theory between what someone ought to do in 'objective' and 'subjective' senses. Roughly, you ought not, in the subjective sense, to bet on zero on the roulette wheel since it has only a one in 38 chance of paying out and the payout if you do win is only 35 to 1. But if, against the odds and your evidence, the roulette ball will land on zero, then you should, in the objective sense, bet on zero.

As we are using the terms 'objective' and 'subjective', the distinction between what you objectively and subjectively ought to do is a distinction that is naturally thought to turn on the agent's information or perspective in some way. What you subjectively ought to do is intuitively more closely connected with what it is *rational* for you to do than what you objectively ought to do. But according to a natural view these are not the same. If what it is rational for you to do depends on both your information and your goals, then what it is rational for you to do can come apart from what you objectively ought to do either because your information is imperfect, or because your goals are imperfect. The concept of what you subjectively ought to do, then, tracks the imperfection in your information, rather than any imperfection in your goals.

The contrast between objective and subjective normative reasons, like that between objective and subjective 'oughts', comes from cases in which an agent's reasonable beliefs come apart from the facts. For example, there will be dancing at the party, but Freddie is unaware of this. Since Freddie really likes to dance, the fact that there will be dancing at the party counts in favor, in some sense, of him going there. Because there will be dancing at the party, there is a sense in which he ought to go there, at least if other things are equal. Yet since he doesn't know about the dancing, this fact doesn't make it any more rational for him to go. By contrast, if he does know about the dancing, that is at least the right kind of thing to make it, at least potentially, what he ought to do in the *subjective* sense of 'ought'.

We will say that when something counts in favor of an action, belief, or other attitude by tending to make it *correct*, other things being equal, or what the agent *objectively* ought to do, then it is an *objective* reason, and that when something counts in favor of an action, belief, or other attitude by tending to make it what the agent *subjectively* ought to do, then it is a *subjective* reason. So long as Freddie is unaware of the dancing, it gives him an objective reason to go to the party, but no subjective reason to go.

Objective	Subjective
ought	*ought*
independent of perspective	dependent on perspective
connected to *correctness*	connected to *rationality*
reasons	reasons
correspond to objective *ought*	correspond to subjective *ought*

When philosophers use the expression 'normative reason', they nearly always intend to be talking about objective reasons. And some of the most influential recent discussions of reasons, by Derek Parfit and T. M. Scanlon, take for granted a *theory* about how objective and subjective reasons are related—that subjective reasons are just *appearances* of objective reasons.[15] But in our terminology, both objective and subjective reasons count as 'normative' reasons, because they are both a kind of pro or con, contributing to the case that you should do something without necessarily making it the case that you should, and neither depends on what you actually end up doing (or believing, etc.), nor on *how* you end up doing it (or believing it, etc.). So given how we introduced the contrast between normative and motivating reasons, it follows that both objective and subjective reasons must count as 'normative', in this sense.

---

[15] Parfit [2011], Scanlon [2003, 13]. Parfit and Scanlon might resist this description of their view, denying that there is anything worth calling a 'subjective reason' at all, and maintaining that there are not two kinds of reasons—objective and subjective—but only one kind (intuitively the ones that we are calling 'objective') plus appearances of (objective) reasons. Whether or not you think that this difference is important will depend on how important you think it is that something is dignified with the title of 'reason'.

Moreover, both objective and subjective reasons play both explanatory and deliberative roles. We have already noted that objective reasons tend to make something what you objectively ought to do, whereas subjective reasons tend to make something what you subjectively ought to do. So both have explanatory roles to play, but with respect to the explanation of different things. Similarly, in order to emphasize the deliberative role of reasons, we emphasized the importance of how your motivating reasons and your normative reasons are related to whether you act or think well. But here again, similar remarks go for subjective reasons as for objective reasons. Each will correspond to different dimensions along which you can reason well—whether you are reasoning rationally, or whether you are reasoning correctly.

We should make no assumptions up front about the relationship between objective and subjective reasons. In Chapter 5 we will see that many philosophers believe, like Parfit and Scanlon, that objective reasons are prior to and explanatory of subjective reasons, and that some even believe that subjective reasons are a *special case* of objective reasons. But the contrary view is also possible, as is the view that neither is prior to nor explanatory of the other. Whichever view you find it natural to assume when confronted with this distinction, it is important to keep in mind that that view is not directly forced by the cases, like Freddie's, that we use to introduce the distinction. So we should not build such theories into the terms 'objective reason' or 'subjective reason' up front.

As we have noted, common ways of trying to carve out this or similar distinctions are deeply vexed in the literature. Most of them do have the failing of incorporating theoretical assumptions directly into their terminology or definition. For example, some philosophers distinguish between 'reasons' and 'possessed reasons', intending to mark the same distinction that we have with 'objective' and 'subjective'. But this terminology codifies the theoretical assumption that subjective reasons are just a special case of objective reasons, ones that you 'possess'—and thereby rules out the possibility that just as there can be objective reasons with no corresponding subjective reasons, so also can there be subjective reasons without any corresponding objective reasons. By contrast, our terminology leaves this question open. Maybe subjective reasons are just a special case of objective reasons, and maybe they are not. We will return to this question in Chapter 5.

Finally, before we move on through the remainder of this book, we must call attention to the fact that we have so far been using 'reason' as a count noun, except where we noted historical references to a human capacity, as in 'his reason was impaired'. Count nouns admit of plurals and can be modified by words like 'many', as in 'there are many reasons to read Hume'. But 'reason' is also often used as a *mass* noun.[16] Mass nouns do not have plural forms and are modified by words like 'much'. For example, we sometimes say that there 'is much more reason to do it than the other thing', not clearly meaning that there *are many more reasons*. Again, it would be a stunning coincidence if there were no intimate relationship between mass noun uses of 'reason' and count noun uses, as there is for 'water', 'beer', and 'salad'. Considering the relationship between these uses can place helpful *prima facie* constraints on how we think about many other questions. For example, if normative and motivating uses of 'reason' are just special cases of the explanatory uses of 'reason', then this creates a puzzle about where the mass use of 'reason' fits in.

For the most part, throughout this book we will be concerned with normative reasons as picked out by 'reason' as a count noun. But we will be interested throughout to observe where important issues hang on how we think about the nature of motivating reasons, explanatory reasons, and 'reason' as a mass noun and their relationships. We think you should be, too.

Chapter Summary

In this chapter, we laid out our goals for this book and motivated several distinctions that we will rely on throughout: between normative, motivating, and explanatory reasons, and between objective and subjective normative reasons. We also introduced both the explanatory and deliberative roles for (normative) reasons. Each of the explanatory and deliberative roles for reasons helps us to understand one of the ways in which reasons are important in so many related areas of philosophy, and we argued that understanding how they interact is especially important as well, making it especially important to understand how reasons could play both roles. At the same time, these two roles for reasons will structure our investigation for the remainder of this book.

---

[16] As importantly observed by Fogal [2016].

Recommended Reading

Ross's picture comes from his classic book, *The Right and the Good*, especially chapter two. Broome's contrary picture comes from his paper 'Reasons'. Bernard Williams' idea that reasons must motivate by a sound deliberative route comes from his 'Internal and External Reasons'. The distinction between normative and motivating reasons dates at least to Francis Hutcheson's distinction between 'justifying' and 'exciting' reasons in his 1728 *Essay on the Nature and Conduct of the Passions*, but is made in a particularly forceful way by Michael Smith in chapter five of his classic *The Moral Problem*. Jonathan Dancy's *Practical Reality* is the ur-source for the idea that there must be some close relationship between normative and motivating reasons. In distinguishing between objective and subjective reasons without prejudging their relationship we follow Mark Schroeder's 'Having Reasons', and the idea that philosophers should pay attention to mass noun uses of 'reason' comes from Daniel Fogal's 'Reasons, Reason, and Context'. We recommend pairing this chapter with chapter one of Jonathan Dancy's *Ethics Without Principles*.

Exercises

1.1 *Comprehension*. In section 1.2 we saw that appealing to reasons can help us to explain which circumstances can make it permissible to break which promises. Demonstrate your understanding by working through a similar example involving exceptions to the duty to aid someone needy.

1.2 *Extensions*. In section 1.2, we motivated reasons' explanatory role as right-makers by reference to Ross's diagnosis of the complicated contours of what we ought to do. Ross's diagnosis, we suggested, has the advantage over Sidgwick's of offering the same diagnosis of intuitive counterexamples to utilitarianism as Sidgwick offered of intuitive counterexamples to deontic principles. Utilitarianism is commonly understood, including by Sidgwick, as combining the thesis that you should always do what would have the best results (consequentialism) with the monistic thesis that the only thing that makes results good is how much happiness they involve (hedonism). How could you use act-consequentialism together with a *pluralist* theory of value in order to co-opt these virtues of Ross's diagnosis? Is this alternative superior to Ross's? Why or why not?

1.3 *Extensions.* In section 1.3 we connected moral worth with the deliberative role of reasons by pointing out the apparent connections between acting with moral worth and the reasons for which you act. But we didn't say *which* reasons you must act for in order to act with moral worth. Is it possible to act with moral worth without knowing what makes an action wrong? Why or why not?

1.4 *Extensions.* In section 1.4 we introduced the idea that normative reasons are a special case of explanatory reasons—explanations of a particular sort of thing. How is this view related to the distinction drawn in section 1.2 between two ways of understanding the explanatory role of reasons? Is it compatible with both? Why or why not?

1.5 *Comprehension.* Give your own examples of objective normative reasons that are not subjective reasons, of subjective reasons that are not motivating reasons, and of explanatory reasons that are not motivating reasons, to show that you understand each of these distinctions.

1.6 *Extensions.* Assume for purposes of this exercise that motivating reasons are a special case of explanatory reasons—explanations of a particular kind of thing. What kind of thing should we say that motivating reasons are explanations of? What two conclusions can you draw about motivating reasons from the observation that explanation is *factive*, in the sense that if A explains why B, then A and B must both be true?

1.7 *Extensions.* In section 1.5 we distinguished between the count noun and mass noun uses of 'reason'. Explore the extent to which these two uses come apart by trying to come up with examples of things that there is reason to do, but nothing is a reason to do them. Can you do it? Why or why not?

1.8 *Extensions.* Can you construct a sentence in which 'reason' is used as a mass noun but receives a motivating reading? Can you construct a sentence in which 'reason' is used as a mass noun but receives a purely explanatory reading? What light might your answers shed on the relationship between the mass and count noun uses of 'reason'? What light might they shed on whether the normative uses of 'reason' are just a special case of the explanatory use of 'reason'?

2
What Are Reasons?

2.1 The Substance of Reasons

Our goal in this book is to introduce reasons and show how a wide variety of seemingly unrelated theoretical assumptions about reasons connect issues of substantive import in normative philosophy—in ethics, epistemology, the philosophy of action, the theory of the emotions, and elsewhere. Our plan is to start at the inside and proceed outward—from the nature of reasons themselves and of the *reason* relation, to the roles of reasons, and finally to their connection to other normative concepts and relations.

In order to provide some regimentation for how to think about these questions, we will work throughout with a way of representing the structural questions that we will be asking about reasons by means of a device that we call *reason diagrams*. We will assume, in general, that whenever there is a normative reason, there is always a kind of *support* going on, and that we can therefore distinguish between what is *supported* and what is doing the *supporting*. Intuitively, the thing that counts *as* the reason is the thing that does the supporting, and the thing that it supports is what it *favors*, or what it is a reason *for*.[1]

We can draw this as follows:

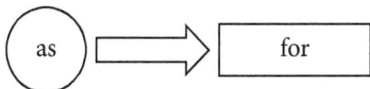

Similar diagrams can be drawn for different kinds of reasons. In particular, Chapter 1 distinguished between objective normative, subjective normative, motivating, and explanatory reasons. We can think of each of these as a different relation between, *inter alia*, something that counts *as* the

---

[1] We need to be slightly careful with 'for' talk; as will emerge in Chapter 3, we can also talk about things being reasons *for* agents *to* do things. Here what is supported is intuitively given by the 'to' clause, not by the agent.

reason, and the thing that it counts as a reason *for*, and so we can draw them with different kinds of arrows, for example, as follows:

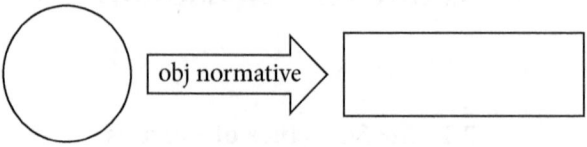

By leaving the circle and rectangle blank in our diagram, we can draw a picture of the objective normative reason *relation*, and by filling them in, we can draw a picture of the state of affairs of some particular thing counting as an objective normative reason for some other particular thing.

On some views, something is a reason for something else only relative to some further parameters. Indeed, as we will see, there are a wide variety of candidates for what these extra parameters might be. We will draw these as extra *relata* of the reason relation by associating them as spokes around the hub that characterizes the thing that counts *as* the reason.

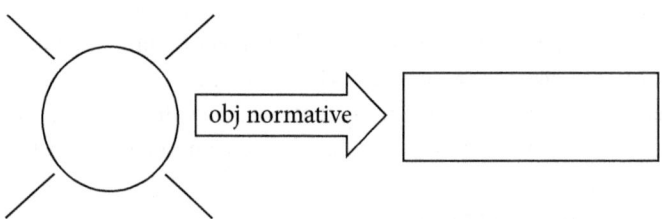

Reason diagrams structure which questions we need to answer in order to understand how reasons work. We need to know, for each kind of reason—objective normative, motivating, and so on—what sort of things go into the circle, counting *as* the reasons. Similarly, we need to know what sort of things go into the rectangle, counting as what the reason supports or favors. And finally, we need to know what other *relata* each relation has—what other spokes are required—in order to complete the diagram.

Throughout we will speak, as we have just done, in the metaphysical mode, of 'the reason relation', and of the relation whose obtaining 'makes' something a reason, or 'makes it true' that something is a reason. We do not mean, however, to be begging any questions against trepidatious approaches to the metaphysics of normativity, such as noncognitivist treatments of thought and talk about reasons. Cognitivists and noncognitivists alike must start with views about the argument structure of the 'reason' predicate, and we trust that noncognitivists will understand how to translate everything that we say into their preferred idiom.[2]

These are all questions that we need to have a firm grip on to think intelligently about *the conditions under which* something is a reason for something else. If we don't know which sorts of things can be reasons or what sort of thing they are reasons for or what else their being reasons for is relative to, then we can't think clearly about further, downstream, philosophical questions like this one. And as we will see, though some people have thought that it is relatively obvious what the *relata* of the reason relation are, different answers have seemed obvious to different people, and they fit into different natural packages whose merits are worth considering as a whole.

We will therefore start at the middle, in this chapter, by exploring what sort of thing goes into the circles in our reason diagrams—the question of what the *substance* of reasons is. This question might be put more naturally by asking, what sorts of things can be reasons? Then in Chapter 3 we will turn our gaze outwards to explore what sort of thing goes into the rectangle—what sort of thing reasons support—and closely related questions about the other spokes of the reason relation that are implicated by this question or are otherwise explicit. Finally, in Chapter 4 we will turn our gaze yet further out to consider other possible candidates for other *relata* of one or another reason relation, which may often not be explicit. We will move back and forth freely in all three chapters between considering answers to these questions for the cases of objective normative, subjective normative, and motivating reasons, though sometimes related issues about the corresponding questions about explanatory reasons will lie closely in the background.

We've already described three places to look for answers to what sorts of things should go into the circle for the case of objective normative reasons. The first place is what we've called normative reasons' *explanatory* role—the role that normative reasons play in their capacity as pros and cons that help to explain what to do, think, feel, etc. Depending on how we understand the explanatory role of reasons, it could place constraints on what sorts of things could play that role. The second place to look for answers to this question is what we've called normative reasons' *deliberative* role—the role that reasons play in their capacity to motivate us to do, think, and feel certain things in

---

[2] Compare Blackburn [1984]. For a general introduction to issues surrounding noncognitivism, see Schroeder [2023].

certain ways. The deliberative role of normative reasons could also possibly place constraints on what they could be.

And finally, a third place to look for answers to what reasons are is the language we use to discuss and ascribe them. 'Reason' is not merely a term of art; although philosophers have found theoretical reasons to be interested in reasons, we have called them 'reasons' because this is a natural word that seems to get at something of pretheoretical interest. Indeed, one piece of evidence that reasons are pretheoretically interesting is that we found it so natural to use the word 'reason' to formulate our last sentence, in talking about 'theoretical reasons to be interested'. So one natural constraint on what sort of thing could be reasons is that it should make sense of how we could have managed to say true things about reasons using ordinary language.

In section 2.2, therefore, we address linguistic evidence about what the substance of reasons could be, or what we will refer to as evidence from natural language *ascriptions*—that is, reports—of reasons. In section 2.3 we'll look to evidence from the explanatory role of reasons, and in section 2.4 to evidence from their deliberative role. It will be one of our major themes that all three of these sources of evidence are at least potentially of great importance, and that it is a mistake to embrace only one to the exclusion of the others.

2.2 Linguistic Evidence

Any attempt to use ordinary language to triangulate on what sort of thing reasons are must begin by coming to grips with the fact that ordinary talk about reasons is ontologically profligate. For example:

1. The reason not to jump off the Empire State Building is its height.
2. The reason not to get rowdy at the bar is Biff, the bouncer.
3. The reason to leave is that it's getting late.
4. The reason to go to the store is to get almond milk.

These claims are naturally read as claims about objective normative reasons. But they each appear to say that a different kind of thing is a reason—a property trope, a person, a state of affairs, and a goal. So taken at face value, these ascriptions suggest that the substance of objective normative reasons is highly permissive.

But it may be that the disunity projected by the variety of expressions used to ascribe reasons is merely illusory. In most or all of these cases, claims that denote a property or object as a reason, like (1) and (2), respectively, can be reinterpreted by a claim with a *that*-clause. For example, (1) can be naturally reinterpreted as the claim that the reason not to jump off the Empire State Building is *that* it's quite tall. Likewise, (2) can be naturally reinterpreted as the claim that the reason not to get rowdy at the bar is *that* Biff will bounce you if you do.

There is also a natural strategy for trying to reinterpret (4), which ascribes a reason to go to the store using a *to*-clause. Unifying (4) with our other uses requires reinterpreting 'to get milk' as expressing something that can also be denoted with a *that*-clause. Fortunately, just such a view is popular in linguistics. Bhatt [2006] argues that non-finite contexts, such as the one introduced by (4)'s *to*-clause, systematically involve covert modality, such as the kind of modality expressed by 'must', 'ought', and 'can' in English. So on this view, (4) may be interpreted as saying that the reason to go to the store is that you must get almond milk, or that almond milk must be obtained.

Since a wide variety of ordinary-language ascriptions of reasons can be paraphrased by citing *that*-clauses, but nothing similar is true for citing persons, property tropes, or the like, that gives us some evidence that the thing that goes into the circle of our objective normative reason diagram must be citable with a *that*-clause. And this is the orthodox view at least tacitly accepted by most theorists. This view can be developed as the claim that it is not literally true that Biff the bouncer is a reason not to get rowdy, but only an elliptical way of saying that the reason is that Biff will bounce you if you do. Or alternatively, it can be developed as the claim that though this *is* literally true, it is true only in some derivative sense of 'reason' that is grounded in the fact about Biff being the reason. The difference between these two views will not be important for our purposes. Both views allow that everything worth saying about reasons can be said about the things named with *that*-clauses.

Nevertheless, there remains room for disagreement about the precise ontology of objective normative reasons, for there are two opposing views about the relationship between reasons and *that*-clauses. The first view is that since the denotation of a *that*-clause is a proposition, reasons are propositions. For example, when the reason to leave is that it's getting late, our reason diagram should be filled in this way:

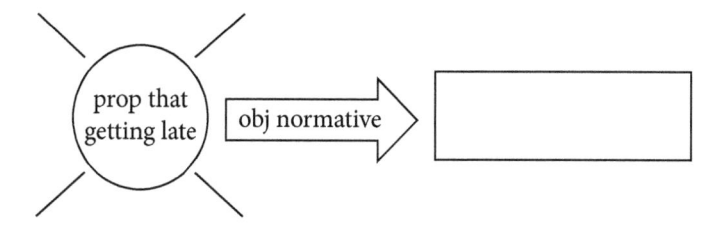

By contrast, on a competing view, reasons are not propositions, but the states of affairs that are the truth-makers for propositions. On this view, our reason diagram should be filled in like this, abbreviating 'state of affairs' as 'SoA':

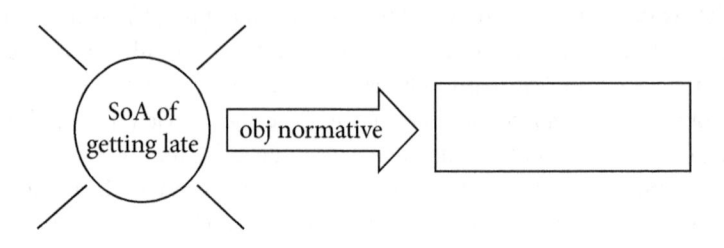

```
        SoA of         obj normative
        getting late
```

The difference between these two views is sometimes occluded by the fact that both can naturally be described as views on which reasons are facts. This is because the word 'fact' is itself contentious in philosophy, used by some theorists to denote true propositions, and by others to denote the states of affairs that make propositions true. Since the dispute between these two views is often orthogonal to other issues, this ambiguity in 'fact' is actually convenient, allowing us to make claims that are neutral between what the propositional view and the state of affairs view disagree about. Nevertheless, a little bit can be said about how to adjudicate their disagreement.

Jonathan Dancy [2000, 114–115] argues that reasons cannot be propositions, because it does not make sense to say that the reason to leave is the proposition that it's getting late. He seems to reason as follows:

P1 If the clause 'that it's getting late' in "the reason to leave is that it's getting late" denotes a proposition, then "the reason to leave is the proposition that it's getting late" is true.
P2 "The reason to leave is the proposition that it's getting late" is not true.
C   Therefore, the clause 'that it's getting late' in "the reason to leave is that it's getting late" does not denote a proposition as the reason to leave.

For Dancy, it only makes sense to say that the reason to leave is the *truth* of this proposition. He takes this argument to be decisive evidence against the propositional view and in favor of the state of affairs view, and it is evidence from ordinary language ascriptions, so it is the right sort of evidence to consider here.

We are not persuaded. Consider an analogous argument, substituting 'the reason (to X) is that' with 'desires that':

P1 If the clause 'that the Habs win the cup' in "Maurice desires that the Habs win the cup" denotes a proposition, then "Maurice desires the proposition that the Habs win the cup" is true.

P2 "Maurice desires the proposition that the Habs win the cup" is not true.

C   Therefore, the clause 'that the Habs win the cup' in "Maurice desires that the Habs win the cup" does not denote a proposition.

The conclusion is false—desires are propositional attitudes—so there must be something wrong with the argument and that something is pretty clearly the first premise. Its flaw is the assumption that because *that*-clauses denote propositions, the expressions 'that *s*' and 'the proposition that *s*' are interchangeable. But they're not. After all, Maurice desires that the Habs win the cup, but he does not desire the proposition that the Habs win the cup.

The flaw in both arguments is the same. While the propositional theory says that every reason claim can be paraphrased in terms of a *that*-clause, and that *that*-clauses denote propositions, it does *not* say that ordinary reason claims can be paraphrased in terms of claims that say that the reason is 'the proposition that…'. On the contrary, the claim that the reason to leave is the proposition that it is getting late is a 'reason' ascription to a noun phrase, and the propositional theory says that all such ascriptions must first be paraphrased in terms of a *that*-clause. These are not inter-substitutable, as we've just shown with Maurice, because they are different parts of speech.

So, it seems to us, Dancy's argument against the propositional view fails. But the propositional view has no great direct arguments against the state of affairs view, either, beyond the advantage that the propositional view treats the role of *that*-clauses in 'reason *that*' ascriptions analogously with those in belief and desire reports. So evidence from ordinary language reason ascriptions leaves a lot of room for both views to be able to make sense of each other.

So far in this section we have focused on ascriptions of objective normative reasons. But the same phenomenon of apparent ontological profligacy with which we began also applies to other kinds of natural language talk about reasons, including about motivating reasons. Indeed, though as written our examples 1–4 are all naturally read as ascribing objective normative reasons, they can all easily be modified to denote motivating reasons, instead:[3]

---

[3] Note that, *pace* Grice [2001], there is nothing special about the formulation of the following sentences that dictates that they must be interpreted as claims about motivating reasons. In suggesting that we read sentences (5)–(8) as motivating reason ascriptions, we are inviting you to imagine them in contexts that make clear that this is the intended interpretation.

5. Haotian's reason for not jumping off the Empire State Building was its height.
6. Haotian's reason for not getting rowdy at the bar was Biff, the bouncer.
7. Haotian's reason for leaving was that it was getting late.
8. Haotian's reason for going to the store was to get almond milk.

The same reason diagrams that we have been using to illustrate objective normative reasons may also be coopted to illustrate motivating reasons. Although it is somewhat misleading to think of motivating reasons as 'supporting' something, we can still distinguish between what counts as the reason and the thing for which it is a reason. So the same reasoning as before might lead us to be tempted to think that motivating reasons are properly ascribed by *that*-clauses, and hence are either propositions or states of affairs:

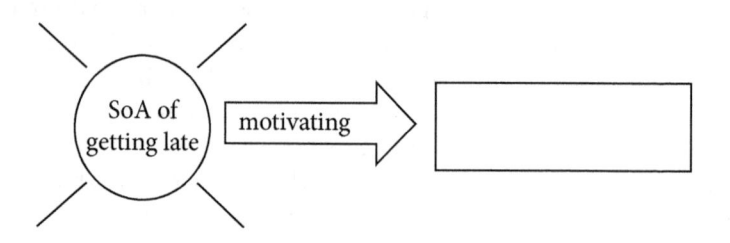

But ordinary talk about motivating reasons carries a crucial further dimension of complexity absent in ordinary talk about objective normative reasons. The first step to identifying this further dimension is to pay attention to the way that we ascribe motivating reasons by describing the agent's attitudes:

9. Haotian's reason for going to the store was that he thought they sold almond milk.
10. Haotian's reason for going to the store was that he wanted to get almond milk.

Challenges to unifying the varied motivating reason ascriptions in (5) through (8) resemble those of unifying the varied ways of ascribing objective normative reasons in (1) through (4). But the mention of attitudes in sentences like (9) and (10) raises new, more complex, issues about the ontology of motivating reasons. Here we'll focus on belief-mentioning ascriptions like (9), though there are potentially analogous issues to be raised about desire-mentioning ascriptions like (10).

At first glance, (9) looks just like any other *that*-clause reason ascription. But in fact this is an illusion, which can be seen by comparing the following:

11. Haotian's reason for baking cookies was that he thought aliens were coming to visit.
12. Haotian's reason for seeing a psychiatrist was that he thought aliens were coming to visit.

In both of these sentences, Haotian's motivating reason is ascribed using a *that*-clause, but they make Haotian's action intelligible in very different ways. (11) describes a belief whose *content* makes his action make sense, while (12) describes a belief whose *existence* makes his action make sense.

Once we grasp the difference between the most natural readings of each of these claims, we can also see that even holding a single sentence fixed, it can be interpreted in either of these two quite different ways.

13. Haotian's reason for seeing his psychiatrist in the morning was that he thought aliens were coming to visit in the afternoon.

On one reading of sentence (13), it describes a scenario in which Haotian wakes up alarmed about his own mental state and sees a need to check in with his psychiatrist as a result. On another, it describes a scenario in which he wakes up concerned to get his psychiatrist visit out of the way in time to make it home for the aliens' visit. These are quite different motives, despite both being ascribable with the same motivating reasons report.

These observations arguably show two things about motivating reasons. First, they show that talk about motivating reasons has an extra layer of complexity that is not exhibited by talk about normative reasons. And second, they arguably show that this complexity arises as a result of the fact that in order to understand a motivating reason claim, we must understand which consideration it is *in light of which* an agent acts—for this is a plausible diagnosis of how the two readings of (13) differ.

A traditional view which is well-motivated by this complexity, dating to Davidson [1963], holds that (9) and (10) are more illuminating about the nature of motivating reasons than (7) or (8), and what they show is that motivating reasons, properly speaking, are psychological states at least partly constituted by beliefs. As a result, this view about the substance of reasons is often called *psychologism*. On this view, saying that Haotian's reason for leaving was that it was getting late is merely an elliptical or indirect way of saying that Haotian's reason for leaving was his belief that it was getting late.

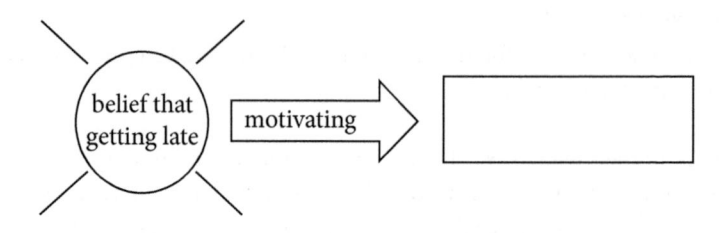

(diagram: "belief that getting late" → motivating → [ ])

It is common for advocates of psychologism to go further, and also follow Davidson in holding that motivating reasons actually have *two* parts—both a belief and a desire. (Similar cases to sentences (11)–(13) can be raised with reason ascriptions involving desire reports.) This theory has the virtue of offering us an alternative treatment of (8). Instead of meaning that Haotian's reason comes from his belief that he ought to get milk, as in the suggestion from Bhatt that we considered a few pages ago, the claim that Haotian's reason for going to the store was to get milk could report that Haotian acted on a desire to get milk.

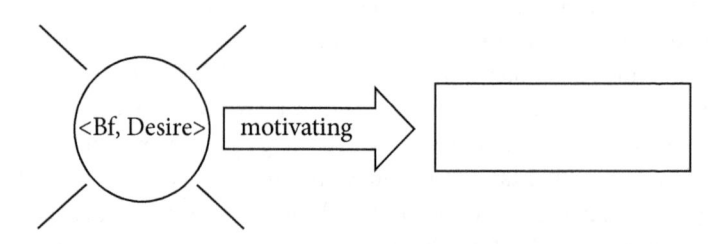

(diagram: <Bf, Desire> → motivating → [ ])

Davidson's view is attractive because it can explain not only the ambiguity in reason reports like (13) but also why different readings are much more eligible in cases like (11) and (12). This is because a *that*-clause which mentions a belief could be a literal report of the belief that partially constitutes the reason, or it could be an elliptical or indirect way of reporting this belief by way of reporting its content, as with the Davidsonian treatment of (7), the claim that Haotian's reason was that it was getting late. It is not the only way of accounting for this ambiguity, but it is a clean and natural one, and an important virtue of this account.

2.3 Explanatory Constraints: Are Normative Reasons Explanatory Reasons?

As we argued in Chapter 1, the fact that someone ought to do, think, or feel something is not a brute fact. It is not a brute fact that you should drive sober. Rather, the fact that drunk driving is dangerous helps to explain why you should drive sober. That much is relatively uncontroversial and flows from reasons' explanatory role. But broad observations such as these leave room for competing conceptions of what that role involves. One such conception deserves special focus for, despite its seeming innocuity, it implies heavyweight commitments about which things can be reasons—commitments about the *substance* of reasons, as we've been calling it.

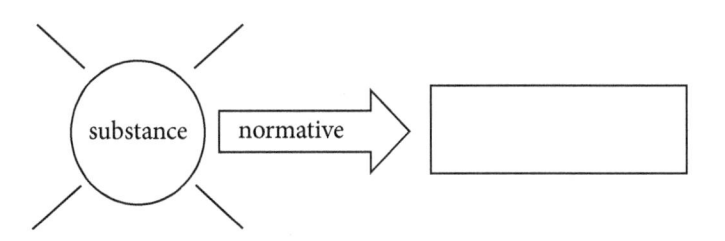

According to this popular thesis, reasons have an explanatory role *because* normative reasons are a special case of explanatory reasons. Earlier, in section 1.4, we discussed explanatory uses of the word 'reason' and raised the question of whether we should think of motivating reasons as a special case of explanatory reasons. In this section, we ask the very same question about normative reasons: are they merely a special case of explanatory reasons, distinguished from other explanatory reasons by *what* they explain?

The thought that normative reasons are a special case of explanatory reasons is appealing partly because 'reason why' and 'explanation why' pattern similarly. For example:

14. The reason why you should not drive drunk is that it's dangerous.
15. The explanation of why you should not drive drunk is that it's dangerous.

At least at first blush, (14) and (15) convey the same thing. Some philosophers, including Walter Sinnott-Armstrong, John Broome, and Stephen Finlay, take this similarity, along with the theoretical unity that comes from subsuming normative reasons under explanatory reasons, as conclusive grounds for thinking that all normative reasons are a special case of explanatory reasons.[4]

Although this thought is natural, it is optional. Recall the case of Haotian's reason to bake cookies for the aliens:

13. Haotian's reason for seeing his psychiatrist in the morning was that he thought aliens were coming to visit in the afternoon.

As we saw in section 2.2, there are two different ways of reading this claim, corresponding to two quite different reasons for Haotian, depending on whether his motive is to seek treatment or to be a good interstellar host. On each of the ways that we saw of making sense of this, strictly speaking a different thing is Haotian's reason in each of these cases. On each such view, the connection between the clauses used to ascribe reasons and the substance of those reasons, strictly speaking, is indirect. So such views open up the distinct possibility that even though (14) and (15) pattern closely, this is not because normative reasons are strictly identical to explanations. Consequently, to properly evaluate the idea that normative reasons are just a special case of explanatory reasons, we must also assess its commitments.

Because the thought is that normative reasons are explanatory reasons, these commitments spring from the nature of explanation. The first such commitment is that it appears that only facts can be explained. For example, there is no explanation of why Paris is in Germany. This isn't because of some inscrutable geopolitical mystery. It springs from the more general observation that only facts can be explained. Since Paris is in France, it is not a fact that Paris is in Germany. Accordingly, there is no answer to why Paris is in Germany.

The factivity of explanation sets an important constraint on what kind of thing normative reasons can be explanations *of*. On the face of it, the explanatory role of reasons that we isolated in Chapter 1 was concerned with explaining what we ought to do. But if reasons for you to do

---

[4] Sinnott-Armstrong [2008], Broome [2004], Finlay [2014]. We will explore a natural way to respect the explanatory role of reasons without identifying normative reasons as explanatory reasons in Chapter 7.

something are explanations of why you ought to do it, then there can only be reasons to do things that you ought to do. But this seems false. The whole point of reasons is that there are typically reasons on *both* sides of important choices—not just on the side of what you ought to do. This pushes proponents of the idea that normative reasons play a role in explanation either toward identifying different candidates for what reasons explain—for example, why there is something *good* about your doing something—or else toward relaxing the tightness of the connection between reasons and explanation, suggesting that normative reasons play some role in explanations of what you ought to do *other than* being explanations of why you ought to do it.[5]

We've just been noting the consequences of the fact that 'explains' is factive in its right-hand place. But similarly, 'explains' is also factive in its left-hand place: only truths or facts can be explainers. That Paris is in Germany cannot explain why there are Francophones in Germany, even though Paris is full of Francophones. If normative reasons are explanatory reasons, then, it appears that *both* the substance of reasons as well as what reasons favor must be facts.

But this implication has important consequences as well, which can be brought out by considering the case of subjective normative reasons. To see how, let's return to the case of Freddie, from section 1.5. Although there is dancing at the party, and Freddie likes to dance, he doesn't know about the party. So though there is an objective reason for him to go to the party—namely, that there is dancing there—he doesn't yet have a subjective reason to go to the party.

This example shows that there are some cases in which there are objective reasons that are not also subjective reasons. Can the same happen in reverse? Can there be subjective reasons that are not also objective reasons? A naïve thought suggests that there are. Subjective reasons have a connection, we suggested in Chapter 1, to what you subjectively ought to do, and what you subjectively ought to do differs from what you objectively ought to do by being filtered through your information. But just as what it is rational for you to do can come apart from what it is objectively correct for you to do because you are *ignorant*, it is natural to naïvely think that these can also come apart because you are *mistaken*. For example, it might be rational for Bernie to sip his drink because he believes that it is a gin and tonic even

---

[5] This is the move of Broome [2004]. We will return to this argument and its consequences at greater length in Chapter 7.

though it is not, and so in virtue of his belief, he seems to have a subjective reason to take a sip. Both ignorance and mistakes are ways in which your subjective beliefs about the world can come apart from the facts.

The idea that subjective reasons are just a special case of explanatory reasons threatens this naïve idea—or at least imposes steep costs to accepting it. This is because the left-hand factivity of explanation means that subjective reasons can be explanatory reasons only if subjective reasons are truths. But cases in which you have a subjective reason without an objective reason—like Bernie's—are cases in which the *content* of your belief—the object of your thought—is false. Consequently, the object of your thought cannot be your subjective reason. This essentially forces on us a dilemma. In order to preserve the idea that subjective reasons are just a special case of explanatory reasons, either we have to conclude that the naïve thought that there can be subjective reasons without corresponding objective reasons is a mistake, or we must conclude that psychologism is true, and that subjective reasons are not the contents of thought or belief, but rather the facts that we have such beliefs.

But both of these conclusions are highly controversial. We've already seen that it is natural to naïvely hold that subjective reasons, like rationality, should depend only on your beliefs, and not on the truth of those beliefs (except in the trivial case that among your beliefs are beliefs about the truth of your beliefs). So it is a bold conclusion to draw—some might say that it is a demonstration of the power of philosophy to teach us surprising things, and others might say that it is a demonstration of the power of philosophers to ignore *reductios*.

But the other conclusion is also striking. On at least one natural interpretation of the deliberative role of reasons, normative reasons are in general our objects of thought when we are deliberating well. If the reason to go to the party is that there will be dancing there, then deliberators will explicitly consider whether there will be dancing, and are moved by the thought that there will be. But psychologists about subjective reasons must give this up. People do not deliberate about whether they believe that there will be dancing at the party, and it can be rational to go to the party if you like dancing and believe that there will be dancing there, even if you do not realize that you believe this.

So this way of understanding the explanatory role of reasons leads to a *prima facie* tension with a natural way of understanding the deliberative role of reasons—a tension that can be resolved only by giving up the naïve idea that there can be subjective reasons in the absence of objective reasons. As with most topics in philosophy, theorists take this problem in all three ways: some reject the idea that the explanatory role of reasons can be captured by the idea that subjective reasons are a special case of explanatory reasons,[6] some reject the idea that the deliberative role of reasons can be characterized by the idea that reasons are appropriate objects of thought,[7] and some reject the idea that there can be subjective reasons in the absence of objective reasons.[8] We will resist the temptation to adjudicate between these views on the basis of these features, in order to turn to the deliberative role for reasons.

2.4 Deliberative Constraints: Are Normative Reasons Motivating Reasons?

We've just briefly explored how the explanatory role of reasons might help us to answer the question of what sort of thing reasons are—the question of reasons' substance. Rather than considering all ways of making sense of the explanatory role of reasons, we focused on one particular way of understanding the explanatory role of reasons, in terms of the idea that normative reasons are just a special case of explanatory reasons. We'll now turn toward the same task for reasons' deliberative role. Again, we hope to use reasons' deliberative role to cast light on the substance of reasons—on what sort of thing reasons might be. And we've already seen, in section 2.3, how one conception of the deliberative role of reasons can be used to push back against one familiar view about what reasons are—psychologism. But rather than consider all possible conceptions of the deliberative role of reasons, in this section we will focus on just one way of trying to make this role precise: the idea that normative reasons can be our motivating reasons.

In Chapter 1 we emphasized that part of what is important about the deliberative role of reasons is that it often matters not just what we do and how it is supported by reasons, but also what the reasons are *for which* we do it. It is morally important to how much credit you should get, for example, if the reason for which you do something is among the most important moral reasons *to* do it, and you don't nearly get as much credit

---

[6] For example, Schroeder [2008], Comesaña and McGrath [2014], and Dancy [2000], who, even though he thinks that reasons must be states of affairs rather than propositions, is led by this combination of views to say that motivating reasons for rational action in cases of false belief can be *non-obtaining* states of affairs.

[7] Davidson [1963].   [8] Lord [2010], Lord [2018], Hawthorne and Magidor [2018].

if you do the morally right thing for the reason that it happens to be in your self-interest. So unsurprisingly, one of the most important ways of trying to make sense of reasons' deliberative role focuses directly on the intuitive idea that in the very best cases, it is possible for the reasons *for which* we act—our motivating reasons—to be the very same as the reasons *for* us to act—our normative reasons.[9]

This idea has much in common with the idea that normative reasons are just a special case of explanatory reasons. Both ideas offer a constraint on the ontology of the substance of normative reasons, by requiring that ontology to *match* the ontology of the substance of motivating reasons. This constraint can be taken in a reductive way, by taking normative reasons to be *analyzable* in terms of motivating reasons, as in Alex Gregory's [2016] thesis that normative reasons just are good (potential) motivating reasons. Or it can be taken non-reductively, by simply offering the constraint that since normative and motivating reasons are *sometimes* identical, their substance must belong to the same kind.

By taking this intuitive idea very seriously, we can derive the hypothesis that every normative reason is identical to some possible motivating reason.[10] Following arguments for this claim from Jonathan Dancy, Philip Stratton-Lake, and others, philosophers have found this interpretation of reasons' deliberative role increasingly appealing, and it puts pressure on views like that of Michael Smith [1994], who holds that normative and motivating reasons have very different substances—adopting a fact-based ontology of normative reasons, and a psychologistic ontology of motivating reasons.[11] But as one might expect, adopting the commitment that normative and motivating reasons overlap affects different accounts of the substance of normative reasons differently.

The most common way of taking the constraint that normative and motivating reasons must have the same substance leads philosophers to draw conclusions about what sorts of things motivating reasons must be from their prior commitments about what sorts of things normative reasons must be. So, for example, Dancy [2000] concludes that motivating reasons must be the facts that we consider in our deliberations, because the facts that we consider are the ones that are the normative reasons on which we act, when we act well. If

---

[9] This identity claim is central in Dancy [2000] and in chapter one of Schroeder [2007b].
[10] Strict identity does not follow from the intuitive thought that we can act for normative reasons—some other intimate relationship may instead be sufficient. Mantel [2018] offers an important account in this vein.
[11] Dancy [2000], Stratton-Lake [2000].

you give someone help because they are in need, the normative reason for you to act, Dancy thinks, is the fact that they need help, and what you are thinking at the time of action is not 'I think that they need help', but just, 'they need help'. So, Dancy concludes, motivating reasons are facts, and they are not, in general, facts about psychology—except in very specific cases such as Haotian's reason to see his psychiatrist.

But the constraint that normative reasons and motivating reasons must have the same substance can also be taken in the reverse direction, whether or not we endorse Gregory's [2016] reductive thesis that normative reasons just are a special case of (potential) motivating reasons. In section 2.2, we introduced Davidson's psychologist idea that motivating reasons consist in belief-desire pairs:

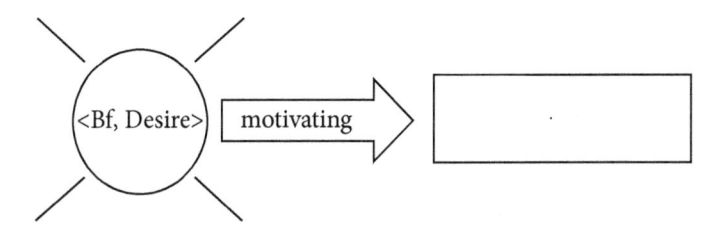

If Davidson's dual-aspect psychologism is right, and normative reasons can also literally be motivating reasons, then normative reasons must also consist in belief-desire pairs:

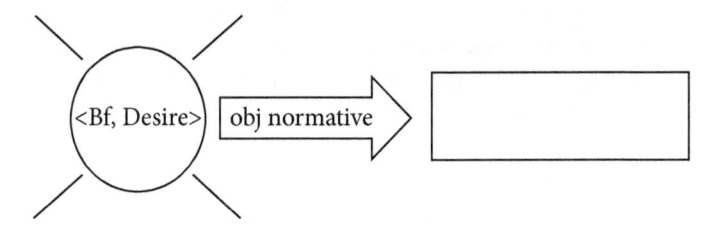

Unfortunately, this leads to an unpromising view of objective normative reasons because there can be an objective normative reason for you to do something even when you lack a corresponding belief-desire pair—either because you are unaware of it, or because you lack the corresponding motivation to care about it. So normative reasons cannot be identical to actual belief-desire pairs.

Nevertheless, there are several ways of retaining something close to this view, while respecting the idea that normative reasons can sometimes also be motivating reasons. One way is to deny that all motivating reasons belong to the same ontological category and to distinguish the reasons for which we act when we act well from those for which we act when we do not. For example, according to Hornsby [2008], Davidson is more-or-less right about the substance of motivating reasons in *some* cases, but not in all. The cases that Davidson is right about are those that we cannot correctly report by saying things like

16. Haotian's reason for baking cookies was that aliens were coming to visit in the afternoon.

Haotian's motivating reason cannot be that aliens were coming to visit, because despite Haotian's beliefs, aliens were not, in fact, coming to visit. So the only thing left for Haotian's reason to be, Hornsby holds, is that he *thought* that aliens were coming to visit.

So Davidson's psychologism, or the similar view that motivating reasons are facts about psychology, can be correct in what we might call the *bad* case, where the agent's belief is not true or at least does not constitute knowledge, but it does not correctly describe the good case. In the good case, motivating reasons have a different substance—they are not psychological states or facts about psychological states (again, except in cases like Haotian's decision to see his psychiatrist, where it matters substantively what his beliefs are), but the kinds of facts that Haotian is explicitly considering when he acts. Since Hornsby holds that Davidson is right about the substance of *some* motivating reasons, we can think of her view as in one way a way of relaxing Davidson's. But since she does not think that Davidson is right about the substance of *all* motivating reasons, that implies that some normative reasons, which are not belief-desire pairs because the relevant belief-desire pairs do not actually exist, might instead consist in facts. Consisting in facts is still being the right kind of thing to be a motivating reason because, on this view, facts can also be motivating reasons.

Another possible response that departs even less from the letter of Davidson's view, attempting to keep even more of its spirit, is to conclude that the substance of normative reasons is not actual belief-desire pairs, but *possible* belief-desire pairs. On such a view it would be possible to act for normative reasons because normative reasons are possibly actual belief-desire pairs. Unfortunately, the metaphysics of this proposal are murky, because if merely possible belief-desire pairs do not actually exist, but only possibly exist, then many normative reasons will not exist, either, but only possibly exist. But there is another, much more straightforward, view in the very close neighborhood: a view that we might call the dual-aspect *content* view.

The dual-aspect content view departs from Davidson by replacing the concrete psychological states of belief and desire with their corresponding contents. Just as the content of a belief is a proposition, we can think of the content of a desire as being a *goal*.[12] So the dual-aspect content view says that the substance of both motivating and normative reasons consists in *proposition-goal pairs*:

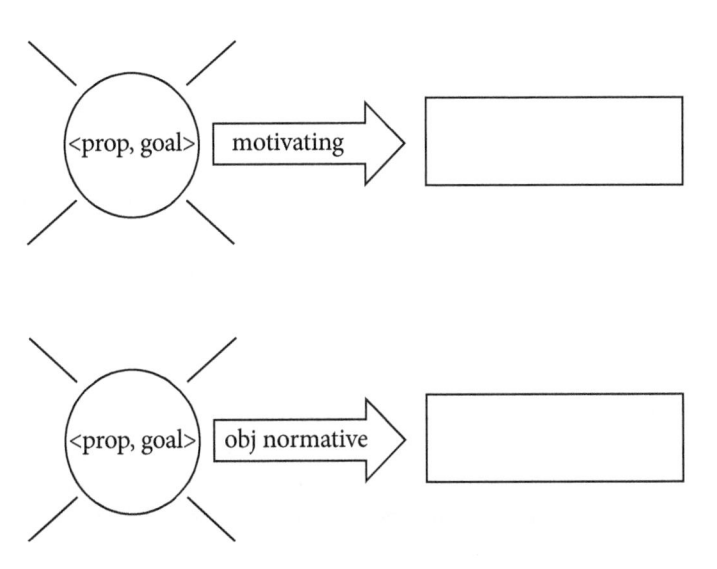

⟨prop, goal⟩ — motivating →

⟨prop, goal⟩ — obj normative →

According to the dual-aspect content view, the same kind of thing can be both a motivating reason and a normative reason, but the conditions under which it is either are different, but overlapping. Just to give a simplistic example of how this might go, a proposition-goal pair might, for example, be an objective normative reason because its proposition is true and its goal is worthy, and it might be a motivating reason because the agent's belief in its proposition and desire for its goal satisfy Davidson's condition or one like it.

---

[12] This way of putting things abstracts from the further question of whether goals are themselves just propositions, or are instead something else.

The dual-aspect content view is novel and surprising. But it has other virtues, as well. Recall from section 2.2 the case of sentences like 'The reason to go to the store is to get almond milk.' In order to interpret ascriptions of objective normative reasons like this one as picking out a true proposition, we saw that they need to be paraphrased in terms of the reason being that we *should* get almond milk or that almond milk *must* be obtained. But now note that *to*-clauses are also often used to ascribe desires, such as the desire *to get milk*. If goals, the contents of possible desires, are parts of normative reasons, as the dual-aspect view contends, then it's no mystery why reasons are commonly ascribed using *to*-clauses. Those ascriptions pick out normative reasons by calling attention to their constituent goals, the things that we desire when we act for those reasons, rather than to their constituent propositions, the things that we believe when we act for those reasons.[13]

We've seen in this chapter that questions about the substance of reasons pit a popular way of interpreting reasons' explanatory role, the thought that normative reasons are explanatory reasons, against a popular way of interpreting their deliberative role, the thought that reasons are what we think about when acting well. The tensions between these two central roles for reasons, and especially between different prominent ways of making them more precise, will continue to inform our discussion throughout this book.

We also haven't decided on any final answer here, either as to the substance of objective normative reasons, the substance of subjective normative reasons, or the substance of motivating reasons. Instead, we've been trying to explore some of the range of possible answers, and how each of those answers fits into natural pictures, together with other packages of commitments. It will be our view throughout this book that philosophy is not best served by us deciding in advance which of these packages is the true one to be assumed everywhere, but instead by a greater appreciation of how different theorists are taking on board different background assumptions. And it is our goal to help us see how those background assumptions fit together.

---

[13] Davidson has a word to say about the pragmatics of such ascriptions: "A primary reason consists of a belief and a pro-attitude, but it is generally otiose to mention both. If you tell me you are easing the jib because you think that will stop the main from backing, I don't need to be told that you want to stop the main from backing; and if you say you are biting your thumb at me because you want to insult me, there is no point in adding that you think that by biting your thumb at me you will insult me" [1963, 688].

Chapter Summary

In this chapter we have been concerned with what kinds of things count as reasons—a question that we have glossed stipulatively as what the *substance* of reasons is. For each of objective normative, subjective normative, and motivating reasons we have seen that there is disagreement about what sorts of things can be each kind of reason. And we have shown how to use evidence from the language of reason ascriptions as well as the explanatory and deliberative roles of reasons in order to get leverage on which of these views is correct. Although we did not settle on a decisive answer to this question, we saw that for some purposes the exact answer may not be terribly important, but for others, such as the question of whether subjective reasons must be facts, the answer can be quite important for understanding what is rational, and why.

Recommended Reading

The debate over whether objective normative reasons are propositions or states of affairs is advanced in chapter five of Jonathan Dancy's *Practical Reality*. The classic source for psychologism about motivating reasons is Donald Davidson's seminal 'Actions, Reasons, and Causes'. The idea that reasons of all kinds are unified around explanatory reasons is in Walter Sinnott-Armstrong's 'A Contrastivist Manifesto', and the classic sources for the debate over whether normative and motivating reasons are totally independent or must be closely related are chapter five of Michael Smith's *The Moral Problem* and chapter five of Dancy's *Practical Reality*. The idea that the dual-aspect theory can help to reconcile Smith's and Dancy's differences comes from Nathan Howard's 'Primary Reasons as Normative Reasons'. We recommend reading this chapter alongside chapter six of Susanne Mantel's *Determined by Reasons*.

Exercises

2.1 *Comprehension*. Describe two competing views about the substance of motivating reasons, and highlight one distinctive virtue of each view.

2.2 *Extensions*. In section 2.2 we considered the possibility that sentences like 'the reason to go to the store is to get milk' could be paraphrased in terms of a 'that' clause by replacing 'to get milk' with an associated modal content, such as 'that milk must be obtained'. So the hypothesis is that 'one reason to go to the store is to get milk' is true just in case 'one reason to go to the store is that milk must be obtained' is true. Test this hypothesis by looking for counterexamples to both the left-to-right and right-to-left directions of this biconditional. Which direction is easier to counterexample? Can you eliminate these counterexamples by substituting a different candidate modal claim? Why or why not? How promising do you think this strategy is for subsuming these sentences to 'that'-clause reason ascriptions?

2.3 *Extensions.* In section 2.2 we considered and rejected Jonathan Dancy's argument that objective normative reasons cannot be propositions. For this exercise, show how the relationship between noun-clause and that-clause attributions of reasons parallels the relationship between noun-clause and that-clause attributions of desire and seeing, by paraphrasing each of the following attributions in the form, 'the reason is that...'.

    1a   The reason to leave is the time.
    1b   The reason to leave is the proposition that the time is late.
    2a   He wants a cup of coffee.
    2b   He wants the proposition that he has a cup of coffee.
    3a   She sees a buffalo.
    3b   She sees the proposition that there is a buffalo.

Are your paraphrases of the (a) sentences equivalent to the (b) sentences? If not, which one should we interpret the "propositional" theories of reasons, desire, and seeing as committed to? Explain how this undermines Dancy's argument.

2.4 *Extensions.* In section 2.2 we rehearsed linguistic evidence about the substance of objective normative reasons, and about motivating reasons. For this exercise, try to marshal similar evidence about the substance of subjective normative reasons. Can you generate the same kinds of ambiguity for subjective reasons reports as for motivating reasons reports? What does your answer tell you about whether subjective reasons are more like objective normative reasons or more like motivating reasons?

2.5 *Extensions.* In section 2.3 we considered the ambiguity in (13) and saw how it can be explained by the idea that subjective reasons show us the light in which someone acted. Try to explain why this ambiguity happens. Does any view about the substance of motivating reasons make it easier to explain?

2.6 *Extensions.* Suppose that Anushka says, 'the reason that Frederika left was that it was getting late'. Then we point out that it was not actually getting late, though Frederika's watch was running fast. Anushka says, 'well, she thought that it was getting late'. Should Anushka admit that she has changed her mind about what Frederika's reason for leaving was? What does your answer tell us about the ontology of motivating reasons?

2.7 *Extensions.* In section 2.3 we considered the view that normative reasons are just explanatory reasons why you ought to do something. For this exercise, explore what follows from this view if explanation obeys the transitivity-like principle that if Q is the reason why R is the reason why S, then Q is the reason why S. Does this consequence seem true? Should we accept or reject the claim that explanatory reasons obey this principle?

2.8 *Extensions.* In section 2.4 we considered whether we could use Hornsby's disjunctive account of the substance of motivating reasons in order to motivate a corresponding disjunctive account of the substance of normative reasons, as a way of reconciling the view that some normative reasons are also motivating reasons with at least part of the spirit of Davidson's account of motivating reasons. For this exercise, evaluate the prospects for this account by comparing two different but similar views like Hornsby's. Some people think that motivating reasons are psychologist unless the agent acts on *knowledge*, while others think that motivating reasons are psychologist unless the agent acts on a *truth*. Which of these views fits better with explaining why some normative reasons are facts, while others are belief-desire pairs? Which do you think is the correct position for those sympathetic to Hornsby's position to take?

2.9 *Extensions.* According to the dual-aspect account from section 2.4, neither 'the reason to go to the store is that we are out of milk' nor 'the reason to go to the store is to get milk' is a complete statement of what the reason to go to the store is, but both can be ways of identifying the very same reason, which has two parts—both the fact that we are out of milk, and the objective of getting milk. Why might it be adequate to mention only one part of this reason, instead of mentioning the whole thing? Does your explanation suggest any concrete predictions about in which contexts it might be more appropriate to describe it in one way rather than the other? Is it ever natural to mention both parts?

3
Arguments

3.1 The Meinong-Chisholm Account

In the last chapter, we considered the substance of reasons—that is, the nature of the things that are properly said to be reasons. But those things are only properly said to be reasons when they are appropriately related to other things in what we might call the *reason* relation. So we now work outward, moving on to consider the structure of the reason relation itself, which, when it holds among the right things, makes it true that some individual substance is a reason. Our goal is not yet to try to understand the *nature* of the reason relation, but just its structure—the number of argument places it has and what kinds of things fill those argument places—throughout focusing on the case of objective normative reasons. In this chapter, our task is to consider the nature of the arguments of the reason relation that may be revealed explicitly by ascriptions of reasons, and in the next we will turn to interesting and natural views about other, non-explicit, arguments of the reason relation.

The distinction between the topics in this chapter and those in the next is somewhat arbitrary. Even arguments of the reason relation that are often explicit can sometimes be made implicit, and even surprising conclusions about the implicit argument structure of the reason relation can be supported by locutions that attempt to make those arguments explicit. Nevertheless, this very rough distinction between implicit and explicit arguments of the reason relation will help to structure our discussion. It is worth a brief reminder that, as in the last chapter, although we will speak throughout in the metaphysical mode, of 'the reason relation', and of the relation whose obtaining 'makes' something a reason, or 'makes it true' that something is a reason, we do not mean to be begging any questions against noncognitivist treatments of thought and talk about reasons. We continue to trust that noncognitivists will understand how to translate everything that we say into their preferred idiom.

We start with a simple and obvious question. Reasons are also often said to be reasons *for agents*. For example, we say things like that there is a reason *for Ryan* to help Katie. Every view of reasons needs to explain why reaching for claims that describe reasons as reasons *for agents* is so natural when talking about them. But explaining how reasons are for agents is not straightforward. That's because 'for' plays two distinct syntactic roles in English. In 'this gift is for Bob', 'for' is a preposition—the same grammatical category as 'on', 'of', and 'at'—which typically combine with a noun phrase, such as 'Bob'. However, in 'what Cela wants is for David to say something nice', 'for' is a complementizer—the same grammatical category as 'that', 'whether', and 'if'—which typically combine with a sentential phrase, such as, roughly, 'David says something nice'.

A particularly straightforward explanation of how some reasons are reasons for agents treats 'for' as a preposition. It holds that a consideration is a reason for an agent to do something when the agent stands in the reason relation along with the consideration and the thing to be done, so that 'there is a reason for Ryan to help Katie' can be glossed as 'there is (for Ryan) a reason to help Katie':

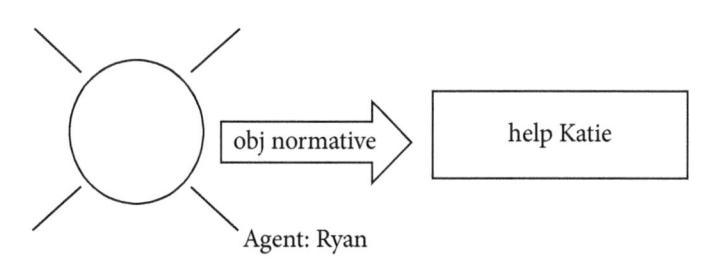

```
         \     |     /
          \    |    /
           \   |   /
            ( O ) ──[ obj normative ]──▶ [ help Katie ]
           /   |   \
          /    |    \
         /     |     \
              Agent: Ryan
```

But this appearance of relativity to agents—of the reason relation holding between, *inter alia*, considerations and agents—which is projected by taking 'for' in natural ascriptions of reasons to be a preposition, could easily be an illusion. In particular, on the quite different view endorsed by Thomas Nagel in *The Possibility of Altruism*, reasons count in favor of *outcomes* or *propositions*.[1] This idea fits naturally with the interpretation that 'for' in the claim 'there is a reason for Ryan to help Katie' is a complementizer taking a sentential clause. So on this Nagelian interpretation, 'there is a reason for Ryan to help Katie' can be glossed as 'there is a reason for (the outcome that) Ryan helps Katie'.

Thus, instead of locating Ryan as a *relatum* in the reason relation, Nagel's explanation locates Ryan in the outcome or in the proposition allegedly

---

[1] Nagel [1970, especially at chapter six].

favored by the reason. Nagel explains the sense in which the reason is a reason *for Ryan* by arguing that the reason favors the outcome where *Ryan* helps Katie. If, suppose, there is a reason for Ryan but not for Ralph to help Katie, then that's so because the reason in question favors the outcome or proposition that Ryan helps Katie but not the outcome (or proposition) where Ralph helps Katie. So, on this view, there is no argument of the reason relation for agents at all—merely the illusion of one.

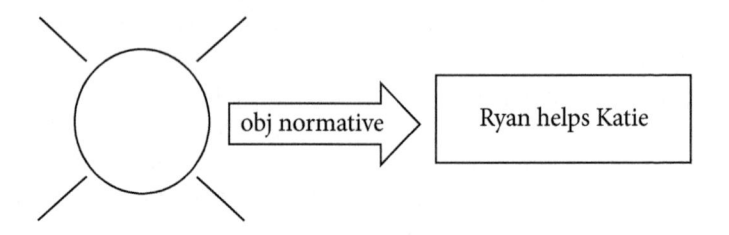

This view about the role of agents in reasons is analogous to the role of agents in what is known as the *Meinong-Chisholm Reduction* in deontic logic, and so we may call it the *Meinong-Chisholm account of reasons*.² In deontic logic, we are interested both in what agents ought to do, and in what ought to be the case. What the Meinong-Chisholm Reduction claims is that the former reduces to the latter. What it is for it to be the case that Jim ought to jam is just for it to be the case that it ought to be that Jim jams. Similarly, the Meinong-Chisholm account of reasons says that what it is for there to be a reason for Jim to jam is for there to be a reason counting in favor of the outcome or proposition that Jim jams.

Each of these interpretations of 'for' suggests a corresponding conception of what reasons favor, and of how Jim is related to the arguments of the reason relation.³ Taking 'for' in these constructions as a complementizer entails the view that the relation directly expressed by 'reason' in English is a relation to propositions, because it requires that 'for John to go to the store' is a semantic unit, and this expresses what appears to be a complete proposition—complete with John. There is correspondingly no need to understand John himself to fill a separate argument of the reason relation. In contrast, the view that 'for' is a preposition separates the roles of 'for John'

---

² Chisholm [1964]. For a history of the Meinong-Chisholm Reduction and its role in deontic logic, see Ross [2010, footnote 3].

³ Hieronymi [2005] claims that reasons do not count in favor of things at all, but rather "bear on a question". But because reasons still, on Hieronymi's view, support particular answers to questions over other answers, we will explore this view in Chapter 4.

and 'to go to the store' into separate units. On this view, John *is* an argument of the reason relation, and opens up the possibility that since 'to go to the store' does not mention John, it is natural to read it as expressing an act-type—the act-type of going to the store. When John exemplifies this act-type by acting this way, we have the state of affairs where John goes to the store. On this view, the reason favors the act-type of going to the store, relative to John.

Meinong-Chisholm View Agents figure in what is supported by reasons rather than as independent arguments of the reason relation.

Whether reasons favor act-types or outcomes affects what they can explain. For example, if the Meinong-Chisholm account of reasons is right, then we can rapidly reason ourselves into what has come to be known as the paradox of deontology. The reasoning goes like this: Ally shouldn't kill, even if she could prevent two other killings—those of Hally and Sally—by doing so. Since Ally shouldn't kill, there must be some excellent reason for her not to kill. On Nagel's view, this implies that there is a very strong reason that supports the outcome that Ally doesn't kill. But Ally is not special; Hally also ought not to kill, even to prevent Ally and Sally from killing—and similarly for Sally. So there must also be an equally good reason supporting the outcome that Hally does not kill, and another supporting the outcome that Sally does not kill. But now of the three reasons that we have discovered, only one counts on the side of Ally's not killing—the other two lie on the side of Ally's killing, for that is the choice on which the outcomes of Hally and Sally not killing are achieved. So far from explaining why Ally ought not to kill, it looks like the balance of reasons weighs in favor of Ally's killing, since there are *two* reasons for doing so, which are each of apparently equal strength to the reason for her not to kill.

This is supposed by some to be a paradox, and by others to be an argument against the possibility of so-called 'agent-relative constraints'— actions that one agent ought not to do, even in order to prevent two others from doing the same action. Traditional deontological ethical theories all allow for the possibility of agent-relative constraints, and so the paradox is supposed to be a puzzle for them. Traditional act-consequentialism is an ethical theory that is distinguished by denying the possibility of agent-relative constraints, and hence the paradox of deontology is often thought to support act-consequentialism or undercut one of the most general arguments against it. So understanding the paradox of deontology is important for one of the most fundamental dividing lines in ethical theory.

But crucially, the reasoning behind the example turns on Nagel's assumption that reasons are reasons for agents in the sense of being reasons for outcomes involving those agents. If we assume instead that reasons favor act-types, like *going to the store* or *not killing*, then from the fact that Ally ought not to kill even in order to prevent Hally and Sally from doing so, we may infer that there is a reason for Ally that counts in favor of the act-type of *not killing*. Similarly, since Ally is not special, and Hally and Sally also ought not to kill, we can again infer that there is a reason for each of Hally and Sally that counts in favor of the act-type of *not killing*. Consequently, when we consider Ally's action, which involves a choice between killing and preventing killings, we only get a reason against killing. So the reasoning behind the paradox of deontology doesn't work at all on the view that reasons count in favor of act-types.

The paradox of deontology derives from the assumption that agents' moral reasons put them in a kind of competition. If Ally does what she has most moral reason to do, then Hally and Sally will not do what they have most moral reason to do since the outcome for which Ally has most reason—that Ally does not kill—is logically incompatible with the outcome for which Hally and Sally have most reason—that Ally (and someone else) kills. It is this structural feature that creates the trouble, because on the outcome view, all reasons for *different* people are special cases of which outcomes there are reasons for. You might think that this is a special feature of so-called agent-centered constraints. But once we see where this tension comes from, we can generate the tension even without assuming that morality allows for agent-centered constraints.

Surely, for example, it is morally indifferent which of Ally, Hally, or Sally wins the weekend 5K run/walk. Nevertheless, each of them might have reasons to win, since it comes with bragging rights. But if each has a reason to win, then when Ally is considering whether to try to win, she is faced with one reason on the side of the outcome where she wins the race (or where she tries to), and two equal reasons on the side of outcomes where she doesn't win—reasons that favor the proposition that Hally wins and the proposition that Sally wins, respectively. Assuming that all of these reasons are of relatively equal strength, then it seems that no one should try to win a race when competing against two or more people, since the reasons against the outcome where they win will be stronger than the reasons for the outcome where they win. But that's absurd.

3.2 Act-Types

We suggest, then, that *if* reasons count in favor of outcomes, then they must still count in favor of outcomes differently, for different agents. This is required in order for us to accommodate phenomena like the paradox of deontology that fall under the rubric of 'agent-relativity' in ethics—cases in which different agents are in some way in competition with one another, having reasons to act in ways that cannot all be jointly realized. Granting agents their own argument space in the reason relation allows us to accommodate these phenomena.

But doing so does not require deleting agents from the outcomes that reasons allegedly favor. We can retain Nagel's claim that reasons count in favor of outcomes or propositions, and allow that what counts in favor of one outcome relative to *one* agent may not do so, relative to another. A reason that counts in favor of an outcome for one agent but not for any agent is what has come to be called an *agent-relative* reason. The natural way to motivate this view, starting from the syntax, is with the assumption that phrases like 'to go to the store' are actually propositionally complete, requiring tacit reference to an agent who does the going to the store. On this view, 'John' does double duty in 'there is a reason for John to go to the store', because he is both the argument of the preposition, and also the person whose going to the store is supported by the reason for John. This view of reasons is analogous to the views about 'ought' defended by Ralph Wedgwood [2006] and John Broome [2013].

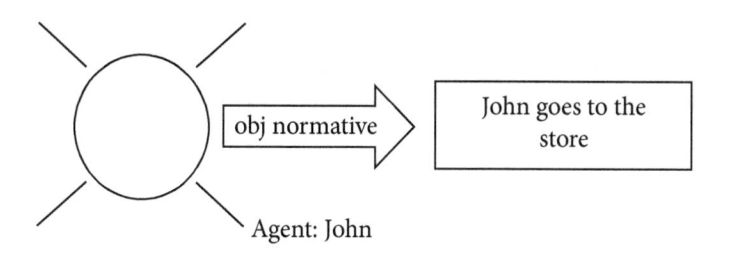

If this account is right, when there is a reason for John to go to the store, it is a reason for John that John goes to the store. This view faces challenges. If 'John' is doing double duty in this way, naming both the agent to whom the reason applies and the agent who completes 'to go to the store', then it should be possible for these two roles to come apart. And so in particular, it should make sense to talk about reasons for John in support of outcomes that involve someone else doing something. For example, maybe we could say 'there is a reason for John that Sally goes to the store'. We don't think, however, that such claims make sense. And if they do not, then if normative reasons are relative to agents, they do not count in favor of arbitrary propositions, but only in favor of propositions concerning *that agent*. There is, at best, a reason for John to ensure that Sally goes to the store, where John ensuring that Sally goes to the store and Sally going to the store are distinct outcomes.

There is a one-to-one correspondence between the class of propositions about an agent and the class of properties—for each property, there is the proposition that the agent has that property, and for each proposition about the agent, there is the property which abstracts the agent from that proposition. So it is at least natural to think of reasons as counting in favor of agential *properties*.

It just so happens that act-types are agential properties—the act-type of going to the store, for example, is what everyone who is going to the store has in common—they are all going to the store. So once we accept that the outcomes in which a reason can count in favor, for an agent, are restricted to outcomes about that agent, there is little to be lost or gained, we suspect, from thinking of reasons as counting in favor of act-types, in this very broadest sense—of agential properties.

A different issue concerns *which* kinds of agential properties there can be reasons for. On the face of it, there can be reasons to do things, reasons to believe things, reasons to intend things, and reasons to feel one way rather than another. So one model takes the parity between each of these claims at face value, and holds that *running, believing that Lisa will run, intending to run*, and the like are all agential properties for which there can be reasons. On a prominent contrasting view, however, which is assumed by Scanlon [1998] and defended by McHugh and Way [2022a], reasons never strictly speaking count in favor of *actions*, but only in favor of *attitudes*.[4] On this view, when we talk about a reason to do something, we are really talking about a reason to *intend* to do it. The contrast between these two models is important for many philosophical issues, but in our terms, both can be described as views on which reasons support agential properties—one merely has a more restrictive view about which agential properties can be supported by reasons.

---

[4] Though Maguire [2018] actually argues that *no* reasons are reasons for attitudes.

3.3 Circumstances

We have seen how the Meinong-Chisholm account of reasons is a way of resisting the idea that the reason relation has a genuine place for an agent. But we have argued that its denial that the reason relation has an argument for agents gives rise to the paradox of deontology, and suggested that once we accept that reasons are relative to agents, it is more natural to think of them as supporting act-types, rather than propositions. By contrast, if 'the fact that Katie needs help is a reason for Ryan to help Katie' expresses a relation between, *inter alia*, the fact that Katie needs help and the act of helping Katie, then it is natural to think that it is *Ryan* to whom it relates these two things. On this view, agents *are* one of the *relata* of the objective normative reason relation.

Including agents in the reason relation allows theorists to model how the balance of reasons can change between individuals. Since it's relatively uncontroversial that at least some reasons vary between individuals—recall Ally's, Hally's, and Sally's reasons—it should be correspondingly uncontroversial that *some* parameter in the reason relation explains that variance. But it turns out that more controversy remains over exactly how this variation happens. In this section, we turn our attention to a different way of resisting the idea that reasons are relative to agents.

In *The Moral Problem*, Michael Smith prominently takes reasons to be relative not to agents, but to something that he calls *circumstances*. Every reason, on Smith's view, is a reason to φ in c, for some act-type φ and some circumstance c. Circumstances are not agents, but rather, situations in which agents can find themselves. Intuitively, on Smith's view, the claim that the fact that Katie needs help is a reason for Ryan to help Katie is true, just in case for some c, the fact that Katie needs help is a reason to help Katie in c, and Ryan is in c.

The difference between these two models is subtle. One holds that the objective normative reason relation looks like this:

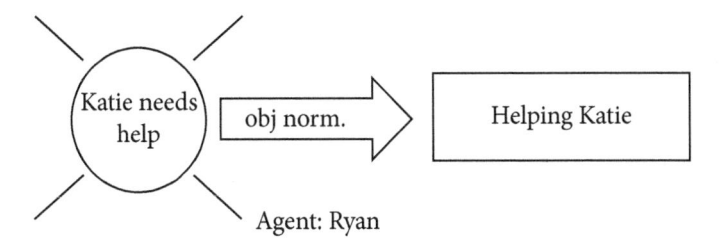

While the other holds that it looks like this:

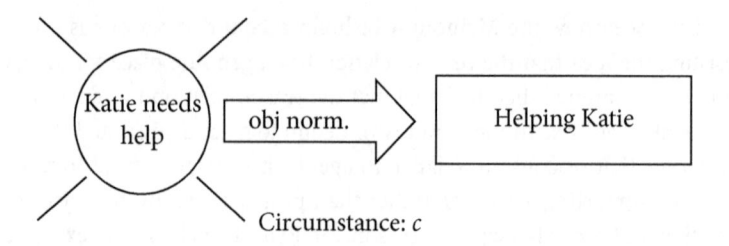

```
          Katie needs  ──obj norm.──▶   Helping Katie
            help
              ↘ Circumstance: c
```

These two ways of thinking of the reason relation are in some ways very similar. Indeed, if we help ourselves to the idea that circumstances can be so fine-grained as to include properties like *being identical to Ryan*—known as *haecceitistic* because they are properties that can be instantiated by only one thing—then everything that can be said on the agential view can be rephrased on the circumstantial view. But proponents of the circumstantial view like Smith are not simply trying to say the same thing in a different or more flexible way. They do not intend haecceitistic properties to count as possible circumstances, because the motivation for accepting this view is that it builds into the very structure of the reason relation the idea that whenever people have reasons, it is in virtue of some *general* property that they have.

We saw in the last section that the question of whether reasons favor propositions or act-types is very closely related to the paradox of deontology, which is one of the fundamental issues at stake between traditional deontological ethical theories and traditional act-consequentialism. The distinction between interpreting the reason relation as having an argument for agents or instead an argument for circumstances is closely related to a different fundamental dispute in ethical theory—between *generalism* and *particularism*.

Ethical generalism is the idea that general *principles* play a central role in ethics—that the answers to what we ought or ought not to do in any particular situation must be somehow derived from more general principles that cover not just this particular situation but also any others that are relevantly like it, and that the order of explanation is from the general to the particular. (Generalists also often hold that the epistemological *order of discovery* proceeds from the general to the particular, but that is a separate issue that is less closely related.) By contrast, ethical particularists hold that the answer to what we ought or ought not to do in some situation is not beholden to or explained by any general principle. Ethical particularism is what we get if we start from Sidgwick's criticisms of general ethical principles and then take that line of reasoning to its limit, without accepting either Sidgwick's or Ross's diagnoses of *why* each general principle is prone to counterexamples.

If generalists are right, then if there is a reason for Ryan to help Katie, there must be some general principle that explains why relevantly similar agents, in relevantly similar circumstances, would also have a reason to help Katie. Nothing follows about the structure of the reason relation, but the reverse is not true. Smith's circumstantial view codifies ethical generalism by requiring that reasons are, in the first instance, relative only to circumstances (which are general—sorry, no haecceities). On this view, the reason why it seems like different people have different reasons is just that some people are in the circumstances to which the reason is relative and some are not. So apparent differences in reasons between different people are always explained by something general. That is why, on this view, the answer to what someone ought or has reason to do is always explained by a general principle. Reasons themselves *are* general principles—not just something that there can be general principles about.

Smith's contemporary articulation of the idea that reasons are not relative to agents at all, strictly speaking, has precedents throughout much of the history of moral philosophy. Many of the British moralists of the seventeenth and eighteenth centuries, led by Ralph Cudworth and Richard Price, denied that obligations or duties were relative to agents in any deep sense, holding instead that what differs between agents is what they have to do in order to fulfill what is obligatory without qualification.[5]

Since Smith's circumstantial account of reasons is a kind of generalism *par excellence*, we could try to argue against it by arguing for ethical particularism. On the other hand, we cannot argue *for* the circumstantial account by arguing for ethical generalism, because the agential account is also compatible with moral generalism—it just doesn't bake it into the structure of the reason relation. On the agential view, it could very well be that every time there is a difference between Ryan's reasons and Rhonda's, there is a general principle that explains why in terms of general properties of Ryan that Rhonda does not share. But the circumstantial view implies more than this—it implies that whenever there is a difference between Ryan's and Rhonda's reasons, there is a single reason that applies to both,

---

[5] Cudworth [1731], Clarke [1706], Price [1748].

but that Rhonda is simply not in a position to act on. It turns out that this further commitment is something that we can try to evaluate—a task we turn to in the next section.

3.4 Reasons in the Absence of Reasons

So far in this chapter we've been exploring the relationship between our answers to what reasons count in favor of, and what else they might need to be relative to. Views according to which agents are *relata* of the normative reason relation are best thought of as natural *alternatives* to views according to which circumstances are relata of the normative reason relation, since each of these views aims to explain the seeming variability of reasons between people. And the Meinong-Chisholm view offers a way of dispensing with both the agent and the circumstance arguments by incorporating the appearance of agents into what reasons support, rather than by treating it as a separate argument in the reason relation. In this final section, we'll consider two more ways of trying to dispense with both agents and circumstances as arguments of the reason relation and show how both fit best as pieces of broader groups of commitments which hang together as packages.

The first and more obvious way of dispensing with both agents and circumstances is simply an extension of the same style of reasoning that led to the circumstantial view. That style of reasoning went like this: Ronnie and Bradley, in an example from Schroeder [2007b], seem to differ in their reasons. Whereas Ronnie likes to dance, Bradley does not, and so it appears that there is a reason for Ronnie to go to the party but not for Bradley to go. The agential view models this in the obvious way:

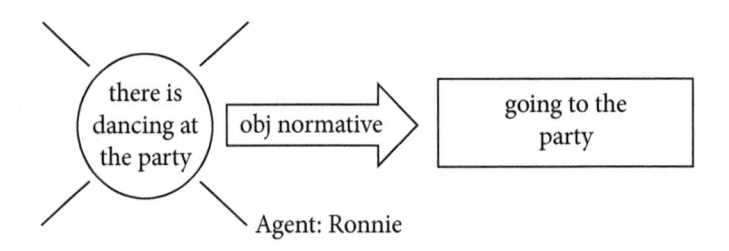

there is dancing at the party → obj normative → going to the party

Agent: Ronnie

However, according to the circumstantial view, the appearance of agent-relativity is explained away by a more general truth that accounts for the differences between agents in terms of a reason that is not relative to agents. For example, Smith would model the same situation like this:

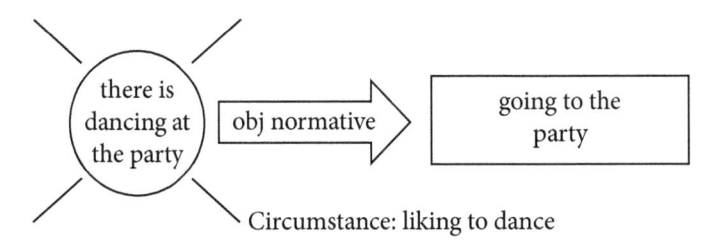

```
  there is                              going to the
  dancing at    obj normative  ⟹          party
  the party
        ↘  Circumstance: liking to dance
```

The difference between Ronnie and Bradley, on this view, is not whether there is any reason that one has and the other does not, but simply a difference in whether they are in the circumstances to which this reason applies, which is a general truth that holds for all agents.

But if we are tempted by this reasoning, why stop there? Notice that once we open up this possibility, we can dispense with circumstances altogether by putting them into what is *supported* by reasons:

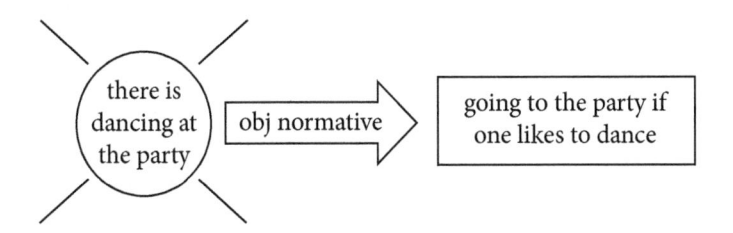

```
  there is                              going to the party if
  dancing at    obj normative  ⟹         one likes to dance
  the party
```

On this picture, as on the circumstantial view, there is no difference in what reasons there are for Ronnie and for Bradley. The difference is simply in the empirical question of what Ronnie and Bradley need to do, in order to act on this reason. Since Ronnie likes to dance, in order to comply with this reason he must go to the party. But since Bradley does not like to dance, he can comply with this reason by staying home.

Now, it might be unclear why the fact that there is dancing at the party is a reason in support of the act of (going to the party if you like to dance) or the outcome where you go to the party if you like to dance. And in fact, most philosophers who take this sort of view treat the things that one has reason to do not as things like (going to the party if you like to dance), but instead as things like (do what you like).

56 THE FUNDAMENTALS OF REASONS

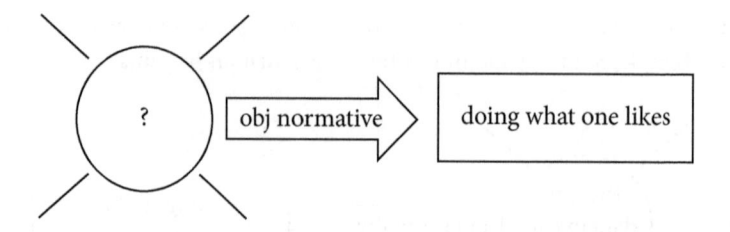

[diagram: circle labeled "?" with arrows, pointing via "obj normative" arrow to box "doing what one likes"]

Like the view immediately above, this view also eliminates the need for an agent or circumstance argument. However, it offers a different account of which reasons there are. On this view, the difference between Ronnie and Bradley is not between what they must do in order to go to the party if they like to dance, but rather a difference between what they must do in order to do what they like. And it is a major explanatory virtue of this view that it sweeps up explanatory generalizations that the previous view leaves on the table like why there is a reason for Bradley but not Ronnie to go to Shatto 39 Lanes when only Bradley likes bowling.

On the flip side, it is much less obvious *which* consideration or considerations give(s) a general reason to do what one likes. The answer cannot, presumably, be that you like it. Nor can it be any of the other specific features that we might otherwise think are reasons to do any of the specific things that you like if one likes sufficiently different things. But if there is any reason to do what you like, in general, then it seems that there must be some good answer to what it is. Strikingly, one possible way of defending this view is simply to deny that the fundamental reason relation requires any substance at all. Intuitively, there can be a defeasible obligation to be generous without any further question about what the reason that supports the obligation to be generous is, except one that is answered by 'to be generous'. Similarly, there can be a requirement not to kill without any further question about what the requirement not to kill is, except one that is answered by, 'not to kill'.

If the fundamental reason relation is like these, then it has no substance at all:

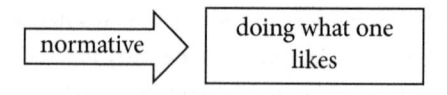

[diagram: box "normative" with arrow pointing to box "doing what one likes"]

This view can be unpacked as the view that it is an illusion that anything ever seems to do the supporting, that there is a substance to reasons. But alternatively, it can also be paired with the view that the sense in which some things—the reasons—support other things is derivative, so that the *reason* relation that has an agent for one of its arguments is simply to be understood as a roundabout way of telling us what the agent needs to do in order to do what the fundamental reason relation supports, which includes *neither* the agent nor what we might think of as the substance of the reason.

There are different ways of theorizing about this more fundamental reason relation. For example, in *The Possibility of Altruism*, Thomas Nagel effectively defined what it is for something to be a reason *for someone* in terms of the conditions under which *there is* a reason for something. If 'there is' expresses a quantifier, then this is a mistake, but we might read Nagel as endorsing a view on which 'there is a reason' talk is not quantificational, but picks out a different, and more fundamental, *reason relation*.

But more plausibly and defensibly, Daniel Fogal [2016] has argued that mass noun uses of 'reason', which we first introduced in Chapter 1 (for example, there is most reason for Jim to jam), do not require a substance of reasons, and pick out a more fundamental *reason* relation than count noun uses (for example, there is a strong reason for Jim to jam). As we've just seen, this makes it much easier for such uses to dispense with agent or circumstance arguments, as well, by adding those details to what the reason favors. Fogal's proposal that mass noun uses of 'reason' are more fundamental than count noun uses is therefore of central importance both for our understanding of the argument structure of the normative reason relation, and also for what it tells us about the prospects of subsuming differences in reasons between agents to an underlying similarity between agents—it is one of the most intriguing and, potentially, pervasively important developments in theorizing about reasons over the last decade.

An alternative, less obvious, way of dispensing with the role for agents in the normative reason relation begins by returning to our question from the previous chapter about the substance of normative and motivating reasons. According to one view—what we called the *dual-aspect content view*—the substance of normative reasons and of motivating reasons for action is the same—it is proposition-goal *pairs*, where a proposition is a potential object of belief that can be true or false and a goal is a potential object of desire that can be worthy or otherwise. On this view, a proposition-goal pair is an objective normative reason for action if its proposition is true and its goal is desirable, and a (potential) motivating reason if its proposition is believed and its goal is desired.[6] So this naturally leaves open the question of what the dual-aspect

---

[6] 'Desirable' expresses a normative quality—roughly, of being good, at least according to Mill. One natural interpretation of the dual-aspect approach thus places special importance on the good. But, as we will see in Chapter 9, being good can be understood as being adequately supported by reasons for desire. So another interpretation of the view places special importance on reasons for desire, which we must hold distinct from reasons for action or run into a

view should say happens when these conditions are combined in various ways. For example, is there anything interesting to say about a proposition-goal pair when its proposition is believed and its goal is desirable? Or if its proposition is true and its goal is desired?

It is highly natural for the proponent of the dual-aspect view to hold that when a proposition is believed and a goal is desirable, that makes the proposition-goal pair a *subjective* normative reason (holding fixed that the proposition and objective are appropriately related). For example, suppose that although Jim *hasn't* ingested a particular poison, Jane believes that he has. The only way to save Jim's life—a desirable goal if ever there was one—when he has ingested this poison is to give him the antidote. Jane knows that only the antidote cures the poison. But she doesn't care whether Jim lives or dies. In that situation, although she harms no one by dumping the antidote down the drain, she is still criticizable for doing so. The dual-aspect view offers a simple explanation: there is a *subjective* reason for her to administer the antidote.

Consequently, one possibility that is worth exploring is that the apparent agent-relativity in objective normative reasons is covered by agent-relativity in whether the agent desires the objective associated with the reason. So, for example, to take the party case, on this view we don't say that whether someone desires to dance changes what they have objective normative reasons to do. Instead, we say that the difference between people who desire to dance and people who do not is that people who desire to dance satisfy one of the important possession conditions on the objective normative reason to go to the party that people who do not desire to dance do not.

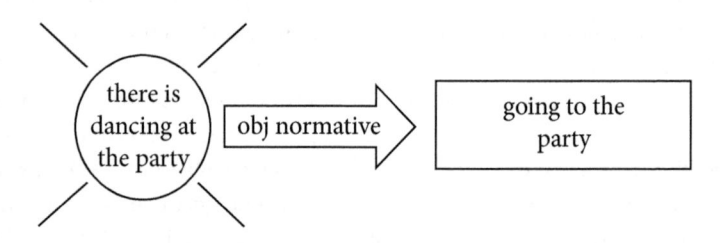

there is dancing at the party → obj normative → going to the party

problematic circularity, suggested at the end of Cunningham [2003] and as we discuss in Chapter 10. Fortunately, we have independent cause to hold reasons for action and desire apart. Not only they are *for* different kinds of things, we *act* for an end but we do not *intrinsically desire* for any further end. So the best version of the dual-aspect account of reasons should be interpreted as putting something else—not the object of a desire—as the second component of reasons for sentiments such as desire, fear, love, and so on.

Like Fogal's idea that count noun uses of 'reason' reduce to mass noun uses, this idea is underexplored, although we will return to it in Chapter 5, and it has the potential to reshape how we think about the differences between agents who seem in some sense to have different reasons. Since much of moral theory and many of the most important skeptical argument in metaethics turn on questions about the relationship between universal and non-universal reasons, it is especially important to work out the implications and prospects of different and potentially surprising ways of thinking about these fundamental relationships.

Chapter Summary

In this chapter we have explored the question of what other things the thing that counts as a reason must be related to, in order to count as a reason, focusing on the most obvious arguments that seem to be implied by the structure of ordinary reason ascriptions. On all natural views reasons count in favor of *something*, and we explored and compared the answer that what they count in favor of is an *outcome* to the answer that what they count in favor of is an *action*. Reasons are also often thought to be relative to agents in some way, with different reasons for different agents, and we considered various ways of resisting this conclusion and how they are connected to different conceptions of what reasons favor.

Recommended Reading

For discussion of the Meinong-Chisholm thesis, see John Horty's *Agency and Deontic Logic*, and for a closer look at different ways of understanding the role of qualifiers like 'for Ronnie' in normative reason ascriptions, seek Mark Schroeder's 'Reasons and Agent-Neutrality'. The idea that reasons are relative to circumstances rather than agents is prominently defended in chapter six of *The Moral Problem* though Smith does not pay explicit attention to its contrasts with the idea that the *reason* relation has a place for agents. The example of Ronnie and Bradley comes from Mark Schroeder's *Slaves of the Passions*. We recommend that this chapter pairs particularly well with a reading about the paradox of deontology—for example, chapter five of Shelly Kagan's *The Limits of Morality* or Christopher McMahon's 'The Paradox of Deontology'.

Exercises

3.1 *Comprehension.* Give examples of three sentences in which 'for' is used as a preposition and of three sentences in which it is used as a complementizer. Be sure to use sentences that do not involve the word 'reason'. How can you tell the difference?

3.2 *Extensions.* Assume that there are reasons for each of Ally, Hally, and Sally to win the race, and that the Meinong-Chisholm view is true. How would you go about resisting the argument that Ally should lose, since two reasons count against her winning, and only one counts in favor?

3.3 *Extensions.* In section 3.1 we observed that in English, 'for' is both a complementizer and a preposition, which is what makes each of two competing interpretations of 'for Jim' initially plausible in 'there is a reason for Jim to jump'. For this exercise, use translation software (if you need to) to try to look at how 'there is a reason for Jim to jump' would be expressed in both French and German. Can you tell whether the word translating 'for' is a complementizer or a preposition? Is the answer the same in both languages?

3.4 *Extensions.* In section 3.2 we considered the view that agents can figure both as relata of the reason relation and as part of what reasons are for, and argued briefly that this is too flexible, on the grounds that it does not make sense for Lucy to have a reason for Larry to do something. For this exercise, give the best examples that you can to try to motivate the view that this actually does make sense. What, if any, features of your examples contribute toward making them more plausible? What moral do you draw about the force of our argument from the text?

3.5 *Comprehension.* Explain why Smith's view that reasons are relative to circumstances rather than agents counts as a kind of ethical *generalism*.

3.6 *Extensions.* In *Being Realistic About Reasons*, Scanlon claims that the fundamental reason relation has four arguments: for a proposition that is the reason, an agent, a circumstance, and an act-type. So every basic reason fact has the form $R(p, x, c, a)$. But in section 3.3 we suggested that the views on which reasons are relative to circumstances and that they are relative to agents are *alternatives* to one another. Construct the best case that you can for why reasons might need to be relative to *both* circumstances and agents. Are you convinced? Or can Scanlon drop one of these relata from his view of the reason relation?

3.7 *Extensions*. According to the views canvassed in section 3.4, the fundamental normative *reason* relation does not have an argument place for either an agent or a circumstance. On these views, the only sense in which something can be a reason for one agent to do something but not another, or a reason to do it with respect to one circumstance but not another, is that the former agent's circumstances contingently require her to do this thing, in order to do something else that there is reason to do. Yet one of the most prominent forms of moral skepticism consists in the claim that there is something deeply puzzling about how there could be anything that is "objectively prescriptive", in the sense that it entails that there are reasons that are shared by every possible agent. What should proponents of these views about the argument structure of the fundamental *reason* relation say about the force of this kind of moral skepticism?

4
Structure

4.1 Explicit and Implicit Structure

So far, we've been examining what we have tentatively called the explicit structure of the reason relation. This kind of structure is often made explicit in everyday ascriptions of reasons, though, as we also saw, on some views those everyday ascriptions can be misinterpreted as suggesting that the reason relation is more complex than it in fact is. In this section, we'll explore how various philosophers have defended space for additional arguments in the reason relation, beyond those made explicit by claims like "the fact that the Cubs are playing the Dodgers tonight is a reason for us to go to Wrigley". These defenses are interesting not just for what they might tell us about the reason relation, but also for what they tell us about the differing methodological presuppositions that underlie different philosophers' theorizing about reasons.

Our main aim in this chapter is not to determine, once and for all, what belongs in the reason relation and what doesn't. Our aim is to uncover some of the implicit methodological assumptions underlying inquiry into reasons by examining how those assumptions motivate the inclusion of non-standard arguments in the reason relation. Nevertheless, this discussion is not entirely uncritical. We will present arguments for and against thinking of the reason relation as these philosophers do, hoping to illuminate various ways to approach questions about reasons.

4.2 The Strength or Weight of Reasons

As we've seen, Ross held that our moral duty—our 'duty proper'—is the product of competing moral forces which he called *prima facie* duties. According to the view described in *The Right and the Good*, something is one's *prima facie* duty just in case it tends to be one's duty proper. But things can tend toward an outcome to different degrees. Failing to write the final exam tends to make it the case that one fails the class more than failing to study for it does. Moral duties are similar. That you've promised your fiancé to show up to the wedding tends to make it the case that you should keep the promise more than promising a friend to meet them for tennis. And that there is a violent catastrophe in the small town where you are the only emergency room physician tends to make it the case that you shouldn't show up for either the wedding or the tennis more than either promise to show.

Philosophers now call these elemental normative forces, which sometimes pull us in opposed directions, 'normative reasons' and many think that facts about the competition between them explain what you should do, in various senses. But to explain what you should do on the basis of the relevant reasons, we need to explain how competition between reasons works. This latter explanation requires a measure of the degree to which a group of reasons favors an option to be able to adjudicate whether those reasons win the competition with countervailing ones.

Philosophers increasingly discuss the degree to which a reason tends to make some option one's duty proper using the term 'weight'. The more a reason tends to make some option one's duty proper, the more weight that reason has or the weightier that reason is. Thus, in this terminology, outcomes of competitions between reasons turn on facts about their weight. As we will see, the term 'weight' carries some misleading implications, such as that the normative forces associated with reasons are additive in the manner of mass.

The importance of weight to reasons' use in moral philosophy foregrounds the central questions of this chapter and the last one: what belongs in the reason relation and why? On the one hand, we don't need to refer to a reason's weight to ascribe it. When I claim that a reason to visit France is that it is literally illegal to sell sub-standard baguette there, I haven't 'left something out' of my claim. I could add that it's a strong (or weak) reason to visit, but that would be an addition to what I've already said, not an elucidation of it. Similarly, if Wilma runs to the store, then she either runs quickly or slowly, and either with a limp or without one, but these are extra things to say about how she runs, not extra *relata* of the *running to* relation.

On the other hand, however, we may think that the role of the reason relation is to keep track of important dimensions of variation between reasons. Weight is an important dimension of variation between reasons. On these assumptions, weight's importance to a theory of reasons earns it a place in the reason relation. This is the approach taken by John Skorupski in his book *The Domain of Reasons*.¹ Skorupski claims that one of the *relata* of the reason relation needs to be occupied by a *weight*, and his view seems to be motivated by a general concern to represent each dimension of variation between reasons as an argument in the reason relation.²

According to Skorupski, when the fact that it is illegal in France to sell sub-standard baguette is a weighty reason for Nathan to visit France, that is because the reason relation holds between Nathan, the fact that it is illegal to sell sub-standard baguette in France, a time, a degree of weight, and the act of visiting France:

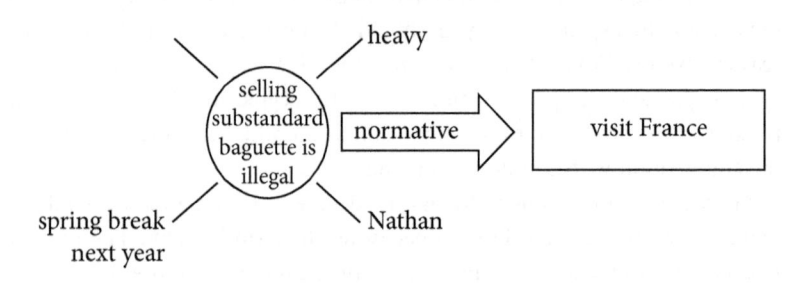

In addition to this metaphysical view about the occupants of the reason relation, Skorupski also holds the corresponding semantic thesis that the semantics of the predicate 'is a reason' reflects the metaphysical structure of the reason relation. The predicate 'is a reason for' is true of some fact, agent, act, time, and degree just in case the fact is a specific reason that favors that agent performing that act at that time to that degree.

These semantic claims are optional and do not follow from Skorupski's metaphysics of the reason relation. We've seen how Smith's view can make sense of the ascriptions of reasons to individual agents even though his reason relation expresses the property of a fact being a specific reason of a certain strength relative only to a circumstance. By the same token, the structure of Skorupski's semantics for 'is a reason' needn't perfectly mirror the structure he imputes to the reason relation. The semantic view does not follow from the metaphysical one. As a result, we'll focus on the metaphysical thesis.

As we've suggested, Skorupski's conception of the reason relation seems motivated by the concern to collect all the important dimensions of

---

¹ Skorupski [2010].
² Scanlon [2014] similarly distinguishes the reason relation from the *conclusive* reason relation.

variation between reasons. For example, his reason relation represents the agent-relativity of certain reasons through the agent argument. Likewise, he recognizes variation in what reasons favor or support through the response argument. But if we are going to represent *all* dimensions of variation between reasons in the reason relation, then we have to go further. Variation across times and variation across worlds is often treated similarly in logic and language—indeed it is common in formal semantics to lump values for both times and worlds into a single 'index', which covers both for the purposes of assigning truth to a sentence.

Likewise, reasons for action can differ in their normative 'flavor': there are moral reasons for giving to charity—it will help the needy—and prudential reasons for doing so—it will earn me praise. This is an important difference between reasons, but not one represented in Skorupski's vision of the reason relation. As a result, we are left to wonder whether Skorupski would expand his relation to include these new arguments, or whether there's a principled reason for excluding them—that is, whether every dimension of variation between reasons merits recognition in the reason relation or only some.

Assessing Skorupski's proposal also requires understanding the gradable nature of weight for reasons. But you might worry that his proposal codifies a strange and unattractive way of thinking about units of measurement on the one hand, and the relations that they represent, on the other. We can see just how strange it is by comparing other cases of things that come in degrees. A reason's weight, like a person's height, comes in degrees. Just as some reasons are *weightier than* others, some people are *taller than* others. There are two ways to understand the relationship between monadic properties like weight and height and dyadic gradable properties like weightier than and taller than. One is to understand these monadic properties as derivative on the dyadic ones, understanding being tall in terms of being taller than and understanding a reason's weight in terms of what it outweighs. Or we could reverse this relationship, understanding the dyadic properties in terms of the monadic ones, e.g., understanding the fact that Mark is taller than Nathan as derivative on the fact that Mark is 6'3" and Nathan is 5'9". It is this second option that Skorupski's view encodes into the structure of the reason relation.

But the problem with the second method of defining the gradable in terms of the absolute is that we must identify the unit that qualifies the absolute property. In the case of height, the choice between units is arbitrary: do we use metric or imperial? Perhaps Planck lengths? It would be an odd bit of imperial parochialism if the fact that Mark is taller than Nathan depended on the fact that Mark is 6′3″ and Nathan is 5′9″ but not on the fact that Mark is 190.5 cm and Nathan is 175.25 cm. Correspondingly, understanding the relational property of one reason being weightier than another in terms of the non-relational weights of the first and second reason, we end up in an odd situation where arbitrary facts about weight—arbitrary because they involve an arbitrary choice of unit of measurement for reasons' weight—underly non-arbitrary facts about which reasons are weightier than others.

When you win the race, *perhaps* there's some philosopher's sense in which you stand in a relation to the number one. Perhaps there are contexts where it's useful to foreground your relation to that number. But you're not the winner in virtue of standing in that relation. Rather, the fact that you come out on top in each pairwise comparison with your competitors explains why you stand in that relation. If a reason's weight is anything like the properties of being tall or of being the winner, then facts about weight are explained by an anti-symmetric, irreflexive, transitive ordering on the total set of reasons for an agent to do (or feel or believe) something, representing the winner in each pairwise competition between reasons for someone to do something. Given that *competition* is fundamental to reasons' explanatory role, we should not be surprised that the relational property modeling that competition is fundamental to a reason's weight.

According to a contrary methodological perspective, a kind of entity deserves an argument place in the reason relation when that entity is fundamental to explaining a consideration's status as a reason. But if the comparison with other gradable properties is sound, then facts about weight are less fundamental than facts about reasons and how they compete. So it does not make sense to put weight in the reason relation: weights don't exist prior to reasons; weights exist only as a derivative abstraction away from metaphysically prior facts about reasons and how they compete. Reasons come in different weights, and cats come in different colors. But the fundamental explanation of what it is to be a cat does not need to mention what color it is. Likewise, the fundamental explanation of what it is to be a reason does not need to mention what weight it is.

4.3 Sets of Alternatives?

The previous chapter examines whether reasons favor act-types or whether they favor outcomes, propositions, or the like. Acts and outcomes have something in common. They are simple objects, which is why we can use the word 'option' while remaining neutral between the two. We haven't offered much explanation of what it is for a reason to favor an option—indeed, it's one of the most disputed questions about reasons. Nevertheless, philosophers generally find it apt to describe the relation between a reason and an option as the former "counting in favor" of the latter.

One of the prominent forms of resistance to the idea that reasons "count in favor" comes from the work of Pamela Hieronymi [2005], who argues that talk about reasons counting in favor is unacceptably imprecise in a way that leads to avoidable mistakes. According to Hieronymi, reasons don't just count in favor of options; they *bear on a question*.[3] But because reasons still support particular answers to questions, Hieronymi's view should not be interpreted as the view that reasons count toward questions *instead* of actions or outcomes, but rather as the view that questions are one of the necessary relata of reasons—that what a reason counts in favor of is always closely connected to one of the answers to a question on which that reason bears.

For example, Hieronymi says that because the only way to form a belief about whether p is to settle the question whether p, reasons to believe that p must bear on the question whether p.

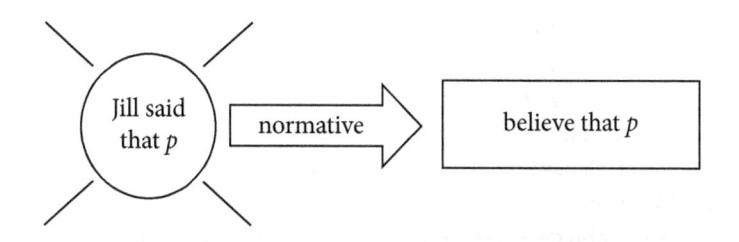

[diagram: "Jill said that p" →(normative)→ "believe that p"]

A significant part of the motivation for Hieronymi's view is to explain the difference between the way that my offering you one million dollars to believe that I am poverty-stricken counts in favor of your believing that I am living below the poverty line, and the way that learning that I am eligible for SNAP benefits counts in favor of it.[4] Both intuitively in some sense "count in favor", but this is misleading because these are two very

---

[3] Artūrs Logins [2022] develops this approach in detail, identifying an ambiguity in the question of whether to φ that, he argues, accounts for reasons' two roles.

[4] SNAP is the United States' Supplemental Nutrition Assistance Program for providing in-kind food benefits to those in poverty, commonly referred to as "food stamps".

different ways of counting in favor. Only the latter bears on the question of whether I am living below the poverty line.

It turns out that this is not the only reason why we might want to add questions as one of the *relata* of the reason relation. Suppose that we continue to talk about reasons as counting in favor of—or *favoring*—actions or outcomes. Characterizing the relation between a reason and an option this way makes certain principles seem natural. For example, it's natural to assume a principle often called *Exclusivity*, according to which if a reason favors an option it cannot also *disfavor* it.[5]

Exclusivity For all facts r, agents s, and actions φ, if r is a reason for s to φ, then it's not the case that r is also a reason for s not to φ.

If the fact that the restaurant is serving Cobb salad gives a reason, that reason *either* favors going or it favors staying away. Even if the avocado in the salad attracts you and its eggs repel you, the attraction or repulsion exerted by those ingredients compete to determine a single answer for what the reason favors. Or so it seems natural to assume.

However, the principle appears vulnerable to counterexamples. Dancy offers the following.[6] Suppose you really like meeting famous people. In that case, if the person sitting at the bar is famous, that's a reason to introduce yourself to them. However, you also know that famous people snub people like you. You hate getting snubbed. In that case, that the person at the bar is famous is a reason *not* to introduce yourself to them. The fact that someone is famous in Dancy's scenario appears to be both a reason to introduce yourself to them and a reason not to introduce yourself to them.

Exclusivity also faces a second challenge. It's not only natural to claim that the fact that I'm sleepy is a reason to drink coffee, it's also natural to claim that the fact that I'm sleepy is a reason to drink coffee *rather than tea* and it may favor getting a good night's rest rather than drinking either. So it's natural to use *contrastive* expressions such as 'rather than'. These expressions might not seem especially troublesome to the simple conception of the 'favoring' relation captured by Exclusivity. It might seem that "the fact that I'm sleepy is a reason to get coffee rather than an uncaffeinated beverage" is

---

[5] Snedegar [2013, 236] notes that Nagel [1970], Raz [1999], and Crisp [2000] appear committed to *Exclusivity*. Here we are deliberately being somewhat casual about whether it is worth distinguishing between a reason disfavoring some option or counting in favor of not taking it, but we will return to this issue in some detail in Chapter 9.

[6] Dancy [1993, 62].

true just when and because the fact that I'm sleepy favors getting coffee more strongly than it favors getting any uncaffeinated beverage. More generally, we might think that "P favors o rather than o_1 or o_2 or ... o_n" is true just when and because the degree to which P favors o is greater than the degree to which P favors any of the alternatives.

But contrastive uses of reasons present a deeper challenge to Exclusivity. Consider the following pair of claims:

1. "The fact that campus is twenty miles away is a reason to drive to campus rather than bike there."
2. "The fact that campus is twenty miles away is a reason to bike to campus rather than run there."

According to the simple explanation of contrastive reason ascriptions, (1) is true because the fact that campus is twenty miles away favors driving there to a greater degree than it favors biking there. If Exclusivity is true, the reason why that fact favors driving rather than biking is that it does not favor biking at all. Otherwise, if favored biking to any degree, we'd have a violation of Exclusivity, for there would be a fact that favored an option (driving) and favored something incompatible with that first option (biking, a way of not driving). The trouble emerges when we run the very same argument again on (2), which implies that the fact that campus is twenty miles way is a reason to bike to campus. So combining the simple explanation of (1) and (2) with Exclusivity produces the contradiction that the fact that campus is twenty miles away is both a reason to bike to campus and not a reason to bike to campus.

As a result, we have *two* distinct challenges to Exclusivity. And so its initial intuitive plausibility gives us a new tool with which to probe the argument structure of the reason relation. Perhaps by adding arguments to the reason relation, we can sufficiently fine-grain reasons so that Exclusivity turns out to be true after all. This is what Justin Snedegar argues. He claims that the reason relation contains an argument space for *sets of alternative options*.[7] He calls this view a contrastive theory of reasons, or *reasons contrastivism*.[8] Contrastivism about reasons

---

[7] Philosophers appeal to contrasts to help answer a wide range of questions. See Sinnott-Armstrong [2008], Schaffer [2004], Hitchcock [1996].

[8] Snedegar [2013], expanded on and defended in more detail in Snedegar [2017]. In [2014], [2017] Snedegar develops other arguments for contrastivism about reasons.

is particularly natural given reasons' explanatory role, because contrastivist accounts of explanation are popular outside of ethics.

According to a common view in the philosophy of language, questions are just sets of alternatives—alternatives that are given by the possible answers to a question. For example, the question of whether the cat is on the mat is the set {the cat is on the mat, the cat is not on the mat}, and the question of who stole the cookies is some set like {Alice stole the cookies, Bob stole the cookies, Catherine stole the cookies...}. So the view that reasons favor options only relative to the sets of alternatives to which they are being compared turns out to be another version of Hieronymi's thesis that reasons are relative to questions—simply motivated in a different way.

Snedegar's contrastivism is compatible with any of the views from Chapter 3, but here is what it looks like on one of those options:

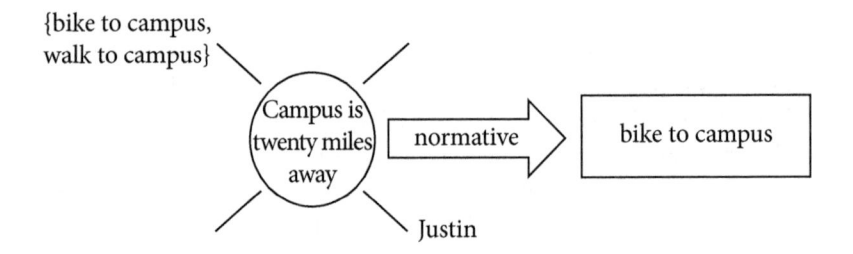

{bike to campus, walk to campus}

Campus is twenty miles away → normative → bike to campus

Justin

Snedegar's contrastive approach is designed to handle puzzles like the one presented by (1) and (2). The fact that campus is twenty miles away favors biking when the alternative is running but not driving—a straightforward solution.

However, the contrastive reason relation does not present a clear solution to Dancy's famous person case. After all, there seem to be only two alternatives: to introduce yourself or to refrain from doing so. The fact that the person is famous can't be a reason for both if Exclusivity is true. If favoring is a brute, unanalyzable relation holding between facts, agents, and options, then it's somewhat mysterious how one fact can favor an option and simultaneously disfavor it. But it's less mysterious if whether a fact favors an option is explained in other terms, say, in terms of whether it helps to produce some value or tends toward the satisfaction of a desire. On these kinds of views, which we will explore in Chapter 7, it's unmysterious how situations like Dancy's famous person can arise, so long as there are at least two values or desires that explain why certain considerations give reasons. If a reason favors an option only relative to a value or desire, then the same fact can favor an option relative to one value or desire and favor an incompatible option relative to a different value or desire. In Dancy's case, the fact that the person at the bar is famous favors introducing yourself relative to your objective of meeting famous people but it favors refraining from introducing yourself relative to your objective of not being snubbed. This explanation of Dancy's case permits us to articulate a different way of capturing Exclusivity:

Weak Exclusivity For all facts r, agents s, actions φ, and objectives o, if r is a reason for s to φ relative to o, then it's not the case that r is also a reason for s not to φ relative to o.

Objectives play an irreducible role in reasons' favoring certain options. This warrants including them in the reason relation, even if explicit mention of objectives is not necessary for making sense of everyday reasons ascriptions. The resulting view looks like this, where 'to get bragging rights' is one possible candidate for the objective relative to which the fact that the person at the bar is famous is a reason for Jonathan to introduce himself:

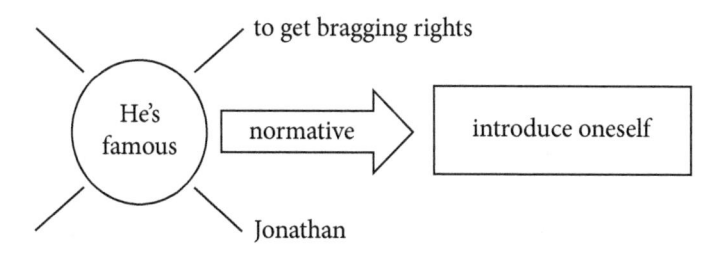

It turns out that the idea that the reason relation has an argument place for objectives has also been independently motivated. But it also turns out that its answer to Dancy's counterexample to Exclusivity can be coopted by other views, as well.

4.4 The End-Relational Theory of Reasons

One reason to suspect that the reason relation itself has a place for objectives comes from Stephen Finlay's *end-relational theory* of normative concepts. According to the view that Finlay defends in *A Confusion of Tongues*, every word that can be used with a normative meaning expresses a relation with a place for what he calls an *end* parameter, where an end is basically what we have called an *objective* or a *goal*—a possible object of desire.[9] Since the word 'reason' can be used with a normative meaning—to make claims about normative reasons—Finlay holds, in our terms, that the reason relation has an argument place for an objective. It is therefore worth looking in more detail at Finlay's view, in order to get a better look at how we might independently motivate the view that the reason relation has an argument place for objectives.

Finlay's own motivation for holding this view about reasons is slightly indirect, because he endorses the claim that normative reasons are just explanatory reasons of why an act would promote some good—and he has a prior motivation for endorsing an end-relational theory about 'good'. Finlay's argument that 'good' expresses a relation to ends starts with the hypothesis that a single concept is expressed in myriad uses:

1. "Chocolate is good."
2. "Isaac Albéniz's piano compositions are good."
3. "Friends are good."
4. "Jim's escape plan is good."
5. "Voting is good."

Finlay argues that the best, and perhaps the only, way of unifying these diverse uses of 'good' under a single concept is to suppose that 'good' expresses a many-place relational concept. 'Good' sometimes appears to be a monadic predicate, such as in (1), only because context implicitly supplies the values of its other parameters.

Of these, Finlay argues that one is a parameter for ends for, he argues, we can only make sense of the full range of evaluative ascriptions by supposing that something is good only relative to the promotion of certain ends. So on Finlay's view, (1) may express, in an appropriate context, the claim that chocolate is good *for people to eat in order to have pleasure*. And (5) may express, again in an appropriate context, the claim that voting is good *for eligible voters to do in order to sustain a healthy democracy*. These ways of making claims about what is good make explicit what is only implicit or supplied by context in sentences (1) and (5)—namely, that claim (1) is to be understood relative to the arguments *for people to eat* and *in order to have pleasure*, and similarly for (5). The 'in order to' clauses express what Finlay calls the *end* arguments of 'good'.

---

[9] Finlay [2014].

Because 'good' is relative to ends and normative reasons are just explanatory reasons of what is good, Finlay argues, normative reasons must be relative to ends as well—they will inherit their end parameter from the 'good' claim that they are understood in relation to. So, for example, 'the fact that the dessert contains chocolate is a reason to order it' can be true because it explains why ordering the dessert promotes your eating it, and it is good for you to eat chocolate in order for you to have pleasure. So the relevant end in this case would be *that you have pleasure*. In Finlay's hands, the hypothesis that both 'good' and 'reason' claims as well as 'ought' and 'must' claims are relative to ends in this way is a powerful explanatory hypothesis that he goes on to use to explain many other features of moral thought, communication, and motivation.

We saw in the last three chapters that many of the structural questions about the arguments of the reason relation are closely related to important questions from many different areas of normative ethics and metaethics. The question of whether the substance of a subjective normative reason is a fact is closely related to the question of whether rationality is internal. The question of whether normative reasons support propositions or act-types is closely related to the debate between traditional act-consequentialism and deontology. The question of whether reasons are relative to agents or to circumstances is closely related to the debate between generalists and particularists. And likewise in Finlay's hands, the question of whether reason claims are relative to ends is closely related to the question of whether normative claims can all be exhaustively conceptually analyzed in fully naturalistic, non-normative terms—the thesis known in metaethics as *analytic naturalism*.

The reason that Finlay holds that his end-relational theory of normative concepts constitutes a defense of analytic naturalism is that he thinks that all that it takes for chocolate to be good for you to eat in order for you to experience pleasure is just for it to be true that if you eat chocolate, that makes it more likely that you will experience pleasure. Once we clarify all of the *relata* of 'good' claims, Finlay argues, the sense of normativity drops out, and what makes this claim feel normative is just the conversational background in which we *adopt* the objective of your experiencing pleasure as one of our aims. So Finlay's thesis that normative concepts are end-relational does not by itself entail analytic naturalism, but it is the central ingredient in his defense of analytic naturalism.

Finlay's end-relational theory of value provides an indirect argument for an end-relational theory of reasons, especially to analytic naturalists.

Consequently, there is some reason to think that there is a place in the reason relation for an objective, especially if one is an analytic naturalist attracted to Finlay's style of analysis. But defending this claim of Finlay's view involves defending not only his analytic reduction of goodness but also his method of analyzing reasons using goodness. Finlay's view therefore provides only weak support to Exclusivity, and therefore only weak support to a contrastivist account of the reason relation according to which alternatives not options are the things that reasons favor.

4.5 The Dual-Aspect Theory of Reasons, Redux

An alternative motivation for finding objectives in reasons is much more direct. We've seen that Finlay's theory locates objectives in reasons by arguing that objectives are an independent argument place of the reason relation. But there is a different possibility for how objectives could figure in reasons. And it is that objectives are already present as part of one of the uncontroversial constituents of the reason relation. This is what is held by the dual-aspect theory of reasons, first introduced in Chapter 2.

According to the dual-aspect theory, normative reasons for action are the contents of the belief-desire pairs that Davidson took to be our motivating reasons. So, on this view, the substance of normative reasons already has objectives or goals built into it. So the dual-aspect theory makes room for objectives in reasons without the need to postulate objectives as an extra argument of the reason relation.

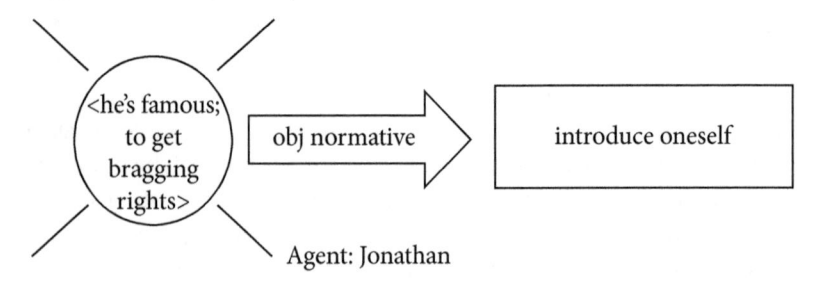

<he's famous; to get bragging rights> → obj normative → introduce oneself

Agent: Jonathan

But we can now see that this view allows for a simple explanation of Dancy's objection to the principle of Exclusivity. Recall the intuitive formulation of this principle:

Exclusivity For all facts r, agents s, and actions φ, if r is a reason for s to φ, then it's not the case that r is also a reason for s not to φ.

Dancy's case of meeting the famous person appears to be a counterexample to Exclusivity. However, the counterexample depends on assuming that the dual-aspect view of normative reasons is false. As Snedegar rightly observes, Dancy's case succeeds as a counterexample to Exclusivity because a single fact can favor one act relative to one objective, and disfavor that act relative to a different objective. In Dancy's case, the fact that the person is famous favors introducing yourself relative to your objective of meeting famous people but disfavors introducing yourself relative to your objective of not getting snubbed. But this case succeeds as a counterexample to Exclusivity only by assuming that reasons are facts. Consider a closely related principle, which is neutral about the ontology of reasons:

Exclusivity* For all objects r, agents s, and actions φ, if r is a reason for s to φ, then it's not the case that r is also a reason for s not to φ.

Dancy's case is a counterexample to Exclusivity* only if one and the same reason both favors and disfavors introducing yourself. But it's clear that, according to the dual-aspect view, there are at least *two* reasons given by the fact that the person is famous. The first is the pair of the fact that the person is famous and your objective of meeting famous people. And the second is the pair of that same fact and your objective of not getting snubbed. But neither of these pairs counts both in favor of and against introducing yourself. On the contrary, while the first pair favors introducing yourself, the second favors not introducing yourself. Because on this view reasons are pairs and the first and second reason are distinct objects, there's actually no violation of Exclusivity*. So the dual-aspect theory offers a different way of preserving the intuitive idea of exclusivity that does not require postulating extra parameters—just taking on specific commitments about the substance of reasons.

In this chapter, we've seen that very different kinds of methodological considerations can be marshaled for and against including different extra arguments of the reason relation. This might be motivated, as in Skorupski's case, by trying to capture all of the ways in which reasons can be different. But we have seen some reasons to be skeptical about whether this is a sound basis for adding potential arguments to the reason relation, as well as about some of Skorupski's particular applications. We have also seen how Finlay triangulated on the argument structure of reasons by independently arguing for conclusions about the argument structure of goodness, and appealing to a bridge principle about the relation between reasons and goodness. And we have seen how to leverage putative counterexamples to *a priori* highly plausible general principles about reasons.

We don't claim that these methodologies are exhaustive—only that they show that there are many potential ways to try to get leverage on this question, and that answers to questions about the argument structure of reasons have a surprising range of applications to independently important questions from a wide variety of areas of ethical theory.

Chapter Summary

In this chapter we have extended our gaze to consider the possibility that some things mentioned explicitly only sometimes in reason ascriptions might also be important *relata* of the reason relation. The main possibilities that we considered are *weights*, *questions*, and *objectives*, though there remain other possibilities that we did not consider here. We argued against the view that the reason relation needs to include weights in order to allow for the fact that reasons do have weights. But both the view that reasons are relative to questions and the view that they are relative to ends are the kinds of views that will pervasively shape how we think about other questions about reasons.

Recommended Reading

The introduction to Lord and Maguire's *Weighing Reasons* offers a still-current overview of many of the issues surrounding reasons' weight. Skorupski's discussion of the weight of reasons is in his master monograph *The Domain of Reasons*, and Mark Schroeder argues against absolute weights for reasons in chapter seven of *Slaves of the Passions*. The classic statements of Hieronymi's question view are in her papers 'The Wrong Kind of Reason' and 'Controlling Attitudes'. Snedegar develops contrastivism about reasons in a series of papers and in his book *Contrastive Reasons*, and Finlay discusses the end-relativity of reasons in chapter four of *A Confusion of Tongues*. Howard's dual-aspect theory of reasons is stated in his 'Primary Reasons as Normative Reasons'. This chapter pairs particularly well with reading chapter one of Snedegar's *Contrastive Reasons*.

Exercises

4.1 *Comprehension.* Some reasons are for people in North America, while others are for people in Australia. Should there be an argument place for continents in the objective normative reason relation? Why or why not?

4.2 *Extensions.* A swimming pool (at a time in a circumstance) has a certain temperature; this fact is not brute—something explains it. Do features of temperature explain why the temperature of the pool is the way it is? Do features of the pool explain why the pool is the temperature that it is?

If you answered yes to only one, which and why? Repeat the questions replacing 'pool' and 'swimming pool' with *reason* and 'temperature' with 'weight'. Do we get the same answers? Why or why not?

4.3 *Extensions.* In section 4.3 we noted that on Hieronymi's view the thing that the reason counts in favor of must be "closely related" to an answer to the question that the reason bears on, but in the reason diagram that we drew, they are not identical. On her view, the attitude that is supported by a reason is the one such that coming to form it is constituted by answering the question that the reason bears on. So, for example, the fact that Jill said that p counts in favor of believing that p because it supports the p answer to the question whether p, and believing that p is settling on that answer to the question of whether p. Notice that on this view, the question that each reason is relative to comes from a feature of the kind of attitude that it is a candidate to support. Can you extend this thesis to apply to reasons for action? Why or why not? What should Hieronymi say about the nature of reasons for action?

4.4 *Comprehension.* In section 4.3 we claimed that Snedegar's argument for contrastivism requires an appeal to exclusivity. Explain why it is not enough for Snedegar's argument to rely on the premise that both of sentences (1) and (2) are true.

4.5 *Extensions.* What do we lose if we give up exclusivity? We saw in Chapter 1 that it is attractive to explain what someone ought to do in terms of the relative weight of the reasons for them to do it and not to do it—weighing pros on one side of the balance and cons on the other side. Do such weighing explanations require exclusivity, or not? Use an example to make your discussion concrete.

4.6 *Extensions.* Dancy's famous person case challenges exclusivity for reasons for action. We can address the challenge by appealing to objectives. Do analogues to Dancy's case arise for reasons for belief? For reasons for feelings like fear or love? If not, why not? If so, should these latter challenges also be resolved with appeal to objectives? Why or why not?

4.7 *Extensions.* Finlay's indirect motivation for the end-relationality of normative reasons is very different from the dual-aspect theory's direct observation of apparent reports of reasons using 'to' clauses. What should Finlay say about the cases that motivate the dual-aspect theory?

PART 2
THE *PROVINCE* OF REASONS

5
Objective and Subjective Reasons

5.1 Two Dimensions of Assessment

In Part 1: *Parts*, we began to close in, investigating contrasting views about the substance of reasons and which sorts of things being a reason involves being related to. We haven't resolved any of these questions, though clearly we are more sympathetic to some answers than to others. In Part 2: *Province*, we turn our gaze outward, to look in more detail at the roles played by reasons. We will pay close attention, in particular, to the connection between objective and subjective reasons in Chapter 5, and the connections between reasons and evidence, explanation, and deliberation, in Chapters 6, 7, and 8, respectively.

We first introduced the distinction between objective and subjective reasons in Chapter 1. As we glossed it, the distinction between these reasons mirrors a distinction often made for 'ought'. Freddie, recall, likes to dance. If there's dancing at the party, and nothing else is at stake, then there's clearly a sense in which he ought to go—this is the objective sense. But 'ought' can also be used in a less objective way. If Freddie doesn't know that there will be dancing at the party, the lure of dancing has no pull. And if Freddie is under the false impression that there will be charades at the party and he *hates* charades, there's clearly a sense in which he *shouldn't* go—by his own lights he'd be pursuing misery. Cases like this support the common claim that 'ought' (like 'should') has a more subjective use as well, which is tied in some way to what's rational.

We can think of the objective and subjective uses of 'ought' as expressing two dimensions of normative assessment, which diverge when an agent's perspective diverges from the facts. When these diverge, what it makes sense for the agent to do can differ from what it is most advisable for her to do. Distinguishing these senses of 'ought' allows us to acknowledge both the respect in which an action can be a success, even though it was unwise, or can be a failure, even though it made sense.

How well each of these two uses of 'ought' are grounded in ordinary linguistic use is controversial. And philosophers also disagree much about which is more important, or the proper subject of ethical inquiry.

But the philosophers' distinction between subjective and objective need not depend on ordinary English. So long as it is genuinely useful to distinguish between two dimensions of normative assessment, we can make sense of what moral philosophers mean by 'objectively ought' and 'subjectively ought', even if it turns out that the word 'ought' in natural language can only be used in one of these ways. So we can think of this distinction as motivated *either* by the need for normative concepts to play each of two complementary roles in philosophy *or* by a natural language distinction.

As we saw in Chapter 1, this distinction between *ought*s seems mirrored by an analogous distinction between subjective and objective reasons. Like the distinction for 'ought', objective reasons are typically taken to come in some way from the facts, while subjective reasons are typically taken to come in some way from the agent's perspective. And like the distinction for 'ought', we can make the distinction for reasons *either* by the need for normative concepts to play each of two complementary roles *or* as motivated by a natural language distinction.

To make the distinction from conceptual roles, it suffices merely to begin with objective and subjective *ought*s and conjecture that if *ought*s are explained by reasons, then we will need two sorts of reasons to explain these two sorts of *ought*s. We can seemingly explain why Freddie ought to go the party, in the objective sense, by drawing attention to the fact that there will be dancing at the party. And we can seemingly explain why Freddie ought to avoid the party, in the subjective sense, by drawing attention to his belief that there will be charades at the party.

Although both kinds of reasons play similar roles in recommending some course of action in one way or another, they differ in that one in some intuitive sense reflects the facts while the other in some equally natural sense reflects Freddie's perspective on the facts. Because normative reasons can be either objective or subjective, an adequate understanding of the relationship between objective and subjective reasons must unpack this metaphor of reflecting a perspective, as well as answer what the priority relationship is between objective and subjective reasons. So it is to these two questions that we turn in the remainder of this chapter.

5.2 Reasons and Perspective

We can begin unpacking the metaphor of 'one's perspective on the facts' with two seemingly uncontroversial claims. First, if Freddie has *no idea* that there will be dancing at the party, the consideration that there will be dancing there is not part of Freddie's perspective on the world. Conversely, if he knows that there will be dancing at the party, the consideration *is* part of his perspective. So, somewhere between knowing a consideration and having no idea of it stands the psychological state responsible for a consideration being a subjective reason for Freddie to go to the party in virtue of being part of his perspective.[1] Unpacking the metaphor of perspective requires identifying this threshold epistemic condition that you must satisfy in order for something to be your subjective reason.

But on some views, unpacking perspective requires more. After all, knowing that there will be dancing at the party is not enough to make it rational to go there. This very same knowledge instead makes it rational for people who dislike dancing to stay away from the party, rather than to go to it. According to the *Humean Theory of Reasons*, both an agent's objective reasons and her subjective reasons depend on her desires—and in exactly the same way. Proponents of the Humean Theory will deny that Freddie's desire to dance is any part of his perspective on reasons—they will say instead that his perspective just comes from his awareness that there will be dancing, and his desire to dance plays the orthogonal role of making the fact that there will be dancing at the party a candidate to be either an objective or subjective reason for him to go there.

But the Humean Theory of Reasons is highly controversial, for reasons that we'll see in Chapter 7. And those who reject it may find it natural to allow that what it *makes sense* or is *rational* for someone to do depends on what she cares about or desires, while insisting that what it is *advisable* for her to do does not, or does so to a lesser extent. Indeed, historically far more philosophers have found it plausible that rationality depends on preferences than that advisability does. And even if both depend on preferences, it is plausible that rationality depends *more* on preference. If this is so, then we need to make room for something like desire as a component of the perspective in virtue of which you have the subjective reasons that you do.

So we should allow, at least in principle, that the kinds of perspective that give rise to subjective reasons are composed of two different kinds of states: one that comes from someone's having at least some idea of how things are, and one that comes from her goals. The standard way of distinguishing between these two kinds of state comes from Elizabeth Anscombe, who asks us to

---

[1] Compare Whiting [2014], who raises and answers broader problems about how to keep subjective reasons sufficiently dependent on the agent's perspective.

imagine a shopper filling his grocery cart according to a shopping list. On his list are the things he *wants* to buy. So if there is something in the cart that is not on the list or something on the list that is not in the cart, the error is the shopper's and not the list's. Desires are like the shopper's list; they have, in Anscombe's terminology, a 'world-to-mind' direction of fit.[2]

By contrast, Anscombe has us imagine that a detective is following the man around, recording what he buys in order to report back to his superiors. Now if there is something in the cart that is not on the detective's list or something on the list that is not in the cart, the error is the list's, not the shopper's. For unlike the shopper's list, the whole point of the detective's list is to match the world. Beliefs are like the detective's list: they have, in Anscombe's terminology, a 'mind-to-world' direction of fit.

So summing up, understanding subjective reasons requires cashing out the metaphor of perspective, and an agent's perspective must draw on at least one important condition on the mind-to-world component of her psychology, and likely (according to many views) on a separate condition on the world-to-mind component of her psychology. For simplicity, we'll refer to these as the 'mind-to-world' and 'world-to-mind' conditions on perspectives, respectively.

Lord [2018] identifies eight possibilities for the 'mind-to-world' condition on perspectives, which he calls the 'epistemic condition', by drawing three binary distinctions:

1. Does satisfying the mind-to-world condition require some high degree of evidence or justification for the consideration that gives a subjective reason?
2. Does satisfying the mind-to-world condition require having attitudes whose content is the reason's substance?
3. Is the mind-to-world condition factive—i.e., does holding that relation to p imply p?

Each of these questions is a matter over which theorists have often disagreed. We have already encountered the third question in Chapter 1, where we saw that thinking of subjective reasons as a special case of explanatory reasons lends itself to the 'yes' answer, but the 'no' answer fits better with the intuitive judgment that a false perspective can make inadvisable actions rational. But the other two questions are important as well.

---

[2] Anscombe [1957].

The first question asks about the point at which we are irrational for failing to take a possibility into account. Being completely unaware of the possibility or being certain that the possibility is not actual makes it rational, at least in many cases, to ignore it. If I left the stove on full blast, then I should rush home to turn it off. But if I'm certain that I turned it off or if I recall that the stove is broken so that it *can't* be on, then I'm not irrational for ignoring the possibility that it's on when deciding what to do. But at what point does one's justification for a claim make one irrational for failing to treat it as a reason? *High-bar* views hold that this point is reached only given a relatively high degree of justification—perhaps strong enough to put you in a position to know the claim. By contrast, *low-bar* views hold that little or even no justification is required—bearing a doxastic attitude to the claim, even an unjustified one, suffices.

The second question asks whether satisfying the 'mind-to-world' condition requires having some attitude whose content is the subjective reason's substance. For example, if the subjective reason for Freddie to avoid the party involves his impression that there will be charades at the party, must Freddie have some attitude whose content is the proposition that there will be charades at the party?

As we've seen, it's clear that some such attitudes, such as knowledge, *suffice* for possession. But can other psychological states that lack content or whose content is other than the reason's substance suffice? Lord thinks so. He is moved by cases like the following. Suppose you head to the new bar on the block, the Petrol and Tonic. Its main room is decorated with jerry cans and an assortment of gas pumps from yesteryear. Chevron and Shell logos are displayed prominently along with a sign that reads: NO MATCHES. NO LIGHTERS. NO SPARKS. NOT EVER. You can hear Bowie's "Putting out the fire (gasoline)" over the din and the air is thick with nostalgia, somehow reminding you both of a mechanic's shop and your bygone summers mowing lawns in the neighborhood. You sidle up to the bar and ask for a "G&T", somehow missing the bartender's question, "Leaded or unleaded?" Are you necessarily irrational if you take a sip?

The case elicits conflicting intuitions. Some, like Lord, think that taking a sip is irrational in this situation, regardless of whether you have noticed any of these clues.[3] So he takes cases like these to show that having perspective

---

[3] Compare Kiesewetter [2017].

on a reason does not require bearing an attitude toward the substance of the reason. According to Lord, whether the reason affects your rationality is not a matter of whether you *actually* have the relevant attitude; it's a matter of whether you're *in a position* to have it. Lord happens to think that the relevant attitude is knowledge. So, according to him, you satisfy the 'mind-to-world' condition on having a reason just when you're in a position to know the fact that is the reason's substance.

Appeal to cases like the one above is core philosophical methodology. We test principles against cases either to ensure that they have the right predictions or to reform our intuitions about cases. However, when it comes to the relationship between reasons and rationality, it's surprisingly contentious what to say about the cases. When philosophers disagree, it's very hard to determine whose intuitions are theory-driven and whose intuitions are "pure" without begging the question.

Indeed, some philosophers have strongly *internalist* intuitions about rationality. According to them, rationality, very roughly, depends only on what's going on in one's mind. Given this conception of rationality, agents' subjective reasons differ only if their minds differ. To illustrate, suppose you go to a new bar after reading a riveting article in *The Philosophy Journal*. You are so distracted by the article that you take no account of the bar's name, decor, ambiance, odor, etc. If you order a gin and tonic to quench your craving for one, is it rational to take a sip from what the bartender gives you? Some think, *of course*, why not? This remains true, according to internalists, even if you're at the Petrol and Tonic. According to them, you can still be rational if you sip from the glass so long as you remain blamelessly unaware of the abundant red flags about the contents of the Petrol and Tonic's cocktails.

Sure, the red light from the flashing neon "NO MATCHES. NO LIGHTERS." sign reaches your eyes; perhaps it is registered by your visual cortex. But that doesn't ensure that you're aware of what's written, much less of what it implies; the sign's message may not make its way into your perspective on the world. And if you are too preoccupied by *The Philosophy Journal* to take note of the bar's abundant warnings, you are not irrational for taking a sip of a gasoline and tonic—or, at least, so advocates of this internalist view think. Their internalism makes it attractive to think that whether there is a subjective reason for you depends on whether you have an attitude whose content is the reason's substance. Merely being in a position to know that your drink is a gasoline and tonic, for example, does not suffice for possessing the relevant reason without the relevant attitude.

5.3 The World-to-Mind Condition

Until recently, philosophers seemed to agree that an agent's perspective on her objective reasons is exhausted by the 'mind-to-world' condition. But this point of agreement has come into doubt. For example, if I have a headache, then the fact that the pills in the bottle are acetaminophen is a reason for me to take one. I may see the label and know that the pills are acetaminophen. But if I don't believe that acetaminophen is an analgesic, then it is perfectly rational for me to decline taking one despite, it seems, satisfying the 'mind-to-world' condition on a consideration being an objective reason for me to take the pill. So it looks like there's more to a consideration's being a subjective reason than one's satisfying the 'mind-to-world' condition on possessing it.

Some may resist this challenge to the 'mind-to-world' condition's sufficiency. They may deny that the fact that the pills are acetaminophen is an objective reason to take one when you have a headache, insisting instead that the real reason is a *conjunction*: it's that the pills are acetaminophen *and acetaminophen is an analgesic* that's the reason. I don't have that fact as a subjective reason, according to them, because I don't believe that acetaminophen is an analgesic. So the challenge is merely apparent.

But we can recreate the initial problem if we imagine that, just as in the first case I didn't know that acetaminophen is an analgesic, in this second case I don't know that analgesics are painkillers. In that case, it still looks rational for me to decline to take a pill when I have a headache. If the conjunctive strategy is to work, therefore, it must keep going—the real reason must be the fact that the pills are acetaminophen and acetaminophen is an analgesic and analgesics are painkillers. But the view that the perspectives that give us subjective reasons have a 'world-to-mind' as well as a 'mind-to-world' component can explain this case without resort to such measures. To do so, we say that to have this reason, you must simply be disposed toward acetaminophen in the right way.

We've been using 'perspective' as a visual metaphor to help illuminate subjective reasons. But this description may be more than just metaphorical. J.J. Gibson's *affordance theory* in the science of visual perception holds that, roughly, an animal's capacities and intentions partly determine how they visually perceive their environment.[4] According to the theory, very roughly, whether I visually represent the stacked wooden boxes leading to the next

---

[4] Gibson [1979].

floor as *stairs* depends, in part, on whether I know how to climb them to reach that floor. Since I know how to climb the boxes, I represent them as stairs. To an infant who cannot climb them, the boxes that constitute the stairs may be part of the infant's visual perception, but they are not represented as stairs. Affordance theory thus suggests that our visual perspective is partly shaped by our know-how.

Some theorists, including Lord, think something similar about reasons. According to Lord, just as our visual perception may be shaped by our know-how, our perspective on reasons is shaped by whether we know how to use them in reasoning. His explanation of why there is no subjective reason for me to take a pill in the above case is that I don't know how to use the relevant facts as reasons in my practical reasoning. From my limited perspective, the fact that the pill is acetaminophen or that it's an analgesic are simply not reasons to take the pill since I don't know how to use them as premises in practical deliberation. This lack of know-how doesn't inhibit me from knowing the relevant facts, but it does inhibit those facts from figuring as subjective reasons for me to take a pill. Thus, my perspective on objective reasons is shaped by my knowledge of how to use various considerations as reasons in my practical and theoretical reasoning.

Apart from know-how, we might also enrich an agent's perspective on reasons by including 'world-to-mind' states, such as desires, intentions, preferences, etc. For example, if Ronnie and Bradley both know that there's dancing at the party but only Ronnie likes to dance, then only Ronnie has a reason to go. This difference in their reasons is most naturally explained by a difference in whether they like to dance.[5]

Some British sentimentalists such as Lord Shaftesbury and Francis Hutcheson, and their contemporary exponents such as Christine Tappolet and Michael Milona, hold that, very roughly, emotional reactions are analogous to perceptual experiences of value properties.[6] If something disgusts us, our disgust is a (perhaps misleading!) perception of that object's badness. If something attracts us, our attraction perceives goodness in what attracts us. So just as differences in *visual* perception between agents affect their subjective reasons—if only I see the tiger, only I have a reason to run—differences in our desires, understood broadly, *qua* differences in *emotional* perception, also do.

---

[5] Compare Schroeder [2007b, chapter one].
[6] Shaftesbury [1999], Hutcheson [1728], Tappolet [2016], Milona [2017].

If the sentimentalists are right, then we have independent reason to believe that our noncognitive states partly constitute our perspective on the world, affecting which reasons we possess. We can explain why it's rational only for Ronnie to go to the party despite the fact that both he and Bradley know that there will be dancing through a difference in their respective perspectives on reasons. From Ronnie's perspective, which is informed by a desire to dance, that there will be dancing *is* a reason to go to the party. From Bradley's perspective, which is not informed by such a desire, that there is dancing is not such a reason.

Accepting that desires inform agents' perspectives on reasons allows us to resist a subtle but powerful argument for the Humean Theory of Reasons. As we saw earlier, the Humean Theory holds that both objective reasons, as well as subjective reasons, depend on the existence of an appropriate desire. For example, on one natural formulation of the Humean Theory, a fact is a reason for an agent to do something just when and because it helps explain why doing that thing promotes the object of one of the agent's desires.[7] A fact is a reason for an agent, according to this view, when it shows the means to one of the agent's ends.

Seemingly innocuous cases like Ronnie and Bradley provide some intuitive support for the Humean Theory. It is plausible that only Ronnie has a reason to go the party *because* only Ronnie has the right desires. And the Humean Theory says that this is right—Ronnie's going to the party is more *advisable* than Bradley's going, and the difference is that because Ronnie and not Bradley desires to dance, the fact that there is dancing there is an objective reason for Ronnie but not for Bradley to go there. But according to an alternative view, the same reason is an objective reason for both Ronnie and Bradley, but their difference is that Ronnie comes closer to the perspective that is required to make it his subjective reason.

The Humean interpretation of Ronnie and Bradley's case may seem banal. But it isn't. It's the thin edge of a wedge that reduces *all* reasons to desires. The wedge argument is simple. If it is clear and uncontroversial that some objective normative reasons are explained by desires, then this is an explanation that we can generalize to explain all reasons—and it will be attractive to do so, unless we can find a more powerful, more general, explanation.

However, we can resist the Humean's totalizing explanation of reasons' normativity by resisting it at its root, at its explanation of the

---

[7] This formulation comes from the version of the Humean Theory dubbed *Hypotheticalism* by Schroeder [2007b].

difference between Ronnie and Bradley. If we think that desires constitute our perspective on reasons, we can deny the Humean claim that Ronnie's desires *make* certain considerations into reasons. Rather, according to the competing sentimentalist explanation being proposed, Ronnie's desires grant him perspective on certain reasons, like the fact that there will be dancing at the party. The difference between Ronnie and Bradley is the 'world-to-mind' analogue to the 'mind-to-world' difference between Ronnie, who knows there will be dancing at the party, and Freddie, who does not. In short, whereas the Humean account gives desire a broadly *metaphysical* role in making some consideration into a reason, the sentimentalist account gives desire a broadly *epistemic* role in fitting a reason into an agent's perspective.

The sentimentalist account is particularly natural if we assume the dual-aspect theory of reasons from Chapter 3. The dual-aspect view, recall, holds that reasons have two parts. In the case of reasons for action, for example, they are composed of proposition-goal pairs, where the proposition corresponds to the content of the 'mind-to-world' condition on subjective reasons, and the goal corresponds to the content of the 'world-to-mind' condition. If reasons for actions comprise not just propositions but also goals, then it's clear why bearing the appropriate doxastic attitude to a given proposition is insufficient for fitting it into your perspective. You must also desire its goal. In Ronnie and Freddie's case, the reason to go to the party isn't simply the fact that there will be dancing there; the goal of dancing is part of the reason to go. So the reason to go to the party is <there will be dancing at the party, to dance>. To have this reason in one's perspective, it does not suffice to believe that there will be dancing at the party; you must also want to dance. Only Freddie wants to dance. So only *he* has perspective on the reason. That's why it's rational for him to go but not Ronnie.

5.4 Objective Priority

We've been employing the metaphor of one's perspective on reasons and the idea that one's subjective reasons correlate with one's perspective on objective reasons. This metaphor is expedient but limited. It's now time to be a little more explicit about the relationship between subjective and objective reasons.

It seems fairly plain that there must be some such interesting relationship. Normally, when some consideration is an *objective* reason to do some action, gaining perspective on the consideration tends to make it more rational to act that way. Of course, subjective and objective reasons can come apart: the fact that your bartender has handed you a tasty G&T is a reason to gratefully accept the drink, but it might be irrational for you to do so on that basis if you think the bartender is out to poison you with gasoline. The point is that when an agent's subjective and objective reasons diverge, we can usually point to a quirk of their psychology that explains why—in this case, thinking that the bartender wants to poison you.

Given that subjective and objective reasons seem closely related, it should not be surprising that many philosophers have tried to understand one in terms of the other. According to some philosophers, facts about subjective reasons are just a certain sort of fact about actual or possible objective reasons. And according to others, facts about objective reasons are just a certain sort of fact about actual or possible subjective reasons. In this and the following section, we'll explore the strengths and weaknesses of both of these orders of explanation and then propose a different approach to explaining the relation between subjective and objective reasons.

Probably the most common order of explanation comes from theorists who have taken objective reasons to be primary and understood subjective reasons in terms of them.[8] According to the simplest version of this view, subjective reasons are just a special case of objective reasons—objective reasons toward which the agent, in addition, satisfies the appropriate perspective conditions. It is natural for proponents of this kind of view to say that satisfying the perspective conditions on the objective reason is what it takes to count as *possessing* the reason. On this picture, objective reasons are like books, and your subjective reasons are like your library. There are a lot of books that are not in your library, but every book in your library is a book, and having it in your library is just a matter of owning it. Similarly, on this view, there are a lot of objective reasons that are not your subjective reasons, but every one of your subjective reasons is an objective reason, and having it as your subjective reason is just a matter of possessing it.

The theory that subjective reasons are just possessed objective reasons valorizes one of the very natural ways that we have of drawing the distinction between objective and subjective reasons in the first place—by means of the possessive construction. So, for example, if we ask Ronnie why he

---

[8] Scanlon [2003], Schroeder [2007b], and Parfit [2011] are all prominent examples of this approach.

showed up to the party when we thought he had other plans and he responds, "Well, this party has dancing!", we can identify something worth calling "Ronnie's reason for going to the party". We can contrast Ronnie's reason for going to the party with Jimmy's reason for going to the party, which was to meet new people. When Ronnie names dancing as part of the explanation of why he showed up, he's reporting his perspective on objective reasons; that is, he's reporting the subjective reason for him to go that made it rational for him to go and that moved him to show up. And when we draw the distinction between Ronnie and Freddie, we can say that there was a reason for both to go to the party, but Ronnie had this reason and Freddie didn't, because he had no idea that there was dancing going on.

This view is commonly known as the *factoring account*, because it factors subjective reasons into two components—being an objective reason, plus a further possession condition.[9] And it offers a simple, appealing account of how changes in one's perspective affect what one ought to do: since our perspective rarely comprises all the facts, it rarely comprises all of the objective reasons for various actions, beliefs, and feelings. Learning new facts thus causes one to acquire new reasons, thereby changing what their balance requires. Nevertheless, the factoring account also builds in some heavy commitments. It claims that one's subjective reasons to do something are a subset of the objective reasons for one to do it. So from this it follows that if some consideration is not an objective reason, it is, *ipso facto*, not a *possessed* objective reason, so it is not a subjective one.

It is a consequence of this that if we build constraints into our account of objective reasons, subjective reasons will inherit them. For example, we've been suggesting throughout that only truths can give objective reasons. But the factoring account entails that subjective reasons will also have to be truths. So when Billie shows up to the party when we thought she had other plans and she explains herself by responding, "Well, this party has guacamole!", the factoring account implies that Billie is mistaken about her reasons to come to the party if, unbeknownst to her, we've run out of guacamole. So because the factoring account restricts subjective reasons to truths, it may seem to allow too few subjective reasons.

Advocates of the factoring account are typically unfazed by this worry. After all, false beliefs are most often accompanied by supporting true beliefs.[10] If you falsely believe that there will be guacamole at the party,

---

[9] This terminology comes from Schroeder [2008]. [10] Compare Lord [2010].

that may be because your friend misled you either about the quantity of guacamole on offer or about the level of general enthusiasm for guacamole. So while the belief or consideration that the party has guacamole may be ineligible to be a reason because it is false, there's a "backup" fact to serve as your reason: the fact that your friend said that there will be guacamole at the party. So long as there's always a backup fact to play the role that a false belief plays in constituting your perspective, then the presence of the corresponding backup reason softens some counterintuitive implications of the factoring account. This strategy's success depends on whether these backup reasons are always there when needed.[11]

A different challenge to the factoring account questions its assumption that 'reason' in 'Billie's reason' denotes an objective reason. Instead of being like books in your library, subjective reasons might be like golf partners. There is no general stock of golf partners out there among whom are those to whom you, in addition, bear the right possession relation in order for them to count as *your* golf partners. On the contrary, being a golf partner *just is* being someone's golf partner—being a golf partner is inextricably relational. So, according to a competing hypothesis, being a subjective reason is also inextricably relational. The possessive construction in 'Billie's reason' is not a separable component on top of there being a reason; instead, it is just specifying whom this reason is the reason *of*, and reasons are, like golf partners, inextricably reasons *of* somebody.

If this hypothesis is correct, then when we contrast the reason "there is" for both Ronnie and Freddie but that is not one of "Freddie's reasons", the important contrast is not between whether we use the possessive construction, but over whether we are talking about objective or subjective reasons—either of which we could do with the possessive construction. And because the possessive construction is very permissive in natural language, it does in fact make it very easy to talk about objective reasons. For example, we can quite easily say that the fact that there is dancing at the party is a reason for Ronnie but not for Bradley to go there, and paraphrase this by saying that it is a reason that Ronnie has but not Bradley, or that it is one of Ronnie's reasons but not Bradley's—all the while stipulating that neither Ronnie nor Bradley knows about this reason.

---

[11] It also requires that these backup reasons be suitably weighty, which is far from obviously true.

If subjective reasons are not a special case of objective reasons, then you might think that they are considerations that *would* be objective reasons, were they true. For example, we might say that:

O to S r is a subjective reason for s to φ just when and because (a) r is part of s's perspective, and (b) if r were true, r would be an objective reason for s to φ.

Clause (a) is not our focus, so we can understand it schematically. Various accounts of the psychological state responsible for subjective reasons can be plugged into (a), yielding different accounts of one's perspective on reasons. Rather, we're primarily concerned with (b), the part of O to S that proposes to analyze the *categorical* property of being a subjective reason with a *conditional* claim about counterfactual objective reasons.

In his important paper 'The Conditional Fallacy for Contemporary Philosophy', Robert Shope argues that there is a pervasive problem that arises when philosophers try to analyze categorical conditions in conditional or counterfactual terms. This pervasive problem has come to be known following Shope as the *conditional fallacy*.[12] The core of the problem is that categorical properties often *ground* the truth of counterfactual conditionals. For example, because I am tall, it is true that if I jumped, I could reach it. But being tall is not the same as its being true that if you jumped you could reach it. On the contrary, maybe I really don't like jumping because I am deathly afraid of hitting my head, and so I would only jump if I were shorter. If the closest jumping world were a short world like this, then it is not true that if I jumped I could reach it, even though it is true that I am tall. The problem is that even though the categorical property *normally* grounds the conditional property, careful choices of cases or setting of background conditions can make the conditional shift whether the categorical property is present or not.

As we've observed, O to S seeks to analyze subjective reasons in conditional terms. So it is important to check and see whether what we know about the conditional fallacy helps construct counterexamples to O to S. And indeed it does. Suppose that I have a strong craving for New York pizza, and I rationally believe that I am in New York. It is plausible, in this case, that I have a subjective reason to get pizza. Getting pizza is the rational way, given what I reasonably believe, to satisfy my craving.

---

[12] Shope [1978].

But suppose that I am not in New York, as is consistent with the kinds of non-factive accounts of the perspective condition (a) that motivate counterfactual accounts like O to S in the first place. And suppose that because I am rarely in New York, I never crave New York pizza when I am in New York—instead, when I am actually there, I find myself attracted to everything else that New York has to offer. So if my belief that I am in New York *were* to be true, I would not actually be interested in getting pizza, and hence there would not be an objective reason for me to get pizza. So in this case O to S says that there is no subjective reason for me to get pizza even though I do crave it and rationally believe that I *am* in New York, simply because, were I to actually be in New York, there would not be an objective reason for me to get pizza.

This counterexample to O to S works exactly as the conditional fallacy predicts it does: by considering cases in which the antecedent of the conditional analysis shifts one of the conditions on whether you have a subjective reason, the truth of the counterfactual conditional can come apart from whether you have a subjective reason. And the reason why we get counterexamples of this kind is because the order of explanation between subjective reasons and the truth of these counterfactual conditionals goes the other way around—the fact that you have a subjective reason typically grounds the truth of closely related counterfactuals in the sort of way that many other truths ground closely related counterfactuals.

5.5 Subjective Priority

If subjective reasons cannot be analyzed in terms of objective reasons either as a special case of such reasons or counterfactually, then we might turn instead to the idea that objective reasons can be analyzed in terms of subjective reasons. Some moral philosophers and philosophers of practical reason find this order of explanation to be alien. To them, subjective reasons seem like mere appearances of objective reasons—indeed, subjective reasons are sometimes called "apparent" reasons.

But other philosophers, especially those raised on a healthy diet of decision theory, find this alternative order of explanation to be the most natural. Decision theory is particularly useful as a theory of rational choice given imperfect or incomplete information. It tells us how to rationally rank choices for agents given their varying *degrees* of confidence in each possible scenario that they can't definitively rule out. These degrees of confidence are typically modeled by a probability function, and are commonly referred to as *credences*.

So decision theory is, in the first instance, a theory about what is *subjectively* rational, given your credences—that is, given your *perspective* as determined by how confident you are in each possible scenario. Consequently, it's natural for decision theorists to understand 'objective' normative notions as subjective ones augmented with perfect, complete information. This interpretation holds that r is an objective reason just in case r is a subjective reason to φ for a perfectly informed agent—that is, for an agent who has full credence in truths and no credence in falsehoods.

Indeed, there is a powerful argument that this order of explanation must be the correct one—an argument based on *fineness of grain*.[13] According to this argument, the facts about what objective reasons you have and what you objectively ought to do are relatively *coarse-grained*, because they correspond to what is or is not the case, which is a binary distinction, whereas it turns out that the facts about what you subjectively ought to do are relatively *fine-grained*. This is because they depend instead not only on the binary of what you believe or don't believe is the case, but also on how *confident* you are that it is the case, which is more finely individuated. From the perspective of decision theory, the possible facts about what you objectively ought to do correspond only to what it is decision-theoretically rational to do given probability functions that assign every proposition to 1 or 0. But the possible facts about what you subjectively ought to do correspond to the full range of possible probability functions.

Proponents of this argument therefore say that there are not enough possible facts about what your objective reasons might possibly be in order for an analysis like O to S to work. You might have a subjective reason to place a bet because you are 50 percent confident that you will win, but there is no corresponding condition of this confidence being *true* under which you would have an objective reason to win. But this is no obstacle to its turning out that we can flip the analysis the other way around, and analyze objective reasons in terms of subjective reasons. Because it is clear (even clearer than the other way around) that not all objective reasons are actual subjective reasons, it is typical, again, to turn to counterfactual analyses, which typically take something like the following form:

S to O r is an objective reason for s to φ just when r would be a subjective reason for s to φ were r part of s's perspective in condition c.

---

[13] Compare Wodak [2019] and Schroeder [2018].

Unfortunately, however, we already know enough about the conditional fallacy to be able to predict how analyses like S to O are going to go astray. These are found in cases where a consideration's being an objective reason is affected by whether or not it is part of a perfectly informed perspective. Counterexamples are simple: that I'm not thinking about elephants is never part of a perfectly informed perspective, for the moment it's part of my perspective, it's false. But that I'm not thinking of elephants could be an objective reason to, say, push a button. For example, an eccentric billionaire could have set up a button that pays out to all and only people who aren't thinking about elephants. So some considerations can be objective reasons even though they cannot be subjective reasons at all.

This elephant counterexample, like New York pizza, can feel cheap and cheesy. You might think that it exploits an inherent instability between the belief and a natural way of understanding the 'perfectly informed perspective': when the belief is not part of a perfectly informed perspective, it should be, and when it is part of the perspective, it shouldn't be. So you might try to reject the counterexample as based on a misinterpretation of what perfection demands of an informed perspective. We might think instead that the beliefs that are part of such a perspective are not just truths, but beliefs that remain truths when you believe them—alethically stable beliefs, let's call them.

Nevertheless, even alethically stable beliefs can expose the conditional fallacy inherent to *S to O*. Suppose you love nothing more than a surprise birthday party and, because of this, you hate nothing more than having that surprise ruined. The heretofore unexpected birthday party in the next room is, therefore, an objective reason for you to go into the next room. However, including the corresponding belief in your perspective ruins the surprise, so it fails to be a reason for you to go into the next room.[14]

Now, even if objective reasons cannot be analyzed in terms of subjective reasons and subjective reasons cannot be analyzed in terms of objective reasons, it does not follow that objective and subjective reasons are not analytically related to one another. A third possibility is that each can be analyzable in terms of a common core. Indeed, this is precisely what is suggested by the general diagnosis of the source of the conditional fallacy counterexamples. There is some condition under which something is a core reason, and then adding *truth* to this condition makes it an objective reason, and adding *perspective* to it makes it a subjective reason. Exactly how to formulate the

---

[14] For the surprise party case see Schroeder [2007b, chapter two].

core reasons view will depend on how we answer the questions from Part 1, but a simple version of this view would look like this:

Core Reasons   (1) r is an objective reason for s to φ just when r is a core reason for s to φ and r is true.
(2) r is a subjective reason for s to φ just when r is a core reason for s to φ and r is part of s's perspective.

As predicted, Core Reasons elegantly explains why the biconditionals in S to O and O to S are generally but not counterexample-proof-ly true. The biconditional from S to O is generally true because *generally*, when r is true and a core reason for s to φ, r could have been part of s's perspective without ceasing to be a core reason, and so if r *were* part of s's perspective, then r would have been a subjective reason as well. But it is not universally true, because sometimes the nearest world in which r was part of s's perspective is one in which it would have ceased to be a core reason. Likewise, the biconditional in O to S is generally true because generally, when r is part of s's perspective and a core reason for s to φ, r could have been true without ceasing to be a core reason, and so if r *were* true, then r would have been an objective reason as well. But it is not universally true, because sometimes the nearest world in which r is true is one in which it would have ceased to be a core reason.

The decision-theoretic picture described earlier can be co-opted to have this sort of structure. Instead of thinking of decision theory as primarily a theory of rational choice under uncertainty, so that it privileges the subjective over the objective, we can instead think of it in generic terms simply as issuing prescriptions conditional on information states in terms of a function from preference/probability function pairs to act choices. This function is itself neither objective or subjective, but it can yield objective outputs when we plug in the objective probability function that assigns 1 to all truths and 0 to all falsehoods, and it can yield subjective outputs when we plug in the probability function that describes the agent's credences.

We can reach another way of thinking about the idea of core reasons that is less beholden to decision theory, by going through the semantics of modal expressions. It is a familiar observation from linguistics that modal words like 'ought' can be used to express a family of distinct but related meanings—for example, to make claims about what is likely to be the case, about what someone morally ought to do, or about what they prudentially or legally ought to do. The conventional understanding of how 'ought' is able to express so many related meanings—so many *flavors*, if you will—is that its meaning depends on one or more contextual parameters that can be set differently in different conversational contexts, thus allowing for different thoughts to be expressed in different conversations.

According to the most influential such account, developed by Angelika Kratzer, modals like 'ought' actually require two distinct conversational parameters—one called the *ordering source*, which plays the role of ranking possibilities in some way, and one called the *modal base*, which selects among those possibilities.[15] For example, the sentence, 'you ought not to jaywalk' could be interpreted as either a legal or a moral claim. Each would depend for its truth on a characterization of the facts of some situation, which would be the modal base for each claim. But the truth of these claims can come apart, because they use different ordering sources, reflecting the fact that the law and morality require different things. So this sentence might be true on the legal reading, but not on the moral reading.

Kratzer herself says that the modal base of deontic modals (whether moral, prudential, or legal) is always what she calls *realistic*, meaning that it is used to hold fixed the true facts of the situation, as in our preceding example.[16] This, intuitively, corresponds to the idea that deontic uses of 'ought' express the *objective* ought. But another, we think better-supported, possibility is that deontic modals can take either a realistic *or* an *epistemic* modal base. On this alternative picture, the difference between whether an 'ought' claim expresses an objective or a subjective ought is just the difference between which kind of modal base we select in our conversational context. For example, 'you ought to fold' could be true on the subjective reading, which incorporates only what you believe, including the poor quality of your poker hand, as its modal base, but false on the objective reading, which also includes the objective fact that your opponent's hand is even worse. But both claims depend on the single ranking of outcomes as better when you have more money.

This counts as a common core picture of 'ought', because neither the objective nor the subjective 'ought' is basic. All deontic ought claims are either objective or subjective, but these are just two reflections of a common core that we get by combining the basic Kratzer semantics for 'ought' with the selection of a deontic ordering source. And if all it takes for 'ought' to

---

[15] See, in particular, Kratzer [1977] and [1981] for the classical development of this framework.

[16] Kratzer [1981, 44–45].

express either an objective or a subjective meaning is for it to have a common core, then the same thing goes for 'reason'.

Chapter Summary

In this chapter, we have been concerned with the relationship between objective and subjective reasons. Subjective reasons, we argued, are helpfully thought of through the lens of the *perspective* that an agent must occupy in order to have one or another subjective reason. We spent most of the chapter exploring whether subjective reasons can be reduced in some way to the agent's perspective on objective reasons, or conversely, and we introduced an alternative possibility that is rare in the literature but we argued appears to be better-motivated than more common views: that both objective and subjective reasons can be reduced to what we called *core* reasons.

Recommended Reading

We have drawn heavily in this chapter on Errol Lord's discussion of the 'mind-to-world' and 'world-to-mind' components of the perspective required to count as having a subjective reason in his book *The Importance of Being Rational*, especially chapters three and four. For an introduction to sentimental perceptualism, we recommend Michael Milona's 'Intellect vs Affect: New Leverage in an Old Debate', and for an introduction to the Humean Theory of Reasons, chapter one of Mark Schroeder's *Slaves of the Passions*. For additional problems with objective priority, beyond those discussed here, see Daniel Wodak's 'An Objectivist's Guide to Subjective Reasons' and Mark Schroeder's 'Getting Perspective on Objective Reasons'. The canonical source for Kratzer's treatment of modal meanings is her seminal paper 'What "Must" and "Can" Must and Can Mean'. We recommend reading this chapter alongside chapter three of Lord's *The Importance of Being Rational*.

Exercises

5.1 *Comprehension.* Try to describe an example in which someone has an objective reason to do something but no corresponding subjective reason to do it, and an example in which someone has a subjective reason to do something but no corresponding objective reason to do it. Can you think of cases of both kinds? Which views agree that cases of both kinds are possible, and which deny this? Which one(s) do they rule out?

5.2 *Extensions.* Suppose that Alicia satisfies the 'mind-to-world' but not the 'world-to-mind' perspective condition for a conclusive moral reason to help her friend, but satisfies both conditions for reasons not to help her friend. What is the objectively morally correct thing for her to do? What is the rational thing for her to do? What can we blame her for doing? Does it matter that Alicia satisfies one of the perspective conditions on this reason, if she doesn't satisfy both? Or does it not matter for anything, unless she satisfies both?

5.3 *Comprehension.* Compare the two treatments from this chapter of the difference between the reasons of Ronnie, who wants to dance, and of Bradley, who does not want to dance: the Humean Theory of Reasons, and the view that desires can fulfill the world-to-mind perspective condition. Explain what they have in common, and how they differ in their commitments.

5.4 *Extensions.* Are there any limits on what sorts of desires lead to intuitive differences in pairs of cases like Ronnie's and Bradley's, or do cases like theirs feel intuitively different in the same way no matter what we imagine that Ronnie desires and turns out to be available at the party? What does your answer tell you about the relative advantages of the competing accounts of what is going on in this difference?

5.5 *Extensions.* Can being 75 percent confident that p give you a subjective reason to take a bet that p at even odds? Explain why a 'yes' answer poses a challenge to objective-first accounts of the relationship between objective and subjective reasons. Does a 'yes' answer also pose a challenge to the core reasons view? Why or why not?

5.6 *Extensions.* Reformulate Core Reasons in order to make it consistent with the dual-aspect theory of reasons from Chapter 3, according to which reasons consist in both a proposition and a goal.

5.7 *Extensions.* In Chapter 1 we briefly encountered the view that the mass noun use of 'reason' is prior to and explanatory of its count noun use. On this view, r is a reason to do something just in case it explains why there is reason to do it. Does the mass noun use of 'reason' also admit of an objective/subjective distinction? How would you apply the ideas of this chapter to mass noun 'reason' if so? And what lessons can you take away, if not?

5.8 *Extensions.* If there are both 'mind-to-world' and 'world-to-mind' conditions on the perspective required to have a subjective reason, then we can distinguish between three distinct ways of failing to have a subjective reason. You can satisfy neither perspective condition, you can satisfy the mind-to-world but not the world-to-mind condition, or you can satisfy the world-to-mind but not the mind-to-world condition. For this exercise, consider whether each of these three statuses seems to be different from the others in normatively important ways. For example, would you criticize someone in different ways for not doing something under each of these three different conditions?

6
Reasons and Evidence

6.1 Family Resemblances

In Part 2 of this book our task is to consider the relationship between reasons and other things with which they are particularly closely associated. In Chapter 5 we explored the relationship between objective and subjective normative reasons, and in Chapters 6 through 8 we turn to the relationships between reasons and evidence, explanation, and reasoning.

The closeness of the relationship between reasons and evidence can be brought out by focusing on four of the characteristic features of reasons. First, reasons are *competitors*—they compete or weigh against one another in determining whether some normative status obtains, such as whether you may do something or ought to believe something. If I've made a promise to show up at seven for dinner, but I encounter an injured cyclist on the way, whether I should help will be a function of the strength of the promise and the gravity of the cyclist's injury. These two considerations compete to determine what I should do.

Second, at least some considerations only *contingently* give reasons, because whether a consideration gives a reason can be *undercut* by other considerations. For example, that someone has a headache is a reason to give them an aspirin. But that reason is undercut if the person does not metabolize acetylsalicylic acid, the active ingredient in aspirin. That the person has a headache does not tend to make it right to give them aspirin when they do not respond to it as a painkiller. The consideration's reason-giving status is undercut.

Third, as we explored in Chapter 5, reasons admit of an objective/subjective distinction. In normal circumstances, if it appears to Bernie that his drink is a gin and tonic, then there is a subjective reason for him to take a drink, but the consideration that Bernie's drink is a gin and tonic is not an objective reason for him to take a drink because it is not true, at least in the canonical case. Likewise, that the drink is *actually* gasoline and tonic is an objective reason for Bernie not to take a drink, but it's not a subjective reason because he neither believes nor does it appear to him that there's gasoline in the glass.

Finally, reasons can explain why we've acted in some way, thought something, or felt some way. That is, we can, and often do, have certain attitudes and act in certain ways for reasons—our attitudes and actions can be *based on* reasons. When Bernie takes a sip from the glass, he's responding to the apparent gin and tonic. Or when I choose to help the cyclist out of moral concern, my help is based on their need for help—the very reason why I ought to help, supposing that's so.

It turns out that evidence seems to share all four of these characteristics. Whether a person's belief is justified depends on their evidence and whether that's so depends on competition between the evidence on each side. Evidence can also be undercut: that the wall appears red is evidence that it's red, which can nevertheless be undercut by the news that I'm wearing red-tinted glasses. Evidence also admits of an objective/subjective distinction. Given my knowledge that all cats are mammals, news that Fido is a cat should strengthen my belief that Fido is a mammal when that's all I know about Fido—it's *subjective evidence* that Fido is a mammal. But that Fido is a cat is not *objective evidence* that he's a mammal if Fido is actually a dog. And finally, so long as I'm rational, I'll base my beliefs on my evidence; that is, my evidence will be the basis for my beliefs.

Given that reasons and evidence share these four characteristics, it's natural to suspect that there's some interesting relationship between the two. In this chapter, we'll explore two ways of thinking about the relationship between reasons and evidence, one that explains reasons for action in terms of evidence concerning what you ought to do and another that explains evidence in terms of reasons for you to believe.

6.2 Reasons as Evidence

The first connection we'll explore is prominently defended by Stephen Kearns and Daniel Star in a series of articles that have attracted considerable attention. According to them:

RAE Necessarily, a fact f is a reason for an agent s to φ just when f is evidence that s ought to φ (where 'φ' is a verb phrase).[1]

---

[1] It's worth asking oneself whether Kearns and Star's account can allow that falsehoods are reasons for action, as their account allows that some falsehoods are evidence for what one ought to do, and that is a sufficient condition for being a normative reason to do it.

This account is attractive in a number of ways. It promises a general explanation of how reasons' deliberative role is tied to their explanatory role. It is plausible that the right way to answer questions about what to do or think is by arriving at beliefs about what you *ought* to do or think. And those beliefs, in turn, are appropriately settled by *evidence* about what you ought to do or think. Consequently, if deliberation about what to do or think is always directed toward a question of what ought to be, the relation that Kearns and Star posit between reasons and evidence is extremely natural.

This account offers other explanatory dividends. If all reasons to do or think something are also evidence about what ought to be, then reasons' authority over how to act and think—their "normativity"—is also wholly unsurprising. Reasons derive that authority from their evidential connection to facts about what we ought to do and think, which are uncontroversially authoritative or normative.

Moreover, RAE unifies reasons of different types, like reasons for action and reasons for belief. In either case, a reason to do or think something corresponds to the possibility that you ought to do or think that very thing. More generally, it appears that every reason to do something is explained by an apparent obligation to do that very thing. Kearns and Star's proposal therefore promises to unify the domain of reasons by subsuming it under facts about what ought to be.

And finally, RAE is, along with the Humean Theory of Reasons from Chapter 5, one of the first views that we have encountered in this book that provides the prospects of an answer to what reasons are. In their co-authored work Kearns and Star are carefully neutral about whether RAE constitutes an analysis of reasons, and not just a necessary biconditional. But in philosophy, part of what can make it attractive to accept is the prospect that they might help us to analyze an otherwise intractable concept or property. This is especially true when a biconditional is subject to plausible but not totally compelling counterexamples. The existence of an analysis requires a necessarily true biconditional, and so in pursuit of one we may sometimes reasonably respond to purported counterexamples by explaining them away. But if we do not expect there to be any analysis, or if we already have an analysis of a very different kind, then we may have no *a priori* reason to expect there to be any simple true biconditional in this neighborhood. And so we may be more easily persuaded by purported counterexamples.

And as we'll see, despite its many attractions, RAE is also subject to a number of purported counterexamples. One source of potential trouble for RAE comes not from its letter, but from the interpretation of how evidence works with which Kearns and Star have supplemented it. In particular, Kearns and Star interpret evidence in probabilistic terms. But one salient feature of probabilities is that they can vary in different ways as we collect different kinds of information. So it is particularly natural, once we tie evidence to probabilities, to think that what is evidence for what will also vary according to some body of background information.

Kearns and Star incorporate this assumption into their version of RAE. According to them, a proposition is evidence for a conclusion relative to a body of background information just when the probability of that conclusion conditional on that proposition plus that body of information is higher than the probability of the conclusion conditional on the background body of information alone. For example, the fact that a black cat passed by is evidence of a nearby witch relative to a suitably superstitious body of information just when the probability of a nearby witch relative to the superstitious body of information, increases conditional on a black cat passing by. However, the cat fact will fail to increase the likelihood of a proximal witch relative to a less superstitious body of information. In that case, the very same cat fact is *not* evidence for a proximal witch relative to that less superstitious body of information.

So on Kearns and Star's interpretation, if RAE is true, then considerations give reasons only relative to bodies of information. Consequently, evaluating the plausibility of RAE must ultimately depend on correctly answering a difficult question about which bodies of information matter when determining which reasons exist. At least *some* of the agent's information bears on whether, relative to her, one consideration is evidence for another. For example, that Fido is a mammal is evidence that he's a cat only against a background of information that includes the proposition that at least most cats are mammals. But it can't be *all* of an agent's information: otherwise agents could acquire no new evidence about what they ought to do *and*, correspondingly, no new reasons for doing it when they're already certain about what they ought to do, since nothing can raise a proposition's likelihood above certainty. Both the agent's reasons and her evidence must shift as the moral landscape shifts.

Kearns and Star's answer to this problem is that a consideration's standing as evidence for another consideration is evaluated relative to "some salient relevant subset of one's total body of evidence" (Kearns and Star [2009, 232]). Properly assessing RAE depends on identifying that subset. Unfortunately, Kearns and Star offer no guidance on what makes a subset salient or relevant, and whose evidence matters—the agent or the person evaluating the agent. We don't have answers to these questions. But the structure of the problem is a very general one for probability-raising accounts of evidence—and perhaps RAE can be developed in a way that does not depend on the probabilistic treatment of evidence. So having flagged the seriousness of this problem, let's spot Kearns and Star an adequate solution to this difficulty.

A second high-level feature of Kearns and Star's development of the idea that reasons are a special case of evidence derives from their account of what reasons are evidence *for*. One natural way of understanding the thesis of *evidentialism* in epistemology is as the thesis that the only reasons to believe that p are evidence that p. Evidentialism, so understood, rules out the rationality of believing on the basis of anything other than evidence—for example, on the basis of wishful thinking or of faith, if faith doesn't constitute a kind of evidence. And like RAE, evidentialism postulates a close relationship between reasons and evidence, at least for the case of reasons for belief. But strikingly, whereas evidentialism says that reasons to believe that p are evidence *that p*, RAE says instead that reasons for you to believe that p are evidence *that you ought to believe that p*.

This contrast is striking. Whereas there exists a prominent motivation in epistemology for connecting evidence with reasons, and Kearns and Star connect evidence with reasons, they do so in a very different way. But they don't really have much choice about the matter. Both actions and beliefs are things that it can be the case that we ought to do. But only beliefs, and not actions, have contents. So the connection between evidence and reasons postulated by evidentialism does not exist at the right level to generalize from belief to action. But the idea that a reason for you to φ is evidence that you ought to φ does generalize to both belief and action.

The idea that reasons to believe correlate with evidence that you ought to believe has some unexpected, nice consequences when we turn our attention to reasons not to believe. Many orthodox evidentialists believe not only that the only kind of reason to believe that p is evidence that p, but also that the only kind of reason not to believe that p is evidence that $\sim p$. But often you should not believe that p even when the evidence that p is better than the evidence that $\sim p$, particularly when it is only slightly better. So many orthodox evidentialists are committed to the strange claim that you ought not to believe that p even though the reasons to believe that p are better than the reasons not to believe that p. But RAE has no such strange consequence, or at least, not just because of cases like this one. Because you shouldn't form a belief when the evidence on one side is only slightly better than the evidence on the other side, the fact that the evidence on one side is only slightly better than the evidence on the other side is evidence that you shouldn't believe that p. So Kearns and Star can say that there are reasons not to believe that p that are not evidence that $\sim p$, and hence are not forced along with the orthodox evidentialist to say that you ought to do one thing even though the reasons to do the other thing are better.

Still, we can exploit the difference between RAE and the evidentialist's idea about the connection between evidence and reasons for belief to mine as a source of potential counterexamples to the thesis. For example, the fact that you have evidence that p and the fact that you lack evidence for $\sim p$, are each evidence that you rationally ought to believe that p without being evidence that p, as is the fact that most people in the room with you rationally ought to believe that p. But there is also a much more general set of problems for Reasons as Evidence that are independent of its distinctive treatment of reasons for belief.

6.3 Challenges to Reasons as Evidence

As Kearns and Star take pains to emphasize, their thesis is merely that necessarily, whenever a fact is a reason for someone to do something, that fact is also evidence that the agent ought to do that thing, and conversely—it is a thesis about the necessary coextension of the property of being a reason for someone to act in some way and the property of being evidence that they ought to do it. This thesis is more modest than one might expect. It's natural to wonder *why* the set of reasons for someone to do something is necessarily coextensive with the evidence that they should do it. Since long before even Hume, philosophers have been suspicious of unexplained necessities.

There are three possibilities: it could be that a consideration's being a reason for s to φ explains why it is evidence that s ought to φ. It could be the reverse: a consideration's being evidence that s ought to φ explains why it is a reason for s to φ. Or being a reason for s to φ could name the very same property as being evidence that s ought to φ. Kearns and Star recognize that declining to explain the necessary coextension of reasons and evidence is unsatisfactory, writing "we also believe that the *best* explanation of [RAE] is that the property of being a reason and the property of being evidence of an ought are identical" (Kearns and Star [2009, 218]). Nevertheless, it is worth examining all three possibilities.

Philosophers have offered both extensional and explanatory challenges to Kearns and Star's view. Brunero [2009] challenges the coextension thesis from both directions, offering cases suggesting evidence in the absence of corresponding reasons and others suggesting reasons in the absence of evidence. Brunero's first challenge suggests that there are reasons for an agent to act some way that aren't evidence that she ought to act in that way. Brunero asks us to imagine a case where the following is true:

(A) Buying your mother the gift that your father chose would make him happy.

(A) certainly doesn't *entail* that you ought to buy the gift; perhaps it is too expensive or your mother already received a similar gift. The existence of a good reason to do something is consistent with the fact that you ought not to do it. Nevertheless, making your dad happy tends to be one of the things that you ought to do and reasons to do something characteristically make it the case that you ought to do it. As a result, that it would make your father happy is a reason to buy the gift.

However, your father lacks good taste. When he recommends a gift, your mother inevitably finds it a tacky waste of money. Last year it was an ornamental toilet plunger. Before that it was a sizable, Italian marble bust of noted stand-up comedian Don Rickles ("But it's *vintage!*", he insists). Following your father's advice, therefore, defeats the main purpose of getting your mother the gift. Indeed, so great is your mother's irritation on receiving a gift recommended by your father that, in each case, it's unerringly true that you should not have gotten that gift. Doing so invariably turns out to be a mistake. Consequently, (A) is extremely strong evidence that you should get your mother something else.

The axioms of probability entail that you cannot raise the probability for a proposition without lowering the probability for the contrary proposition. Consequently, this conception entails that (A) is not evidence that you ought to buy the gift—after all, (A) is evidence that you should get something else. So (A) challenges both the extensional claim that reasons are a subset of the evidence and the explanatory claim that p is a reason for s to φ because p is evidence that s ought to φ.

Brunero's challenge turns on the fact that (A) is seemingly both a reason to get the gift and evidence that you ought not to get it. It is because of the general fact that (A) cannot be both evidence that p and evidence that $\sim p$, therefore, that this is a case in which (A) fails to be evidence that you ought to get the gift, and hence it's a counterexample to RAE. This general fact should seem familiar. In Chapter 4, we considered the thesis of Exclusivity according to which nothing can be both a reason to φ and a reason not to φ at one and the same time. But this thesis about evidence is very similar to Exclusivity. It says for evidence what Exclusivity says about reasons. So a natural way of thinking about Brunero's first challenge is that it exploits the fact that Exclusivity is less controversial for evidence than it is for reasons.

Brunero's second challenge suggests that some pieces of evidence that an agent ought to act in some way are not reasons for them to act in that way. Consider the contrast between the following:

(B)   I've promised to show up for dinner at seven.
(C)   There is no reason for me not to show up for dinner at seven.

(B) is a consideration that counts in favor of showing up for dinner. But (C) is not; it merely reports the absence of considerations against showing up for dinner. Nevertheless, (C) can clearly raise the probability that I ought to show up for dinner. So (C) offers a case of evidence of an act's rightness without the corresponding reasons to act in that way.

This argument relies on the premise that a report of the nonexistence of reasons for action is not itself a reason for action. This follows from the idea that some normative claims are merely *verdictive* in the sense that they offer a *verdict* on the balance of reasons. Deontic concepts like *permissible* are often thought to be verdictive. For example, we could claim that an act is permissible just when the reasons for the act are strong enough. On its verdictive interpretation, the deontic concept's role is simply to issue a report of or verdict on whether certain reasons are strong enough. If this interpretation is correct, then the normative significance of an act's permissibility is entirely derivative on the reasons it reports. As a result, it appears to some that treating the act's permissibility as a reason *in addition to the reasons it reports* involves some illicit double-counting.[2]

---

[2] We both reject the idea that verdictive facts—particularly facts about the existence of reasons—cannot themselves be reasons. As Schroeder [2009] argues, the argument we've offered above appears to presuppose that reasons are *additive*, that adding a reason to do something to another reason to do it yields stronger support for doing that action. But that presupposition is false. So there is no threat of double-counting the reasons that the verdictive fact reports since adding the reason given by that fact to the reasons it reports needn't yield stronger support, thereby double-counting. However, our position is consistent with the premise that Brunero's counterexample (C) requires, namely, that reports on the *non*existence of reasons are not themselves reasons.

Despite these challenges, many find Kearns and Star's connection between reasons for action and evidence compelling enough to warrant defense against these and similar challenges. Daniel Whiting attributes the difficulties for RAE suggested by Brunero's cases to the choice to associate reasons for action with claims about what ought to be.[3] Whiting proposes that reasons for someone to act are instead evidence for a different claim: that it is right in some respect that the person acts in that way. Critically, a person's act's being right in some respect does not entail that they ought to act in that way. That wrestling bears is good exercise is a respect in which wrestling bears is good for your health. But we cannot conclude that wrestling bears is good for your health, *simpliciter*. Rather, Whiting claims that 'right in some respect' is a *contributory* notion. The good exercise provided by wrestling bears contributes to its being healthy, but it clearly does not contribute enough to make wrestling bears healthy. So Whiting attempts to fortify RAE by weakening the propositions for which reasons are thought to be evidence.

But once Whiting tells us that being right in some respect is a contributory notion, it is clear that being right in some respect is playing what we have called the *explanatory* role of reasons. The respects in which something is right weigh against one another in order to contribute to the answer to what it is overall right to do. This means that we face a choice in making sense of Whiting's view. Either we must give up the idea that reasons play the explanatory role, postulating something else not called 'reasons' to play this role, or else what we are ultimately claiming is that reasons must be evidence of themselves—that they must be in a certain sense *self-disclosive*. Whiting may prefer the first fork of this dilemma, as Kearns and Star are likely to, but since we began our investigation of reasons looking for what plays reasons' explanatory role, this strikes us as giving up too much.

On the other hand, the thesis that reasons must be self-disclosive is not trivial. For example, the parallel thesis about secret agents is false: a person is a secret agent just when they offer evidence that a secret agent exists. But it seems to us that some reasons can fail to disclose themselves when met with sufficient ignorance. Imagine a society that is bigoted enough that no member of the society recognizes the claims of trans people. The bigots all believe that trans people are mistaken about their genders. Learning that a trans man self-identifies as a man, consequently, does not raise the bigot's

---

[3] Whiting [2018].

likelihood that treating the trans man as a man is right in some respect, owing to the bigot's deep-seated bigotry. Nevertheless, the fact that someone self-identifies as a man is a reason to treat them as a man. So some reasons are not evidence of acts being right in some respect.[4] Whiting might reply that it's not the bigot's body of information that matters, but my own, exploiting the body-of-evidence-relativity of reasons that we have already spotted to Kearns and Star. But unfortunately this will not work, because I could be just as deluded as the bigot about whether trans men are men, so the problem will reproduce itself.

All of these arguments indirectly challenge explanations of one notion in terms of the other by directly challenging their extensional implications. But the explanations can also be challenged more directly. For example, McNaughton and Rawling [2011] remind us of a familiar distinction between how divine judgments about what's forbidden and permissible might relate to obligations:

Divine Command Theory (DCT) holds that φ-ing is obligatory just when God commands it, and that when φ-ing is obligatory, this is because God commands it. God has the power to make acts obligatory.

Divine Advice Theory (DAT) agrees that φ-ing is obligatory just when God commands it. But, according to DAT, when φ-ing is obligatory, God commands it because it's obligatory—God has *infallible* epistemic access to the normative facts.

In both cases, a necessary connection relates God's command that φ-ing is obligatory and φ-ing's being obligatory. DCT offers an explanation of that connection: God's commands *make it the case* that φ-ing is obligatory. The commands are metaphysically prior to the obligations. By contrast, DAT offers a different explanation of why we find a divine command wherever there is an obligation: God is *infallible* and so never fails to command what is obligatory and never commands something that isn't obligatory. According

---

[4] By contrast, Sophie Keeling [2022] provides the resources for an argument that reasons for *belief*, at least, do disclose themselves. The idea that normative reasons have their deliberative role essentially supports the idea that p is a reason for believing that q only if you can believe that p for q. But Keeling [2022] defends a view close to the following: one believes that p for the reason that q only if one's evidence justifies the belief that p is a reason for q. If those two conditionals are right, then it follows that p is a reason for believing that q only if one's evidence justifies the belief that p is a reason for q, which is very *close* to the thesis that reasons for belief are self-disclosive.

to DAT, God's commands do not make any obligations hold. Rather, the obligations are metaphysically prior to the commands. These relations are logically distinct: the first entails the metaphysical priority of commands over obligations, the latter does not.

As we've been stressing, reasons are competitors. Reasons compete to determine the overall normative status of someone's actions, thoughts, and feelings. On this way of thinking, competition between reasons plays the same role that divine commands play in DCT. Just as commands determine obligations, according to DCT, reasons characteristically determine the overall normative status of actions, thoughts, and feelings. This is what we called Ross's Picture in Chapter 1. Evidence, by contrast, plays the role that divine advice plays: it tracks, but does not determine, obligations. While it is important to acknowledge that some things that are evidence for something else are also part of the explanation of why that something else is true, as we have seen this is not *in general* true. So the explanatory version of RAE is incompatible with Ross's picture. As a result, so long as we seek the appeal of Ross's picture, we cannot identify the property of being a reason for someone to act with the property of being evidence that they ought to act in that way.

6.4 Evidence as Reasons for Belief

We've focused in this chapter on identifying difficulties for the view that being a reason for action is being evidence for some ought fact. One way of thinking about the source of the difficulties for this view is by focusing on the observation that it attempts to bridge two gaps simultaneously: not just the gap between reasons and evidence, but also the gap between action and belief, since reasons for action bear on action but evidence bears on belief. So in a way, we should not be shocked that the view faces these difficulties, given its ambition to clear two gaps with a single theory.

But there is only a single, comparatively modest gap between reasons for belief and evidence, since both categories concern only belief. So the opposite order of explanation—taking the parallels between reasons and evidence to derive from the fact that evidence provides a reason to believe—only has to cross this modest gap. Let us call the strategy of appealing to this reversed order of explanation *Evidence as Reasons* (EAR).[5]

---

[5] Compare Schroeder [2021b, chapter one].

It is worth noting that EAR shares with RAE some of the problems that we raised earlier that arise from the assumption that evidence that p must raise the prior probability that p. Once you become certain that p, nothing can raise the probability that p relative to your existing beliefs. Yet it seems that you can have reasons to believe that p and indeed that you may continue to believe that p for those reasons. Both views seem to imply that reasons for belief can do their jobs *too* well, entirely disappearing if they are entirely convincing. Here much of the space for solutions and implications is the same, but not all. On Kearns and Star's version of RAE, the fact that all evidence is relative to background beliefs leads to the conclusion that all reasons are relative to background evidence—including reasons for action. But EAR doesn't tell us anything about reasons for action, intention, or emotions. It only tells us something about the connection between evidence and reasons for belief. So this looks at least like an initial mark in favor of EAR over RAE.

But proposing an alternative order of explanation falls short of articulating any precise alternative thesis. What form should EAR take? A first troublesome thought is that there are significant costs to understanding EAR as offering any kind of analysis of evidence in terms of reasons. If evidence is just a reason to believe, then the evidentialist's thesis that the only true reasons to believe that p consist in evidence that p is trivial, and would be true even if you can give someone a genuine reason to believe that you are poverty-stricken by offering them a million dollars to do so. In order for evidentialism to be a substantive thesis that can rule this possibility out, we need a prior and independent notion of evidence in order to constrain what can count as a genuine reason for belief. And because the debate between evidentialists and non-evidentialists is a substantive one, we need this notion even if we are not ourselves persuaded that evidentialism is true.

Another worry that you might have about EAR derives from the fact that evidence seems to bear equally on the attitudes of doubt and belief. Just as evidence that p is reason to believe that p, evidence that p is also reason to doubt that $\sim p$. There can be both objective and subjective reasons to doubt that $\sim p$, which correspond to objective and subjective evidence that p, respectively, the reasons to doubt that $\sim p$ compete with reasons not to doubt that $\sim p$, and so on for each of the other striking parallels that we have drawn between reasons and evidence. So even if evidence that p is always reason to believe that p, it is also always reason to doubt that $\sim p$. It is not clear why either of these attitudes should play a privileged role in the analysis.

Here is one way that we might go about trying to solve both of these problems. Recall the thesis of *core reasons* from Chapter 5. According to this thesis, objective and subjective reasons are just two different reflections of a core notion of a reason—objective reasons imposing worldly conditions on core reasons, and subjective reasons imposing perspectival conditions. Accepting core reasons allows us to say that just as there is a core concept of a reason from which both objective and subjective reasons are defined, so too is there a core concept of evidence from which both objective and subjective evidence are defined.

It turns out that there is a whole area of inquiry known as *confirmation theory* that is concerned with constructing measures of how much one proposition evidentially supports another proposition relative to some background probability function.[6] Although confirmation theory has explored many different candidates for *how* to measure degrees of evidential support, one thing that they typically have in common is that they assign values to degrees of support to propositions irrespective of whether those propositions are believed or true. So confirmation theory is naturally understood in our terms as measuring degrees neither of objective evidence nor of subjective evidence, but of what we might call *core* evidence.

Consequently if we help ourselves to the thesis of core reasons from Chapter 5 and also to the concept of core evidence as elucidated by confirmation theory, then we can formulate evidentialism as the thesis that core reasons to believe that p must be core evidence that p. On this picture, what constrains whether my offer to give you a million dollars to believe that I am poverty-stricken can count as a genuine reason for belief or not derives from the relationship between core evidence and core reasons, so it is actually consistent with the idea that EAR can be interpreted as analyzing objective evidence in terms of objective reasons and subjective evidence in terms of subjective reasons.

But our second problem still militates in favor of not interpreting EAR as an analysis (or pair of analyses). We might instead interpret it simply as the converse of evidentialism formulated in terms of core reasons:

Evidence as Reasons   Core evidence that p is always core reason to believe that p.

On this picture, objective evidence and subjective evidence can be straightforwardly defined in terms of core evidence in precisely analogous ways to how we define objective and subjective reasons in terms of core reasons, by

---

[6] For an accessible introduction, see Joyce and Hayek [2008].

adding truth or perspective conditions, respectively. But the explanation of *why* we have these concepts of evidence and *why* they are important, as well as of *why* we observe and single out other properties of evidence as important, is that evidence is always reason to believe, and these concepts and distinctions are important to make for reasons. *Ipso facto*, they are important to make for evidence. On this way of understanding EAR, it is no more fundamental a thesis than the corresponding thesis that core evidence that p is always core reason to doubt that $\sim p$.

We do not take this observation to imply that evidence has no deliberative role. Rather, we take it to show that evidence bears on deliberation only through its connection to epistemic reasons. This has important implications for our ontology of reasons for belief. Only propositions, perhaps only true propositions, can be evidence. If evidence figures directly in doxastic deliberation, and if only epistemic reasons figure in doxastic deliberation, then we have a powerful argument for our ontology of reasons for belief: that is, since some epistemic reasons are evidence, plausibly all epistemic reasons are propositions. To be clear, it is almost uniformly assumed that epistemic reasons are propositions. But examining the implications of this position will also have to wait until Chapter 10.

Chapter Summary

In this chapter we have explored the relationship between reasons and evidence. We observed a number of important similarities between reasons and evidence, and we explored whether these similarities could be precisified into a tighter correlation between reasons and evidence, along the lines of Kearns and Star's thesis of Reasons as Evidence. RAE, we suggested following a long line of diagnoses in the literature, loses sight of the explanatory role of reasons because evidence is more promiscuous than explanation. So RAE can plausibly only be defended as part of a package of views that decentralizes the explanatory role of reasons. Still, even if RAE is not exactly true, that leaves open the possibility of other close connections between reasons and evidence.

Recommended Reading

The idea that reasons are closely connected with evidence of what you ought to do is prominently defended by Judith Jarvis Thomson in her book

Normativity and by Stephen Kearns and Daniel Star in a series of papers led by 'Reasons as Evidence' and 'Reasons: Explanations or Evidence?'. We have relied extensively in this chapter on John Brunero's response to Kearns and Star, 'Reasons, Evidence, and Explanations', and on chapter one of Jonathan Dancy's *Ethics Without Principles*. We recommend reading the chapter alongside Kearns and Star's 'Reasons as Evidence'.

Exercises

6.1 *Comprehension.* Construct an example in which evidence that something is true is *undercut* by some further evidence. Then construct an example in which a reason to do something is undercut by some further reason. What makes both of these count as cases of undercutting defeat?

6.2 *Extensions.* In section 6.1 we support the claim that the objective/subjective distinction can be made for evidence as well as for reasons by giving a case of something that is subjective evidence but not objective evidence. Give your own case illustrating this distinction by pulling them apart in the other direction. Which case is more compelling? How does this compare to the grounds for making the objective/subjective distinction with respect to reasons?

6.3 *Extensions.* Earlier we distinguished between objective and subjective *oughts*. Evaluate whether reasons are evidence of what you objectively ought to do or evidence of what you subjectively ought to do by combining each of these answers with the idea that objective reasons are objective evidence and subjective reasons are subjective evidence. Which combination of views is more defensible?

6.4 *Extensions.* Now evaluate the question of whether reasons are evidence of the objective or subjective *ought* by focusing on the case of reasons for *belief*. Help yourself to the assumption that you ought to believe that p just in case it is true that p. What conclusions does this assumption let you draw about what sorts of things are reasons to believe that p? What, if any, analogous conclusions can you draw about what sorts of things are reasons not to believe that p?

6.5 *Extensions.* Continuing from the last exercise, now consider the alternative proposal that objective reasons are evidence of what you objectively ought to do and subjective reasons are evidence of what you subjectively ought to do. Is this an improvement on the views considered in exercise 6.4? Why or why not?

6.6 *Extensions.* It is often thought that what is evidence for one person is not evidence for another, because evidence that p must raise the probability that p, and what raises the probability that p will be different for different priors. So now compare two kinds of evidence that you ought to φ—evidence relative to *your* prior probabilities, and evidence relative to *my* prior probabilities. When I say that there is a reason for you to φ, which of these two kinds of evidence am I talking about? Does it matter whether we are talking about objective or subjective reasons?

6.7 *Extensions.* Part of the appeal of RAE comes from the plausibility that reasoning about what to do will have to involve considering evidence about what you ought to do, and one natural way of supporting this idea is by appeal to the thesis that reasoning about what to do is just reasoning about what you *ought* to do. Test how well this thesis generalizes to other applications of RAE by answering whether the kind of reasoning that leads to beliefs, intentions, or emotions is just reasoning about what you ought to believe, intend, or feel.

6.8 *Extensions.* Is core evidence that p always reason to believe that p? Suppose that you have bought a ticket in a fair lottery with millions of tickets. The fact that the lottery is fair and has millions of tickets is evidence that your ticket will lose. Is it a reason to believe that you will lose? Why or why not? Is it evidence that you ought to believe that your ticket will lose? How do the theses of RAE and EAR fare in light of your observations?

7
Reasons and Explanation

7.1 Introduction

In the last chapter, we considered the important hypothesis that reasons might be analyzable as evidence of what you ought to do. We ended up being cautiously skeptical about the idea that a consideration's being evidence for some fact about what you ought to do (or believe or feel) explains why it gives a reason for you to act or believe in that way. Part of our grounds for doubt comes from the apparent extensional mismatch between being a reason for something and being evidence that you ought to do it, as made vivid by the cases from Brunero.

This mismatch, we suggested, can be partly traced to the fact that *Exclusivity* is more complex for reasons than for evidence. Evidence is exclusive: if a claim is evidence for some proposition p, it is not also evidence for ~p. But, as Dancy shows us, an analogous formulation of Exclusivity for reasons fails. The fact that there's a famous person at the bar is a reason to introduce yourself (relative to the goal of meeting people) and a reason to avoid introducing yourself (relative to the goal of not getting snubbed). So a consideration can be a reason to φ and a reason not to φ, for some action φ. Reasons like Dancy's create a recipe for counterexamples to the idea that reasons are evidence. Whereas a consideration can be evidence either for or against the claim that you ought to do something, but not both, considerations like Dancy's can simultaneously be a reason to do it and to avoid doing it. These reasons guarantee that there's at least one respect in which the consideration is a reason in which it's not also evidence.

A second difference is responsible for the mismatch between explanations and evidence. A fact contributes to an explanation of what you ought to do when it contributes to making it the case that you ought to do it. But a fact can be evidence that you ought to do something without helping to make it the case that you ought to do it when it is merely correlated with the explanatory facts. Being a resident of Montreal makes it the case that you are cold half of the year and that you should root for the Montreal Canadiens. Because other places are not as cold, the fact that you are cold half the year is evidence that you should root for the Montreal Canadiens. But the fact that you are cold half the year is not a reason to root for Les Canadiens because you might be cold half the year because you live in Edmonton. Therefore, the connection between evidence and what you ought to do is more promiscuous than the connection between explanation and what you ought to do, which allows for an extensional mismatch between the two categories.

So it seems clear that reasons are intimately connected with what we ought to do, and it is dubious that they are connected because the latter is evidence for the former. The structure of the cases that bring this out emphasize the contrast between the promiscuity of evidence of what you ought to do in comparison to reasons' role in *affecting, determining*, or *explaining* what you ought to do. And so one very natural moral to take away from these lessons is that instead of being evidence of what you ought to do, the right way to get insight into the nature of reasons is to focus on their role in *explaining* what we ought to do, thus privileging the *explanatory* role of reasons as right-makers first introduced in section 1.3. According to the simplest and most naïve version of this view, a fact is a reason when it explains what we ought to do.

We first encountered a version of the idea that reasons are explanations of what we ought to do in Chapter 1, where we considered whether normative reasons are a special case of explanatory reasons. If reasons are explanations of what we ought to do, then they are a special case of explanatory reasons. So the naïve view simplifies our picture of reasons, by reducing normative reasons to explanatory reasons with a distinctive kind of explanandum (the thing to be explained). Another virtue of the naïve view is that it makes easy sense of why we can sometimes communicate that something is a normative reason for you to do something by saying that it is why you ought to do it. On the naïve view, the relationship between this way of reporting a normative reason and saying that it is a normative reason for you to do it is the relationship between giving a definition and stating the thing defined.

But how do reasons explain what we ought to do? Consider an analogy. When trying to explain why some event took place it's normal to look for its cause. Why did the match light? Because it was struck. This answer may seem simplistic. The explanation of why the match lit might be a more complex fact, of which the fact that it was struck is a mere part along with the fact that the match was dry, that there was sufficient oxygen about, that there wasn't a stiff breeze blowing, etc. Or it may be *an* explanation, one among many. We needn't decide: in all cases, the naïve view holds that the fact that the match was struck is an explainer.

We might be tempted to think something analogous about reasons: the reason why I ought to jump in the lake is that a drowning person needs my help. The naïve view holds that the fact that a drowning person needs my help explains or is part of the explanation of why I ought to jump in. However, this analogy is imperfect. There are no causes without effects—an event is a cause only in virtue of producing an effect. Otherwise, what is the cause a cause of? In contrast, there are reasons for things I ought not to do. After all, the fact that the water is chilly is a *bona fide* reason not to jump in and save the drowning person, even if I ought to save them. More generally, 'explains' is factive in both of its argument spaces. P explains Q only if P and Q. If r is a reason because it explains why I ought to φ, then r is a reason only if I ought to φ. But there can be reasons to do things that we ought not to do. So the simple analogy between reasons and causes cannot hold. Though there are no causes without the corresponding effects, there are reasons without the corresponding *oughts*. So the main problem with this naïve view is that it denies that outweighed reasons are reasons.

Those attracted to the naïve view may respond that the foregoing reasoning is too stingy with the *ought*-facts to be explained, calling attention to the many senses that 'ought' can take in different contexts. After all, perhaps we can say about one and the same situation, depending on which values we are focused on, that Joe ought to be at the movies with us (because he promised that he would join us) or that he ought not to be at the movies with us (because he should be in class instead) or that he ought to be at the movies with us (because he would love this movie). Likewise, it may be that you ought, all things considered, to save the drowning person or that you ought morally to save them. But perhaps that's compatible with the fact that you ought in some other sense not to save them, if your overriding goal is to stay dry and warm.[1] And we can divide senses of *ought* further still. If you *only* care about being warm and not at all about whether you're dry, then you ought to save the drowning person if the water's warm.

So, in addition to the all-things-considered *ought* and the moral *ought*, perhaps there is the *ought* of staying warm, which differs from the *ought* of staying warm and dry, which itself differs from the *ought* of staying warm and dry and respecting human life, and so on. Some philosophers may use

---

[1] One prominent dissenter from this view of 'ought' comes from Judith Jarvis Thomson [2008].

this observation to argue that the limit of this process is that for each reason to do something, there is after all a sense of *ought* in which you ought to do it.[2] As a result, each reason can be the explainer of an extremely narrow *ought*.

Indeed, this thought becomes natural if reasons are the contemporary heirs of Ross's *prima facie* duties. Ross begins *The Right and the Good* by arguing that our duties have different grounds. Sometimes a duty to act some way is grounded in the act's good effects. But some duties, including the duty to keep promises, are not so grounded. Ross thereby posits a plurality of duties from competing sources. Where Ross spoke of *prima facie* duties, we now speak of reasons. But *prima facie* duties, you might think, are expressible with *ought*s. For example, Ross thought that, other things equal, you ought not to lie, you ought to be benevolent, you ought to be grateful and so on. Consequently, since on this way of thinking about Ross's view there is a close correspondence between reasons and *prima facie* duties and a close correspondence between *prima facie* duties and certain *ought*s, it follows that there's a close correspondence between reasons and certain *ought*s.

In order for this defense to succeed, it must turn out to be true that there really are so many different kinds of *ought*. But although it is true that 'ought' can be used to make a number of different kinds of claim, there are also reasons to doubt that it can be so indiscriminate. More importantly, it threatens to lose track of the important distinction between what we ought to do and what we merely have reason to do.

7.2 Weighing Explanations

In the last section we saw that one way of defending the idea that reasons are explanations of what you ought to do in the face of the objection that explanation is factive and there can be reasons for competing options is to weaken the role of *ought* in this account. But John Broome famously takes a different approach.[3] He is attracted to the idea that reasons are explanations of what you ought to do, but acknowledges that there are reasons to do things that it is not the case that you ought to do, and agrees that there are

---

[2] Compare Finlay [2014]. See also Whiting [2018], discussed in Chapter 6, who talks in a similar vein about 'respects' in which something is right.
[3] Broome [2004].

not enough *oughts* to go around in order to evade this difficulty. So instead of weakening the role of *ought* in this account, he instead tries, in effect, to weaken the role of explanation. According to Broome, what makes something a reason is not whether it explains *why* you ought to do something, but instead the role that it plays in explaining *whether* you ought to do it. Explanation whether is weaker than explanation why. In particular, it is not factive.

The way that Broome describes his view is by saying that reasons contribute to a special kind of explanation, which he calls a *weighing* explanation. Weighing explanations allow defeated reasons to play a key role in the explanation of what you ought to do. According to a weighing explanation, you ought to do something just when and because the reasons for doing it are *decisive*. Being decisive is a relational property. The reasons for doing something are decisive, relative to a set of countervailing reasons, just when and because they outweigh those reasons. Consequently, defeated reasons play a key role in a weighing explanation of what one ought to do. Their weight is part of the explanation of why the decisive reasons are decisive and so they are part of the explanation of why you ought to do what they favor.

Weighing explanations are a natural fallback position for those attracted by the naïve view but who also accept that outweighed reasons are reasons. The naïve view is too stingy, falsely requiring that something make it the case that you ought to do something in order for it to be a reason. A natural solution is to weaken the naïve view's analysis and say that a consideration need not make some *ought*-fact true; it need only go some ways toward making it true. So we are led to think that a consideration is a reason for something when it *contributes* to the case for why you ought to do it.

The problem with this approach is that this contributory role is precisely the role in need of characterization.[4] To paraphrase Scanlon, any attempt to explain what it is to contribute to the case for why you ought to do it seems to me to lead back to the same idea: to be a reason to do it. "To be a reason how?" one might ask. "By contributing to the case for why you ought to do it" seems to be the only answer. The weighing explanation does not clarify why some considerations are weighed and others are not—that is, it does not explain why some considerations are reasons and others are not. It merely says that once you have these things, what you ought to do is determined by the decisive set of them. So while weighing explanations find a place for

---

[4] This point has been much emphasized in many responses to Broome, but especially clearly and in great detail in Dancy [2004, chapters 2–4].

defeated reasons in explaining what you should do, they seem to *rely* on a prior notion of reasons rather than give an account of them. So it seems that what is really going on, whether Broome would describe things in this way or not, is that weighing explanations explain *oughts* with claims about reasons, but they don't analyze reasons.

Let's recap where we are so far. We've observed that an important part of the source of potential counterexamples to the thesis of reasons as evidence comes from the fact that evidence is so much more promiscuous than explanation. This motivates the idea that reasons are closely tied to explanation, rather than evidence, and we have been exploring different versions of the idea that reasons are explanations of what you *ought* to do. And we've seen that despite its initial appeal, this idea faces several steep challenges. Still, reasons could be tied to explanation without being tied to explanation of what you ought to do. The nature of reasons might instead be to be an explanation of something else.[5]

For example, according to a common form of the historically popular value-based theory of reasons, reasons are explanations of why there is something *good* about your doing something. We can see that this view retains much of the force of our earlier diagnosis of the counterexamples to Reasons as Evidence by returning to McNaughton and Rawlings' example of the Divine Advice Theory. According to the Divine Advice Theory, God is omniscient about what we ought to do and so out of Their omnibenevolence, They command us to do all and only the things that we ought to do. On this view, God's commands are evidence of what we ought to do, but don't explain what we ought to do, and this made them intuitive counterexamples to Reasons as Evidence. But similarly, on the Divine Advice Theory God's commands also do not explain why there is anything good about doing something—they may be good, but not because of God's commands. So the value-based theorist can maintain that they can give the same diagnosis as the naïve theory of why they get the intuitively right result about cases like this one.

Mediating reasons' connection to what we ought to do through value therefore helps to vindicate their explanatory role. They explain what we ought to do by explaining some different fact on which what we ought to do depends. But this strategy generalizes. For example, according to a natural version of the Humean Theory of Reasons, a second historically popular view that we first encountered in Chapter 5, you ought to do what would

---

[5] This is how one of us, Mark Schroeder, thought about the relationship between reasons and explanation at the time of writing *Slaves of the Passions* (Schroeder [2007b]).

most promote the satisfaction of your desires. This allows reasons to bear indirectly on what we ought to do by explaining what would promote our desires. So even if you have no desire to obey God, God's commands can still be evidence that some actions would promote your desires, making them evidence of what you ought to do without being reasons for you to do it.

Like weighing explanations, a chief advantage of these approaches is that they correctly classify outweighed reasons as reasons. That's because there can be both values and desires on each side of a choice. Moreover, because goodness and desire satisfaction come in degrees, the account is well placed to explain differences between reasons' weights. The greater the good or the stronger the desire whose promotion is explained by a consideration, the stronger the reason given by that consideration.[6]

We have also encountered a third view in this book that is also naturally construed as taking this same form. Recall from Chapter 1 Daniel Fogal's observation that 'reason' can be used as either a count noun or a mass noun. Usually, when a word—like 'beer'—can be used as either a count noun or a mass noun, its mass noun use is analytically and semantically prior. A beer, for example (count noun), is just a serving of beer (mass noun). Similarly, Fogal claims that reasons must be understood in terms of *reason*.[7] But the view that reasons are servings or amounts of reason does not fit well with our best candidates for the substance of reasons from Chapter 2. In contrast, the idea that reasons are considerations that explain why there is reason (mass noun) for you to do something *is* compatible with the leading accounts of the substance of reasons (count noun) from Chapter 2. And this view shares with each of the other views canvassed in this chapter the idea that reasons are explanations of something, simply differing over what it takes reasons to be explanations *of*.

So the idea that reasons can be analyzed as explanations of *something*, just not of what you ought to do, is justly popular. It is shared by a variety of views about the nature of reasons that nevertheless vary considerably along other dimensions.

7.3 Objective and Subjective Reasons

But the idea that reasons are by their nature explanations—of anything, even of *reason* (mass noun)—casts heavy constraints over how we think about

---

[6] Schroeder [2007b] calls this thesis *proportionalism*.   [7] Fogal [2016].

subjective reasons, and about the relationship between objective and subjective reasons. The reason for this is simple, and we already encountered a simple version of it in Chapter 1. Explanation is factive in *both* places. If the explanation of why P is that Q, then it must be true both that *P and* that Q. So if reasons are explanations of anything, then reasons must be truths.

Because explanation is factive, the idea that reasons are explanations is most naturally tied to accounting for the nature of objective normative reasons. We saw in Chapter 1 that on the leading accounts of objective normative reasons, their substance consists, either partly or wholly, of facts—understood either as true propositions, or as truth-makers for propositions. And because true propositions are true and truth-makers make propositions true, both of these accounts of the substance of objective normative reasons build in the assumption that objective normative reasons are closely associated with or identical with truths—they are the right kind of thing to be explanations of something else.

But if objective normative reasons consist by nature in explanations of something else, then they must not be analyzable in terms of subjective reasons, as considered in Chapter 5, either. So if we apply the explanatory account of reasons directly to objective reasons, then it constrains the relationship between objective and subjective reasons—it rules out the idea that subjective reasons come first in priority.

Indeed, it does more. In addition to the views that objective reasons are analyzable in terms of subjective reasons and that subjective reasons are analyzable in terms of objective reasons, in Chapter 5 we encountered the thesis of *Core Reasons*, according to which both objective and subjective reasons are reflections of a common core. According to Core Reasons, there is a core notion of a reason that imposes neither the constraint of truth nor the constraint of perspective, but which, when truth is added to it yields an objective reason and when perspective is added to it yields a subjective reason. Core reasons need not be truths, and so by the factivity of reasons, core reasons cannot be explanations of anything. So the idea that some kind of normative reason can be analyzed as explanations of something is not compatible with the thesis of Core Reasons. Core Reasons tells us that neither objective nor subjective reasons are analyzed in this way, and it requires that core reasons be non-factive. So no kind of normative reasons consists in a kind of explanation.

And of course we already know that if we apply the idea that reasons are explanations directly to subjective reasons, it requires that subjective reasons must be truths. But as we've seen in earlier chapters, the idea that subjective reasons must be truths is deeply controversial. It entails either that you can't have any subjective reasons when your perspective is mistaken, or that your subjective reasons don't match what you are thinking about when you are reasoning, in tension with simple versions of the deliberative role of reasons considered in Chapter 2. And if the idea that reasons are explanations cannot be applied directly to either subjective reasons or core reasons, then it is not just natural to apply it to objective reasons. Rather, it can *only* be applied to objective reasons. So it places a heavy constraint on our account of subjective reasons and on the relationship between objective and subjective reasons.

The main reason why we spent time in Chapter 5 exploring the relationship between objective and subjective reasons, recall, was that there is a close relationship between the kinds of cases in which you have an objective reason to do something and those in which you have a subjective reason to do it. But we also noted in Chapter 5 that there are problems with the idea that subjective reasons can be analyzed in terms of objective reasons, unless we embrace the consequence that subjective reasons must be truths. So it follows that the idea that reasons consist in explanations of something faces a challenge in understanding what the relationship is between objective and subjective reasons that leads them to correspond to the extent that they do.

But perhaps some versions of the idea that reasons are explanations might give us enough additional structure to allow for alternative views about why objective and subjective reasons correspond to the extent that they do. For example, according to the value-based theory of reasons, reasons are explanations of why your doing something would serve some value. Intuitively, this yields an account of objective normative reasons, because if your action truly serves some value, then there is something genuinely advisable about you doing it.

But value-based theorists might contend that there are two kinds of values—both *actual* and *expected*. Whereas receiving money is an actual value, having a *high subjective probability* of receiving money would count, on this view, as an *expected* value. The fact that someone will give you money if you give them your used book explains why giving them your used book will lead to you receiving money, and so it explains why it serves an actual value. So this fact is a reason to give them your used book. But the fact that you are 60 percent confident that someone will give you money if you give them your used book explains why giving them your used book will lead to a 60 percent subjective probability of you receiving money, and so it explains why it serves an expected value. So this fact is also, on the value-based view, a reason to give them your used book.

But the value-based theorist can say that the difference between actual and expected values yields a corresponding difference between their resulting reasons. On this view, explanations of why an action serves an actual value are objective normative reasons, and explanations of why an action serves an expected value are subjective normative reasons.[8] The resulting view endorses the idea that subjective reasons must be truths, but says that they are always the facts about your psychological state that determine what your subjective probabilities are. But it offers a different kind of explanation of the correspondence between objective and subjective reasons that is compatible with the idea that reasons are explanations. This correspondence comes, according to this way of trying to defend the value-based view, from the correspondence between kinds of value—actual and expected.

However, the views that reasons are explanations of what serves your desires or of what there is reason (mass noun) for you to do may not be able to avail themselves of this kind of explanation equally well as the value-based theory. There are not, after all, two kinds of desires—actual and expected—nor are there obviously two kinds of reason (mass noun). So the commitments of the view that reasons are explanations seem to depend on which view we take of what they are explanations *of*.

7.4 Relocating the Role of Explanation

Throughout this chapter we have been exploring the relationship between reasons and explanation through the lens of the idea that reasons are explanations *of* something. On one view, they are explanations of what you ought to do. This view faces problems with the fact that there are routinely competing reasons to do incompatible things, even though there is only one thing that you ought to do, and we saw attempts to address this problem by weakening 'ought' claims or by weakening the kind of explanation that is required. On other views, they are explanations of what would serve some value, some desire, or be what there is reason (mass noun) to do. All of these views face a sharply constrained version of the general problems about understanding the nature of subjective reasons and about how to

---

[8] Compare Wedgwood [2017, chapters 8–9].

understand the relationship between objective and subjective reasons that we explored in Chapter 5, though as we saw, some have more resources to answer these questions than others.

We've focused on these views because the fact that evidence is more indiscriminate than explanation looked like such a plausible diagnosis of the source of counterexamples to the thesis of Reasons as Evidence. A general recipe to find counterexamples to this thesis is to construct cases of evidence that you ought to do something that does not itself help to explain why it is what you ought to do. And so the idea that reasons must be explanations seems like the right kind of thesis to vindicate this diagnosis. And it is natural for proponents of the view that reasons explain value, desire, or reason (mass noun) to hope that their views can retain this diagnosis.

Diagnosis   Examples in which something is evidence that you ought to do something without explaining why you ought to do it work as counterexamples to the thesis of Reasons as Evidence because reasons are closely connected to explanation.

Hypothesis 1   Reasons are closely connected to explanation because what it is to be a reason is to be an explanation of something.

All of these justifications of this diagnosis share in common that they look for the connection between reasons and explanation in the nature of reasons. But it is possible that all of this is a mistake. Instead, the connection between reasons and explanation might come from the nature of *ought*. On this alternative picture, what you ought to do is by nature a matter of what there is most reason for you to do.

Hypothesis 2   Reasons are closely connected to explanation because *ought* facts are facts about the balance of reasons, and so are always explained by the existence of reasons.

This picture inverts Broome's account. Broome's account says that things are reasons because they play the right role in weighing explanations of what you ought to do. But on this alternative picture, things play the weighing role in explanations of what you ought to do because they are reasons, and what you ought to do is by analysis just a matter of what wins the weighing competition between reasons.

This picture justifies our diagnosis of the source of the recipe for counterexamples to Evidence as Reasons at least as well as any of the views on which reasons consist in explanations of something. But it leaves unconstrained the nature of reasons. For all that it says, reasons could have any kind of analysis at all—or none. On the one hand, this means that on this picture we learn less about reasons from the recipe for counterexamples to Evidence as Reasons than we otherwise might. But on the other hand, it lends additional support to Ross's picture from Chapter 1, on which what we ought to do is best explained by the competition between reasons. And it opens up a range of new possibilities for how reasons themselves might be explained—including those we now turn to, in Chapter 8.

Chapter Summary

In this chapter we have been looking for the right relationship between reasons and explanation. We began with the idea that reasons are just explanations of what you ought to do. But this idea ran into trouble with the fact that there are many reasons to do things that it is not the case that you ought to do. This led us to the idea that to be a reason is to be an explanation of something *else*—an idea encoded in many traditional accounts of reasons, value-based, desire-based, and otherwise. But we also observed that the connection between reasons and explanation might tell us nothing directly about what reasons are, and only about *ought*. If *ought* facts *consist* in facts about the balance of reasons, then what you ought to do will always be explained by what reasons you have to do it. This observation opens up many more possible package views about what reasons are that can respect the explanatory role of reasons.

Recommended Reading

In this chapter we have followed Broome's strategy for accounting for reasons as explanations of what we ought to do in his paper, 'Reasons'. Jacob Nebel tries to defend this view without appealing to Broome's strategy in 'Normative Reasons as Reasons Why We Ought'. The idea that normative reasons are by nature explanations of something else—desire, value, or (mass noun) reason—can be found in chapter two of Mark Schroeder's *Slaves of the Passions*, chapter four of Stephen Finlay's *A Confusion of*

Tongues, and in Daniel Fogal's 'Reasons, Reason, and Context'. We recommend that reading this chapter pairs particularly well with Broome's 'Reasons'.

Exercises

7.1 *Comprehension*. Explain why Broome doesn't endorse the simple view that r is a reason for s to φ just in case r is the reason why s ought to φ.

7.2 *Extensions*. In section 7.2 we considered the idea that value-based, desire-based, and mass-noun-first theories of reasons could coopt the same diagnosis of the source of the counterexamples to Reasons as Evidence as the view that reasons are explanations of what you ought to do. Test this idea by exploring whether you can construct a case in which what explains what you ought to do comes apart from what explains what value would be served by your doing it. Is it easier to construct cases in which something explains why you ought (or ought not) to do something without explaining what would be good about your doing (or not doing) it? Or the reverse? Are the cases where these come apart intuitively reasons to do (or not do) it? What does this tell you about whether the value-based view successfully coopts the diagnosis?

7.3 *Extensions*. According to a defense of the value-based theory of reasons considered in section 7.3, actual and expected values are each kinds of value, in the sense in which reasons are explanations of why doing something would serve some value. Evaluate this claim by comparing it to the alternative claim that there is one kind of value—actual value—and expected values are not values at all, strictly speaking, but just expectations about values. Which of these two views seems more defensible to you? Why?

7.4 *Extensions*. If expected values are a kind of value, then is there a third kind of value—expectations of expected value? Why or why not? What does your answer tell you about the plausibility of the view that expected values are a kind of value?

7.5 *Extensions*. Should the mass-noun-first view distinguish between objective and subjective reason (mass noun) in the way that the value-based view distinguishes between actual and expected value? Suppose that we do. Could either be analyzed in terms of subjunctive conditionals about the other, or would we get conditional fallacy style counterexamples (give an example or explain why not)? Are there any new obstacles in this case that we did not encounter when trying to distinguish between objective and subjective reasons (count noun)?

7.6 *Extensions.* Is it intelligible to distinguish between actual and expected desires?

7.7 *Extensions.* In sections 7.1 and 7.2 we considered the diagnosis that the reason why many plausible counterexamples to Reasons as Evidence take the form of evidence of why you ought to do something that does not help to explain why you ought to do it is because it is part of the nature of reasons to explain. In section 7.4 we considered the competing diagnosis that this is because it is part of the nature of *ought* facts to be explained by reasons. For this exercise, test the explanatory breadth of these two diagnoses by comparing how they fare against the observation that reasons can be used to explain not only what you ought to do, but also what is impermissible, what is rational, and what is correct.

8
Reasons and Deliberation

8.1 Introduction

We saw as early as Chapter 1 that reasons have two central roles—an explanatory role, and a deliberative role. Reasons help to explain what we ought to do, but they also play a role in our reasoning about what to do. One way—not the only way, but a common way—to think about the explanatory and deliberative roles of reasons is as follows:

Explanatory role r is a reason for s to φ only if r helps make it the case that s ought to φ.

Deliberative role r is a reason for s to φ only if r can be a reason for which s performs φ.

But we have also seen—as early as Chapter 2—that the explanatory and deliberative roles of reasons can pull in different directions, depending on how we make them more precise. Focusing on the explanatory role of reasons can encourage the idea that reasons must be truths—especially if we assume that the explanatory role of reasons is best cashed out through the idea that reasons must explain. And focusing on the deliberative role of reasons can encourage the idea that reasons must be what we think about when we reason.

In Chapter 7 we explored in detail the idea that the connection between reasons and explanation is that reasons are by nature explanations, and we saw that this idea faces important challenges. In its place, we encountered the contrary idea that the connection between reasons and explanation derives from the nature of *ought*. This picture, we saw, places no constraints on the nature of reasons. It therefore reduces the tension between reasons' explanatory role and any conception of their deliberative role. And it opens up room to respect reasons' explanatory role while exploring the hypothesis that the nature of reasons might be best accounted for by their *deliberative* role. So in this chapter we turn to the deliberative role of reasons, by exploring the relationship between reasons and *reasoning*.

The idea that reasons are explanations was supported by the fact that 'reason' can be used both in normative and explanatory ways. The idea that normative reasons are explanations is in a way just a kind of unity in the count noun uses of 'reason'—that normative reasons are a special case of explanatory reasons. Similarly, the idea that the nature of reasons is given by their deliberative role is supported by the fact that 'reason' is a verb, as well as a noun. By analyzing reasons in terms of their role in reasoning, we find a different kind of unity in 'reason'—between its use as a normative count noun, and its use as a verb.

Privileging the deliberative role of reasons over their explanatory role can also be seen as the natural development of a much longer tradition in moral philosophy. In this tradition, philosophers have long sought to ground morality in what's distinctive about *us*, as moral agents, motivated by the observation that what rocks or tigers do is not morally wrong, even if it kills innocents. What distinguishes us from rocks and from tigers, we might think, is that we and not they are *moral agents*—we have a kind of capacity to engage in practical deliberation, to consider and reject an option even if it serves our interests. We have the capacity, that is, to *reason*, and that is *why* we have reaso*n*s (plural). This line of thought provides additional motivation for the idea that the nature of reasons comes from their role in reasoning or deliberation. In the following section, we'll focus on two characterizations of reasons' relationship with reasoning that privilege their deliberative role over their explanatory one.

8.2 The Reasoning View

Over the last decade or more, the idea that the nature of reasons is given by their role in reasoning or deliberation has come to be known, following Asarnow [2016], as the *Reasoning View*. The Reasoning View has been defended by a number of people, each of whom have elaborated on it in somewhat different ways. But a natural place to start is with Bernard Williams' *internal reasons theory*, developed in his classic [1979] paper 'Internal and External Reasons' and further defended in a series of follow-up articles.

According to Williams, all reasons are *internal*, which for him means that it is always possible for the agent for whom something is a reason to start with the reason and their existing prior set of motivations, and end up by doing the action the reason counts in favor of, through a process that counts as what Williams calls a 'sound deliberative route'. Reasons, that is, must be able to play a role in deliberation—they are the starting points for the actual deliberative processes that agents go through in deciding what to do. The main issue at stake both for Williams and for most of his critics is whether this is a necessary condition on reasons, but it is natural to understand Williams as saying that this condition is also sufficient, as well as necessary—that it tells us what it is to be a reason.

For Williams and for many of his critics, there is a simple reason that this thesis is controversial. Williams reasons as follows: because it must be possible to get from a reason to acting by a sound deliberative route, and because whether you make some transition in reasoning will always depend on facts about your existing psychology, whether you have a reason to do something will always depend in some way on facts about your existing psychology. Williams explicitly notes that this is a kind of generalization on the view that we have earlier called the Humean Theory of Reasons. Recall that according to the Humean Theory of Reasons, every reason depends on or is explained by some desire that it serves. And we noted before that because different agents have different desires, it will follow that different agents will have different reasons.

Williams' view does not require that reasons must depend on actual desires, because he allows that a sound deliberative route does not have to start with your desires. But he does think that a sound deliberative route has to start *somewhere*. So every reason will depend for its existence on the psychological features—whatever those are—that make it possible for the agent to follow a sound deliberative route from the reason to the action that it favors. So Willliams' view, like the Humean Theory of Reasons, raises important doubts about whether there are any reasons that every agent shares—including moral reasons.[1] And these doubts have led some philosophers to conclude that nothing is wrong (because if anything is wrong, then there is a reason for anyone not to do it, Mackie [1977]), that wrongness is relative (because if anything is wrong for someone to do, then there is a reason for them not to do it, Harman [1975]), that morality is not backed by reasons (because if anything is wrong then it is wrong for everyone, and

---

[1] The property of being a reason for everyone, no matter what they want or intend, is commonly referred to following Kant as its being *categorical*. So this doubt can be rephrased as the doubt that any reasons are categorical, in this sense.

so since some things are wrong, these must not be backed by reasons for everyone, Foot [1972]), or that Williams is mistaken (because morality is inherently normative, it is not relative, and some things really are wrong, Foot [2001]).

In perhaps the most important response to Williams, Korsgaard [1986] argued that Williams is right to connect reasons to their role in deliberation, but wrong to think that this places any substantive constraints on what could be a reason for whom. As Korsgaard notes, it is important that the deliberative route that someone follows to act on their reason be a *rational* process—that it be what we could expect a *rational* person to follow. So although it is true, she acknowledges, that if you are not rational, then there are some deliberative routes that you might not actually follow, this does not imply that you do not have the corresponding reasons. Those are still sound deliberative routes for you to follow because a *rational* person would follow them.

Korsgaard concludes that although motivation does depend on psychology, being rational is a psychological condition. Thus, whether you have a reason should not depend on whether you are in fact rational—it should only depend on how you could deliberate *if you were rational*. As a result, she claims, the question of whether there are reasons that everyone shares is independent of the connection between reasons and deliberation—it dovetails with the question of which patterns of reasoning are characteristic of rational thought.

Contemporary versions of the Reasoning View typically follow Korsgaard's suggestion, and appeal to some kind of *ideal* reasoning, abstracting from any agent's *actual* process of reasoning. According to a schematic formulation that fits many versions of this view, a consideration gives a reason because of how it figures in ideal reasoning, variously understood.

The Generic Reasoning View r is a reason for s to φ just when and because r is a premise in *ideal* reasoning toward A's φ-ing.

The Reasoning View has many advantages. Among them is that it offers an appealing explanation of why moral reasons have authority over beings with the capacity to engage in practical reasoning. According to it, what *makes* certain considerations into moral reasons is their distinctive profile in an ideal kind of practical reasoning. So the idea that reasons *come from* reasoning is appealing because it explains not only how reasons and reasoning are connected but also *why* certain considerations give reasons to agents.

We've formulated the Generic Reasoning View to be as neutral as possible between different implementations, but it will require different further qualifications, depending on how we come down on other questions about reasons. For example, a common view about the substance of reasons is that they are propositions. But because there is more than one propositional attitude, this raises the possibility that one and the same proposition could figure as a premise in different forms of reasoning, depending on which attitude we take toward it. So those who say that reasons are propositions will have some more work to do to clarify why the standards of ideal reasoning pay attention to which attitudes we bear toward the premises, or why only belief counts as a way of using something as a premise. We'll ignore this and other important qualifications in what follows, for the sake of focusing on general themes.

Because the Generic Reasoning View does not define 'ideal', every conception of ideal reasoning leads to a corresponding elaboration of the Reasoning View. For example, according to one conception, ideal reasoning follows what your perfectly rational counterpart would advise you to do (Smith [1994]); according to another, ideal reasoning manifests a "good disposition of practical thought" (Setiya [2012]); according to another still, it provides a "good basis" for action (Gregory [2016]); or it satisfies certain norms of practical reasoning (Asarnow [2016]); or it "preserves fittingness" across the premises and conclusion that constitute the pattern of practical reasoning (McHugh and Way [2018]); or it is an instance of "reasoning well" and "well-equips" the agent to act or think (Paakunainen [2017]). So this not only makes room for a diversity of more specific ways of developing the Reasoning View but also validates Korsgaard's claim that we cannot extract substantive constraints on what reasons there are from the connection between reasons and deliberation, unless we import it with a substantive view about which sorts of reasoning count as ideal.

All of these elaborations on when deliberation counts as "ideal" share an important feature in common. They replace 'ideal' in the generic formulation of the Reasoning View with another normative term that elaborates the particular kind of ideality that they take to be constitutive of reasons. They appeal to *normative* distinctions between kinds of deliberation—*rational* advice, *good* disposition, *good* basis, preserves *fittingness*, and so on. So if normative reasons derive from ideal reasoning, these views imply that reasons derive from these other normative properties.

All of these views differ in this respect from Silverstein's [2016] version of the Reasoning Account. According to Silverstein, a consideration is a normative reason just when and because it figures in what he calls "sound reasoning". This makes his view a version of the Reasoning View as we understand it, because the patterns involved in sound reasoning do not need to be actual patterns that anyone ever undergoes, so they are in a sense idealized. But Silverstein says that his account does not involve any essential reference to any other normative property or concept, because soundness can be fully elaborated in non-normative terms as a kind of generalization from the descriptive logical properties of validity and soundness. As a result, Silverstein accounts for reasons in purely descriptive terms—that is, without presupposing any other normative concept—which makes it consistent with reductive definitions of other normative concepts in terms of claims about reasons. We'll review the benefits and costs of this approach in later chapters.

8.3 Problems for the Reasoning View

Unsurprisingly, these different conceptions of ideal reasoning respond differently to various challenges. We'll focus on two. The first concerns the sufficiency of figuring in ideal reasoning for being a reason. And the second concerns its necessity. Both challenges can be overcome, we'll suggest, but overcoming them requires taking on some specific commitments about how we think about ideal reasoning.

We'll start with sufficiency. Eva Schmidt [2021] identifies contents that are seemingly premises of ideal reasoning but not reasons. She describes the case of Peter and Bob. Peter rarely goes to the florist, but every year, he gives Bob a dozen red roses for their anniversary. After a long night of drinking, Peter wakes up and finds himself intending to go to the florist. Peter then infers from his intention to go to the florist to the fact that it's his anniversary via inference to the best explanation. On learning that it's his anniversary, Peter forms the intention to buy Bob a dozen roses, just as he always has on their anniversary. Peter thus reasons as follows:

5   Belief(I intend to go to the florist)
4   Belief(The best explanation of (5) is that today is our wedding anniversary)
3   Belief(So, today is our wedding anniversary)
2   Intention(I will give Bob a dozen red roses for our wedding anniversary every year)
1   Intention(So, I will give Bob a dozen red roses today)

(1–5) is an impeccable piece of reasoning directed at the action of giving Bob a dozen roses. Since Peter rarely goes to the florist except to buy Bob flowers for their anniversary, this really is the best explanation of why he intends to go. The Reasoning View implies that if some content is a premise in ideal reasoning toward agent A's φ-ing, then that content is a reason for A to φ, so it implies that the fact that Peter intends to go to the florist is a reason for Peter to (intend to) give Bob a dozen roses today. But this implication is suspect. Even among those who believe that attitudes can give reasons for action, such as Humeans who believe that reasons for action can be grounded in desires, it is widely doubted that intentions give reasons for action. Otherwise, I can improve the case for performing some action simply by intending to do it, implausibly "bootstrapping" reasons into existence.

Moreover, even if intentions could give reasons for action, it's not at all clear how the intention to go to the florist relates to the intention to get Bob a dozen roses such that the former is a reason for the latter. If anything, the latter is a reason for the former: if we are willing to accept intentions as reasons, then it seems far more plausible that the intention to get Bob a dozen roses provides a reason to intend to go to the florist, rather than vice versa. As a result, we should doubt that (5) offers a reason. This is a problem for the Reasoning View, since we can reason impeccably from considerations that aren't reasons.

This problem can be amplified. Suppose that Peter didn't directly apprehend his intention to go to the florist through introspection. Rather, he deduced it from the fact that he found himself walking south on Westminster Road and the *only* time one walks south on Westminster is to go to the florist. This yields an even longer chain of reasoning:

7 Belief(I am headed south on Westminster)
6 Belief(If I am headed south on Westminster, I must be on my way to the florist)
5 Belief(I intend to go to the florist)
... (and then as before)

Is Peter's belief that if he is headed south on Westminster, he must be headed to the florist a reason for him to give Bob a dozen roses? The implication is hard to accept. We can repeat this process ad infinitum by beginning with an even more tortuous episode of reasoning that has (7) as its conclusion rather than taking (7) as the starting point above. The reasoning view implausibly implies that these new premises also offer reasons for Peter to give Bob a dozen roses today, no matter what they are, provided that they terminate in (7). To solve this problem, the Reasoning View must somehow distinguish between the reasoning that starts with (3) and the reasoning that starts earlier than (3). Whatever makes for this difference, it isn't going to be a difference in whether the reasoning is good, rational, or makes sense.

Moreover, Schmidt's challenge is just a special case of the much more general problem that playing a role in reasoning is a much more promiscuous category than being a reason. Though reasons may rightly play some role in reasoning, we may also engage in prior reasoning to determine what our reasons are, and we may need to note background conditions for some consideration to be a reason, in order not to rely on premises as reasons in cases in which they are not actually reasons or have been defeated. Though each of these things plays some role in the process of reasoning, arguably none of them play reasons' explanatory role. In this way, Schmidt's challenge resembles the problem that we encountered in Chapter 6 for the thesis of Reasons as Evidence, that evidence is much more promiscuous than reasons.

Schmidt's challenge targets the sufficiency direction of the Reasoning View. But there is also a well-known challenge to its necessity direction. This is the problem of what are sometimes, following McKeever and Ridge [2012], called 'elusive' reasons. Elusive reasons are reasons whose existence as reasons is fragile because it depends on their not actually being used in deliberation. For example, Schroeder [2007b] offers an example called 'Surprise Birthday'. Suppose that you love surprise birthdays. Nothing pleases you more than entering a room and being unexpectedly showered with praise. However, you *hate* ruined surprises. Nothing puts a damper on your mood like missing out on a good surprise. Now suppose that, unbeknownst to you, your friend has planned a surprise birthday party for you in the next room. Clearly, that there's a surprise party for you in the next room is a reason for you, a surprise-lover, to enter the room. But that fact *cannot* be part of your reasoning—ideal or otherwise—toward the intention of entering the room. When it is part of your reasoning, it ceases to be a reason, since reasoning with the fact requires being aware of it, and you can't be aware of it without making it false. An unexpected surprise party that you know about is not unexpected after all.

And the problem of elusive reasons is more general. The surprise party reason is elusive because you cannot find out about it without its ceasing to be a reason. But there is an even wider range of cases where *no one* could find out about something without its ceasing to be a reason, because there are unknowable truths. For example, because there are infinitely many prime numbers but only finitely many of them have been discovered, there is a smallest undiscovered prime. Whatever it is, it is a fact that that number is the smallest undiscovered prime. But this is an unknowable fact because learning it makes the prime discovered. The unsuspected surprise party is not unknowable—the people who are planning it know about it. But the smallest undiscovered prime is. And there could even be cases where learning about a reason does not make it cease to be a reason but acting on that reason would.

Some philosophers have been unpersuaded by examples of elusive reasons. They have argued, for example, that elusive reasons are also incompatible with very strong (and commonly endorsed) characterizations of the deliberative role for reasons, according to which nothing can be a reason unless it can be acted on.[2] And they have offered debunking explanations of why elusive reasons can seem to be reasons, because they play some of the explanatory role of reasons without being reasons. Both of these ideas look like the right kinds of things to offer, if you are committed to a view that implies that there are no elusive reasons. But from a more general perspective, these both look to us like desperate defensive moves. The cases of elusive reasons can easily be accommodated in our formulation of the deliberative role for reasons, as we were careful to do in Chapter 1. And so deciding which of the stronger or more cautious formulations of the deliberative role is the correct one is nothing other than deciding whether there are elusive reasons. And as we'll now go on to show, the Reasoning View can itself be refined in a way to make it compatible with elusive reasons.

8.4 Refining the Reasoning View

As with all counterexamples, there are two general strategies for responding to cases of elusive reasons. We could resist the idea that any of these cases actually involve reasons for anyone to do anything. But the range of these cases is broad, and it *is* plausible that you should, for example, enter the room where the surprise party is waiting for you—and that the existence of

---

[2] See, for example, Sinclair [2016], which argues that elusive reasons are not as elusive as they seem, and Paakkunainen [2017, 67–68], which argues that elusive reasons may not be the reasons that they seem to be. Rossi [2021] offers a helpful overview.

the unsuspected surprise party helps to explain why. So because these cases are supported not just by intuitive judgments about the existence of reasons, but by intuitive *ought* judgments and the explanatory role connecting reasons to *ought* facts, resisting the cases is a way of preserving the connection between reasons and their deliberative role that comes at the cost of putting pressure on their explanatory role.

In contrast, we could instead acknowledge the force of elusive reasons cases like that of the surprise party, and resist the conclusion that these are incompatible with the Reasoning Account. It turns out that some ways of unpacking 'ideal reasoning' may be better equipped to pursue this line of defense than others. Consider the following pattern of reasoning:

(1) Belief(There is a birthday party for me in the next room)
(2) Intention(If there is a birthday party for me in the next room, then go into that room)
(3) Intention(go into that room)

Reasoning according to (1–3) follows a kind of pattern. This pattern isn't exactly *modus ponens*—it starts from an intention and ends with an intention, rather than starting with beliefs and ending with beliefs. But it looks much *like modus ponens*. The observation that it follows a kind of identifiable pattern opens up the possibility that we can identify the right kinds of inferences on the basis of the patterns that they follow, independently of whether anyone is ever actually in a position to follow through on any given instance of that pattern. This is just a generalization of the observation that when we do logic, we don't say that *modus ponens* counts as valid because every instance of *modus ponens* is one that would be good reasoning if you did it—on the contrary, some instances of *modus ponens* are *never* ones that it would be rational to engage in.

This is the form of answer to what counts as ideal reasoning that we noted in section 8.2, given by Silverstein. For Silverstein, what makes something a reason is the role that it plays in the right kind of *pattern* of abstract reasoning steps, and identifying a pattern as the right kind is not a matter of verifying that anyone who goes through that pattern reasons well. On the contrary, when people are reasoning well, on this view, it is because they are going through the right kind of pattern and they are starting in the right kind of place—with justified or true premises. This kind of view can explain why it is that the surprise party is a reason to go into the next room. It is because the following schema is a good pattern:

(4) Liking(x)
(5) Believing(going into the next room will get me x)
(6) Intending(to go into the next room)

In the surprise party case, the value for x in this schema is 'being genuinely surprised by surprise parties thrown in my honor'. So it follows this pattern. This is a good pattern, so that is why the premise that going into the next room will lead to me being genuinely surprised by a surprise party thrown in my honor counts as the right kind of thing to be a reason for me to go into the next room, and because I do like being genuinely surprised by surprise parties thrown in my honor and because there really is one waiting for me, this inference is not just a valid one, but a sound one. So it is a reason for me, on this version of the Reasoning View.

This suggests that we can make progress in addressing the elusive reasons problem for the Reasoning View by being careful to distinguish patterns of reasoning from actual episodes of reasoning, and using the forms of the *patterns* to analyze reasons, rather than focusing directly on actual or possible *episodes* of reasoning. This helps with the problem of elusive reasons, because it can turn out that a pattern is a good one even if not every one of its instances can be realized. So this looks to us like progress in finding the best version of the Reasoning View—it should look more like Silverstein's.[3]

It turns out that the same innovation in how we think about the Reasoning View can also plausibly help with Schmidt's objection. The basic structure of Schmidt's objection relies on showing that the Reasoning View is too promiscuous in what it counts as a reason. For any good reasoning that leads to action, we can add earlier steps of good reasoning that get us to the premises of the good reasoning that leads to action. The worry is that the Reasoning View cannot distinguish how far back such reasoning can go before its starting points stop counting as reasons to perform the action in question.

But this challenge should look at least vaguely familiar to those who have read Chapter 6. And that's because the view of *Reasons as Evidence* also faced a very similar challenge.[4] Often, evidence that some potential reason to do something is true will also be evidence that we ought to do what that reason favors. When it is, RAE will predict that the evidence of this potential

---
[3] McHugh and Way [2022b] follow Silverstein in this regard, being careful to distinguish between types and episodes of reasoning.
[4] Schmidt [2017] advances a similar objection to Kearns and Star as well.

reason's truth must itself also be a reason for the action in question. And that likewise seemed too promiscuous. Reasons to believe the things that are reasons for action are typically *not* reasons to perform the action in question, and concluding that they are obscures the important differences between theoretical reasoning about what is the case and practical reasoning about what to do. For example, you might read in the newspaper that there has been a tsunami, and then decide on the basis of the fact that there has been a tsunami to send money to an aid organization. RAE says that the fact that the newspaper said that there has been a tsunami is a reason to donate, while a more plausible division of labor says instead that it is merely a reason to believe in the reason to donate.

It turns out that the connection between the worry for RAE and Schmidt's worry for the Reasoning View is no coincidence. Kearns and Star actually frequently appeal to the thought that reasons are the starting points of reasoning in responding to counterexamples of exactly this form. They reason roughly as follows: reasons to do something are the starting points of good reasoning that results in action. And you are reasoning well if you learn that the newspaper says that there has been a tsunami, form the belief that there has been a tsunami, and then donate to an aid organization on that basis. So, they claim, their view is *not* mistaken in ruling that facts about what the newspaper says are reasons to donate.

Unfortunately, what we've now seen is that this response only shows that Kearns and Star's version of RAE is partners in crime with the flat-footed versions of the Reasoning View that are subject to Schmidt's objection. But we suggest that instead of thinking that this shows that they are right to embrace the counterintuitive consequences of their view in these cases, we should instead conclude that these two views suffer from a common flaw.

But a version of the Reasoning View that focuses on particular patterns of reasoning rather than episodes of reasoning can, we suggest, provide a promising answer to this problem. By distinguishing between patterns of reasoning, we can easily say why the reasons to do something are the starting points of the final *step* that leads to doing something. And by distinguishing patterns of reasons not just by their starting points and ending points but by the steps that they go through along the way, we can say why it is that the starting points of reasoning that leads to the reasons that lead to action do not themselves count as reasons to do that thing.

Take, for example, Schmidt's original florist case. The pattern that goes from (5) and (4) to (3) is a good pattern, and the pattern that goes from (3) and (2) to (1) is a good pattern. But going directly from (5), (4), and (2) to (1) is not itself a good pattern, unless it is mediated by first getting to (3). It would be genuinely weird—if perhaps admirably romantic—for Peter to intend to buy Bob a dozen roses for their anniversary while still being unsure whether it is actually their anniversary. And the cases in which it would make sense would rely on some other form of reasoning not present in the original example—such as a precaution against the possibility of being wrong. Similarly, in the tsunami case, it would be genuinely weird to donate to the aid organization if you don't first believe the reports in the newspaper. This again suggests that there is no good pattern of reasoning that goes directly from believing that the newspaper says that there has been a tsunami to donating to an aid organization—there is only the good pattern to believing that there really has been a tsunami, and the good pattern from there to donating.[5]

If these lessons are correct, then the best version of the Reasoning View will focus on the kinds of patterns exhibited by reasoning in a way that has much in common with identifying the admissible rules of inference in logic. The admissible rules of inference are constituted by patterns that do not depend on whether every instance of the pattern is one that someone might actually apply, and they are constituted by types of *steps* rather than global claims about consequence.

It turns out that this picture actually coheres nicely with the *common core* account of the relationship between objective and subjective reasons from Chapter 5. According to that account, recall, objective and subjective reasons share a common core, and a proposition that is a core reason becomes an objective reason or subjective reason, respectively, by in addition satisfying objective conditions (like truth) or perspectival conditions (like being believed). The connection between the two views is actually quite tight: if what makes something a reason is its role as the premise of certain patterns, independently of whether any particular instance of that pattern is realized, then the condition of being a reason is not constrained either by an objective condition or by a subjective condition. So the most promising version of the Reasoning View is, we have discovered, first and foremost an account of *core* reasons.

Chapter Summary

In this chapter we have explored the relationship between reasons and reasoning, paying special attention to the idea that reasons might be

---

[5] McHugh and Way [2022b, chapter two] explicitly offer this kind of response to Schmidt.

analyzed in terms of their role in reasoning, rather than that reasoning might be analyzed in terms of how it deploys reasons. We saw that there are serious challenges to both the necessary and sufficient directions of this analysis, and that these challenges often lead proponents of the Reasoning View, like proponents of Evidence as Reasons, to reject the explanatory role for reasons. But we argued that there is a promising path for resolving both kinds of challenges, so long as we focus on patterns of reasoning rather than on actual episodes of reasoning, and suggested that the most promising versions of the Reasoning View take this form.

Recommended Reading

The Reasoning View has been recently developed in many different places, but the agenda-setting paper for the recent popularity of this view is Kieran Setiya's paper 'What is a Reason to Act?' In this chapter we have followed Eva Schmidt's instructive 'Where Reasons and Reasoning Come Apart' and extensively discussed the case of the surprise party, which comes from chapter two of Mark Schroeder's *Slaves of the Passions*. Silverstein develops his view in his papers 'Ethics and Practical Reasoning' and 'Reducing Reasons'. We recommend that reading this chapter pairs particularly well with Samuel Asarnow's paper 'Rational Internalism'.

Exercises

8.1 *Comprehension*. Verify that the gloss on the explanatory role of reasons given in section 8.2 is compatible with the conclusions of Chapter 7 by offering an interpretation of what it might mean to "help to make something the case" without actually making it the case.

8.2 *Extensions*. Test the consequences of the gloss on the explanatory role of reasons given in section 8.2 by deciding whether it rules out the possibility that the fact that there is a reason for you to do something could itself be a reason for you to do it.

8.3 *Extensions*. In section 8.2 we saw that Korsgaard's answer to Williams agrees that if there is a reason for you to do something it must be true that you would do it for that reason if you are rational, but says that if you are not rational there might be no process that would motivate you to act for that reason. John McDowell [1995] gave a similar but different answer to Williams, denying that reasons have to motivate rational people but affirming instead that *virtuous* people will be motivated by their reasons. Which of these two answers do you prefer? Why?

8.4 *Extensions.* Schmidt's objection turns on the premise that the early stages of reasoning do not count as reasons supporting the conclusion of these episodes of reasoning. Can you resist this assumption? How would you go about resisting it or debunking the intuitive force behind it?

8.5 *Extensions.* In section 8.3 we said that it is plausible in the surprise party case that because you would be delighted to be surprised by the surprise party, it really is true that you ought to go into the room, and that is evidence that we should not deny that there is a reason for you to do so. Is this an objective or a subjective 'ought'? What does your answer tell you about how easy it will be to resist this argument by denying that you ought to go into the room?

8.6 *Extensions.* What happens to correct reasoning when the standards of correct reasoning are themselves philosophically contentious? For example, the philosopher Vann McGee [1985] has argued that *modus ponens* is not a valid rule of inference, and dialetheists hold that it is rationally acceptable to believe contradictions, because some contradictions are true. How does your answer to what to think about these cases shape how you would develop each form of the Reasoning View? Does it depend on which version of the Reasoning View we go with?

PART 3
THE *PLACE* OF REASONS

9
What Can Reasons Analyze?

9.1 Introduction

The topic of reasons, we warned in our very first paragraph in Chapter 1, is interesting as much for how it relates to *other* topics, as for the interest of reasons in their own right. Reasons have the peculiarly philosophical kind of interest of lying behind or in the spaces in between other concepts and topics in epistemology, the philosophy of action, the theory of the emotions, political philosophy, and moral philosophy—among others. Now that we've spent four chapters exploring the internal structure of reasons (Part 1: Parts) and four chapters on the close associations between kinds of reasons and between reasons and evidence, explanation, and motivation and deliberation (Part 2: Province), we are prepared to explore how what we know about reasons so far puts us in a position to see how they are connected to a much wider web of normative concepts.

In particular, we will use our final four chapters (Part 3: Place) to explore the analytic *priority* relationships between reasons and other normative properties and relations. In this chapter, we will focus on the prospects for analyzing other normative properties and relations in terms of reasons, exploring how the Classical Argument that motivated Ross in Chapter 1 can be extended and where it faces some of its largest obstacles. In Chapter 10, we will turn toward seeing how we might analyze reasons. Although we have already encountered several attempts to analyze reasons by appeal to their connections to evidence, explanation, and deliberation in Part 2, here we will be interested in how these and other attempts to analyze reasons fit into a single space and interact with arguments about what we should use reasons to analyze. In Chapter 11 we'll broach the particularly important and complex but still very underexplored topic of the *weight* of reasons, and in Chapter 12 we'll close by exploring the connections between reasons and a different class of concepts including *moral worth* and *knowledge*.

Recall from earlier chapters that reasons can help us to explain what to do, think, or feel by figuring in what we've been calling weighing explanations. These explanations frame facts about what's good or apt or advisable in a distinctive metaphysical light, as the products of an underlying tug-of-war between reasons. By contrast, many kinds of laws or rules are not obviously subject to this kind of weighing. Consider motor vehicle regulations, which differ by jurisdiction:

1. If you're in North America, then drive on the right.
2. If you're in the UK, then drive on the left.

"Why drive on the right?" someone might ask. Because you're in California is the answer. So it seems that facts about your location along with laws like (1) and (2) determine what side of the road to drive on. Rules also differ between games. In Monopoly rolling a seven means that you move your token seven spaces, but in Settlers of Catan it means that you get to move the bandit anywhere you like.

In short, facts like that you're in California or that you are playing Monopoly seem to determine which particular law applies to your case, e.g., whether to drive on the right or to move your token seven spaces. That is, the facts determine which laws apply. They help to explain what to do by *locating* our situation in a network of conditional rules. Historically, many people have thought that moral facts also play this locative role. For example, if you've promised to meet me at seven for dinner, then it seems that you're under a requirement to meet me for dinner at that time. We might be tempted to understand morality with conditional rules that behave like (1) and (2), such as the following:

3. If you've made a promise, then keep it.

But rules like (3) should give us pause; they are uncompromising. If, after making your promise, you come across a severely injured cyclist on your way to the restaurant, (3) implies that you should ignore the cyclist if helping them will make you late for dinner. That's counterintuitive. Morality seems to grant exceptions to the practice of promise-keeping. Sufficiently needy cyclists are one such exception. So it seems that morality may not share a law-like structure with Monopoly and the vehicular code.

But this challenge is not fatal to our law-like conception of morality; the conflict between your promise and the needy cyclist suggests only that morality's rules are complex, encoding conditions where promises can be broken:

4. If you've promised to meet someone for dinner and no cyclists need help, then keep the promise.
5. If you've promised to meet someone for dinner and a cyclist needs help, then break the promise.

Of course, needy cyclists aren't the only exception to promise-keeping. A great many exceptions exist. It seems, then, that the antecedent circumscribing all exceptions to promise-keeping will need to be very complex. But, nevertheless, facts about your promise or needy cyclists can play a locative role, helping to locate which moral rule applies to your case.

We saw in Chapter 1 that Ross offered a much different diagnosis in *The Right and the Good* of why writing down the rules of morality requires writing down so many exceptions. It is because instead of being baked into exceptionless rules, facts about what you ought morally, or are morally required, to do are ultimately complex facts about the balance of many competing considerations. On this Rossian picture, it is *reasons* that directly determine what to do, without mediation by rules, by *competing* or *weighing* against each other. Insofar as there are moral rules, they are merely tips or guides to picking winners in this conflict.

Ross's diagnosis of the complexity of facts about what you morally ought or are morally required to do is simple, and as we saw in Chapter 1, it yields concrete, testable, predictions that seem to us to be correct and not to be explicable in other ways. For example, it predicts that the more important your promise, the more help the cyclists will have to need in order to justify your missing your dinner, and that it may turn out that you still ought to keep your dinner appointment even when people need a lot of help if there are *other* reasons to be at the dinner—such as that you have advance warning of a cycling crash at the dinner—as well. It does all of these things because it says that facts about what you morally ought to do *just are* facts about the balance of reasons.

In the remaining sections of this chapter we will be concerned with how far Ross's diagnosis might *extend*. Rather than focusing on whether it is the right diagnosis of the nature of moral rules, we will be focused on *which* normative properties might also consist in the relationship between competing reasons.

9.2 Deontic Weighing Analyses

On Ross's picture, as we've seen, facts about what you are morally required to do consist in facts about the balance of competing reasons. But this picture leaves underdetermined just which reasons do the competing and what it takes for them to win this competition. In general, reasons can compete because some reasons are *weightier than* others. So all Rossian accounts of what you are required to do will agree that:

Schematic Requirement   You are required to φ just in case the reasons for you to φ outweigh the competing reasons.

But different views diverge over what the "competing reasons" are. On one simple view,

Otherwise Requirement   You are required to φ just in case the reasons for you to φ outweigh the reasons for you not to φ.

But some authors prefer to compare the reasons to φ pairwise to each of the competing alternatives, as in:

Options Requirement   You are required to φ just in case for every alternative to φ-ing, the reasons for you to φ outweigh the reasons for you to take that alternative.

Now, there is a natural principle about the relationship between reasons that can make it feel like these two ways of making Schematic Requirement more precise are equivalent. According to this principle, if doing one thing entails doing another, then any reason to do the first is an equally weighty reason to do the second. So since no option is a genuine alternative to φ-ing unless it entails not φ-ing, it turns out that the condition specified by Options Requirement entails the condition specified by Otherwise Requirement. However, only Options Requirement turns out to be less committal about the nature of requirement. For example, it leaves open the possibility of what is known as *contrastivism* about requirement. Analogously to contrastivism about *reasons*, introduced in Chapter 4, contrastivism about requirement is the view that *which* options need to be compared can vary from context to context. Contrastivists about requirement can make sense of it being true that you are required to take the second-best option rather than the third-best option, because the 'rather than' clause specifies that only the second and third-best options are being considered and, as we've seen, it has been argued to have many other applications.

Another way of specifying Schematic Requirement is:

Against Requirement   You are required to φ just in case the reasons for you to φ outweigh the reasons against you φ-ing.

Like Options Requirement, Against Requirement can seem to collapse into Otherwise Requirement given the natural assumption that reasons against φ-ing are just reasons for not φ-ing. But it turns out that this equivalence is not obvious. Justin Snedegar [2021], for example, notes that if you must wear a shirt and have only blue, green, and red shirts, it might seem that the reasons against wearing the red shirt *just are* the reasons for wearing either the blue or green shirts. But Snedegar argues that is a mistake. After all, if the blue shirt is wrinkly, then that's a reason against wearing it. But it's not a reason for wearing either the red shirt or the green one if those ones are even wrinklier.

Distinguishing between reasons for and reasons against opens up the possibility that to explain requirement, what we actually need to do is reverse these roles:

Contra-Against Requirement   You are required not to φ just in case the reasons against you φ-ing outweigh the reasons for you to φ.

This is the view advocated by Patricia Greenspan [2005]. Which of Against Requirement or Contra-Against Requirement is more plausible will turn, of course, on what else we can say, in more detail, about the difference between reasons for and reasons against.[1]

One very natural reason to draw on such a distinction in making sense of moral requirements, in particular, is that, as many theorists have observed,

---

[1] Compare also Greenspan [2007] and Snedegar [2016].

ways in which helping others could be personally costly can often justify not helping them, but you are never morally required not to help others on the grounds that doing so would be personally costly. So costs to yourself seem like they need to be the kind of thing that can matter as one of the reasons that determine what you are morally required to do even if they aren't the kind of thing that can ever require you to do something. By distinguishing between the roles of reasons for and reasons against, and by putting only one of those on the side that favors requiring, we can allow for personal costs to play a permitting role with respect to moral requirements without having them play a requiring role. This, more generally, is the approach taken by followers of Greenspan and Joshua Gert [2004], who distinguishes between requiring and justifying reasons.[2]

According to Chris Tucker's recent development of this distinction, there are not strictly speaking two kinds of reasons—reasons for and reasons against, or justifying and requiring reasons—but rather two dimensions of weight possessed by each reason.

Dual Weights Requirement   You are required to φ just in case the requiring weight of the reasons for you to φ outweighs the permitting weight of the reasons for you not to φ.

Like Greenspan and Gert, Tucker imagines that the distinction between two kinds of weight is primitive. But another possibility is that what you are required to do is just what it is correct to *require* you to do, and what you are permitted to do is just what it is correct to *permit* you to do. This treats the '-ible' in 'permissible' and the '-ed' in 'required' as analogous to the '-able' in 'desirable' and the '-y' in 'scary'. On this interpretation, Tucker's view could be true, not because there is a primitive distinction in kinds of weight, but rather simply because what Tucker calls the requiring weight of a reason to φ is just its weight as a reason to require you to φ, and the permitting weight of a reason to φ is just its weight as a reason to permit you to φ.[3]

Regardless of which of these or other ways of precisifying Schematic Requirement we go with, however, the form of Schematic Requirement allows us to distinguish between what we might call different *flavors* of requirement—moral requirement, legal requirement, prudential requirement, rational requirement, sartorial requirement. Each of these forms of

---

[2] Compare Gert [2007], Tucker [2021], and Tucker [2022].
[3] Compare Schmidt [2023].

requirement can be understood in terms of the balance of competing reasons in analogous ways, while paying attention to different *flavors of reasons*. So, for example, while what you are morally required to do is a matter of the competition between moral reasons in favor and moral reasons against, what you are prudentially required to do is a matter of prudential reasons in favor and prudential reasons against, and what you are rationally required to do is a matter of rational reasons in favor and rational reasons against.[4]

It turns out that there have come to be two important competing views about what these flavors of reasons come to, each of which is consistent with the idea that requirements consist in the balance of reasons. On the first view, which we might call the *subset* view, flavors of reasons are just subsets of the set of all reasons. The subset view makes it natural to expect that flavors of reasons could be very easy to come by—all that we have to do is to specify new subsets of reasons that we are interested in. And it makes it natural to expect that in addition to specific *flavors* of requirement, there will also be an all-things-considered requirement, which compares *all* of the reasons, without restriction.[5]

By contrast, according to a competing view of flavors that we might call the *domain* view, different flavors of reasons are not just different subsets of a unified domain of reasons, but instead each reason is tied to its own normative *domain*—where domains include things like *morality, prudence,* and *the law*. One motivation for the domain view is to resist the seemingly inevitable conclusion that there must be such a thing as all-things-considered requirements, by resisting the idea that there needs to be any flavor that encompasses all of the other flavors—whether there is a *domain* that encompasses other domains is a substantive matter and not just a matter of properties of supersets.

But another natural motivation for the domain view is the observation that some reasons are, in the terms of Howard [2021a], *ambidextrous*.

---

[4] As we have noted, the personal costs of doing something with some moral benefit can make it permissible not to do it, but never make it required not to do it. So these personal costs would figure as "moral" reasons only on the permitting side (i.e., as reasons "against" by the lights of Against Requirement or as reasons in "favor" by the lights of Contra-Against Requirement). Some people will find it unnatural to call these personal costs 'moral reasons', but they are of course not morally requiring reasons—they are only morally permitting reasons, and they count as moral in the sense that they figure on the permitting side of this competition to determine what you are morally required to do.

[5] The set of all reasons is, of course, trivially a subset of itself, which is why this picture explains the existence of an all-things-considered 'ought'. See Howard and Laskowski (forthcoming) for an elaboration of this contrast.

Suppose, for example, that Elon offers you $44 billion to believe that he is rich. That is an excellent prudential reason to believe that he is rich—practically any belief would be worth $44 billion, because you could do a lot with that money. But it is also an excellent epistemic reason to believe that he is rich—people who are not rich don't have $44 billion to blow on what other people think about them. So it's a reason twice over—both a prudential reason and an epistemic reason. But on the subset view, we risk it turning out that the fact that Elon has made you this offer is a single reason that should have a single weight whether we are comparing it to other prudential reasons or comparing it to other epistemic reasons, and it should not count twice if we are comparing it to all reasons to determine what you are required to do all-things-considered. But this seems wrong—this fact could carry more weight as a prudential reason or conversely. And the domain view offers one easy explanation of why. There is not a single reason that happens to be in two sets, but rather a single fact that happens to be a reason relative to each of two different domains. We might exploit our tool of reason diagrams to represent this view in terms of an extra *domain* relatum in the normative reason relation as follows:

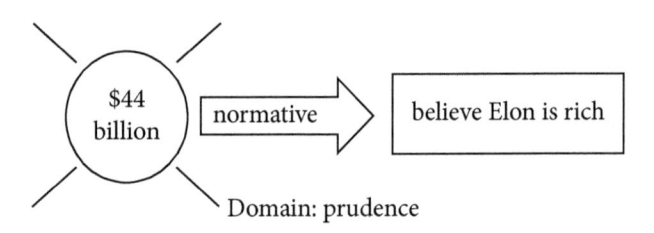

One side note that is worth addressing before we move on is how the issues that we have raised so far are affected when we apply them to what is *rationally* required, in particular. Notice that among our list of domains above was 'rationality'; the structure of each of these comparative accounts of requirement allows both that objective reasons can be compared and that subjective reasons can be compared. And it is plausible that if rationality is a matter of the comparison of reasons at all, it must be a matter of the comparison of subjective reasons. But importantly, significant obstacles still beset using the balance of subjective reasons to account for one very important kind of claim about rationality—what has come to be known as *structural* irrationality. Examples of structural irrationality are widely held to include cases such as holding inconsistent beliefs, having conflicting intentions, intending to do what you believe you will not, failing to intend the means you believe to be necessary to accomplish one of your other intentions, or failing to intend to do what you believe you ought to do.

The topic of structural irrationality is a quite large one in its own right, but the intuitive worry about accounting for it in terms of the balance of subjective reasons comes from the following rough dilemma. We saw in Chapter 5 that there is a perspective condition on having a subjective reason, and that this perspective condition has a mind-to-world component. On some views this mind-to-world component is weak, allowing mere belief to count, while on others it is relatively more demanding, requiring knowledge or justified belief. But cases of structural irrationality can arise even among attitudes that are not in any way justified. You might, for example, wake up one morning confidently believing both that the number of stars in the universe is even, and also confidently believing that the number of stars in the universe is odd. And so if the mind-to-world condition on subjective reasons is too strong, then you can be structurally irrational without having any subjective reasons at all—and therefore without doing anything that is ruled out by your subjective reasons. However, if the mind-to-world condition on subjective reasons is too weak, then you can have weighty subjective reasons simply by virtue of having unjustified or even irrational beliefs. This difficulty in figuring out how strong a condition to place on subjective reasons itself creates a significant challenge for understanding rational requirements in terms of the balance of subjective reasons, and hence for the global project of treating requirements in general in terms of the balance of reasons.

9.3 Ought

In the last section we saw that, although there are a number of choice-points in how to clarify the idea that what you are required to do is a matter of the balance of competing reasons, all of these accounts share some important features. They allow us to compare reasons of different kinds or flavors, and even allow us to give parallel accounts that balance either objective or subjective reasons. And since what is "rational" is just what is rationally permitted, and we can define permission in terms of requirement in the familiar way that what is permitted is just what you are not required not to do, that shows that these accounts can be promisingly extended to account for rationality—at least pending difficult further questions about how structural rationality fits into this picture.

However, yet further challenges to this picture arise once we turn our attention to the difference between what you are required or *must* do and what you ought or *should* do. Saying that you *have to* or *must* wear a tuxedo to the wedding expresses something different from saying that you *ought to* or *should* wear a tuxedo. After all, it's nonsense to say "You must wear a tux but you can wear a suit". Conversely, it is *not* nonsense to say "you should wear a tux but you can wear a suit". So there's a subtle difference in the strength of *should* and *must*. Though it is plausible that *must*, *required*, and *have to* are equivalent, and plausible that *ought* and *should* are equivalent, the former must be clearly distinguished from the latter.

Linguists call this subtle distinction the distinction between *strong* and *weak* necessity modals, and we can mark the contrast in other ways. A sign in a restaurant bathroom might say, "employees must wash their hands, and everyone should, too," which makes perfect sense—everyone is advised to but employees are required to. But in contrast, it does not make sense to say, "everyone must wash their hands and employees should, too." The latter is redundant in a way that the former claim is not. So many conclude that *should* is logically weaker than *must*.[6]

But, *should* is still stronger than *may*. In particular, instructing or advising someone that they should do something licenses criticism if they fail to do it. If you tell your guest that they should wear a tux to your wedding, and they show up in a suit, then you have grounds for criticizing them. If you had merely said that they may wear a tux, you wouldn't have those grounds. So *should* is stronger than *may* in the sense that only *should* licenses criticism.

However, if 'ought' is weaker than 'required', then if both are matters of the balance of reasons, they are going to have to be matters of the balance of *different* reasons. It can't be, for example, that what you morally ought to do is the option that is most favored by moral reasons and also that what you are morally required to is the option that is most favored by moral reasons, because then they would be the same. So anyone who wishes to extend the Rossian diagnosis to both 'ought' and 'required' needs to be able to say something about *which* reasons we weigh for each and how they are related in order to guarantee that 'required' turns out to always be stronger than 'ought'.

The number of options in this space is a little bit hard to keep under control, but one rough strategy is to think about 'ought' not as a way of

---

[6] See, for example, von Fintel and Iatridou [2008].

weakening 'must', but as a way of strengthening 'may'. Suppose, for example, that we think of what you ought to do as a matter of what is best supported, among the options that you *may* do, by the balance of certain further reasons. Since you must do something only if it is the unique thing that you may do, it follows that 'must' entails 'ought' on this view—no matter what sort of strengthening 'ought' gives to 'may'. Consequently, there are going to be a large number of possible views that take this broad form, offering different answers to what sorts of things might matter for what you ought to do that are not themselves requiring reasons for you to do it.

A different problem about 'ought', however, derives from cases involving imperfect information.[7] Suppose that Xiao must choose between four envelopes. One contains $4000, one contains $5000, one contains $6000, and one contains $0. Though Xiao knows that envelope 1 contains the $4000, and she knows the amounts that can be found in the other envelopes, she does not know how the money is distributed between them. Ying is a friend of Xiao's who knows everything that Xiao does *and* that the second envelope holds the $5000. And Zach is a third friend who knows both how the money is distributed and what everyone else knows.

Ying might watch Xiao's choice eagerly, hoping that she takes the second envelope—the one containing the $5000. "She should take the second envelope," he might reason, "after all, the first envelope only has $4000, while the second one has $5000, and the expected value of the third and fourth envelopes is only $3000." And if Xiao had the opportunity to ask Ying for his advice about what she should do, this is certainly the advice that he should give her. But this raises a problem about how to understand Ying's 'ought' or 'should' judgment in terms of the balance of reasons.

	Envelope 1 ($4000)	Envelope 2 ($5000)	Envelope 3 ($6000)	Envelope 4 ($0)
Xiao	Expected payout: $4000	Expected payout: $3667	Expected payout: $3667	Expected payout: $3667
Ying	Expected payout: $4000	Expected payout: $5000	Expected payout: $3000	Expected payout: $3000
Zach	Expected payout: $4000	Expected payout: $5000	Expected payout: $6000	Expected payout: $0

---

[7] The following case comes from Schroeder [2018], inspired by Kolodny and MarFarlane [2010].

The problem is that Ying knows everything that Xiao knows, and so he knows, of course, that the second envelope is not expectedly best from the point of view of Xiao's mind-to-world perspective. She, after all, knows only which envelope has the $4000, so from her point of view, the expected value of each of the other envelopes is only $3,666.67. So it seems that Ying knows full well that his answer to what Xiao ought to do does not match the balance of her subjective reasons. But similarly, Ying also knows that one of the other envelopes has $6000 in it—and indeed, that Zach knows which one it is. As a result, Ying knows that his answer to what Xiao ought to do also does not match the balance of *all* of the objective reasons. So the problem for offering a reasons-based explanation of these uses of 'ought' is that although it can make sense of Xiao's beliefs about what she ought to do as beliefs about the balance of her subjective reasons, and it can make sense of Zach's beliefs about what Xiao ought to do as beliefs about the balance of her objective reasons, it seems that some extra reasons are needed in order to make sense of Ying's beliefs about what Xiao ought to do. It is unclear what exactly those reasons could be, given Ying's intermediate information.

So although in a way, 'ought' has traditionally been part of the home territory for reasons-based analyses of normative concepts, it is also quite slippery territory and there are many still unresolved issues both about the relationship of 'ought' to 'must' and about the role of information sensitivity.

9.4 Fittingness

So far we have seen some of the advantages and obstacles of analyzing various deontic concepts in terms of the competition between reasons. Somewhat more controversial is the case of the concept of the *fitting*, sometimes equated with what is *apt*. Philosophers often talk about what is fitting as if we have an ordinary, pretheoretical grasp of how to assess the intuitive plausibility of claims about what is fitting or not. But it is more helpful to think of the term 'fitting' as used by philosophers as a kind of theoretical term that is tied into a certain understanding of what is going on with a more familiar set of concepts—the admirable, contemptible, scary, awful, annoying, loathsome, blameworthy, and so on.[8] Each of these words

---

[8] Compare D'Arms and Jacobson [2000a].

is formed from a verb root, combined with a suffix. The *fitting* is supposed to be that property that is expressed by each of these suffixes.

The claim that there is a single property that is expressed by each of the suffixes on this list—'-able', '-ible', '-y', '-ful', '-ing', '-some', and '-worthy', at least—is of course substantive and not trivial. And so is the claim that this property is itself normative. But the fact that it is so easy to coin new words using suffixes like this—'re-tweet-able', 're-tweet-worthy', 're-tweet-some'—provides support for the claim that each of these suffixes does something that is at least very similar. And the fact that each of the verbal roots is non-normative but each of these words as a whole seems to express a normative thought is evidence that the property expressed by each of the suffixes must itself be normative. 'Fitting', then, is a fitting name for this property—allowing us to say that someone is admirable just in case it is fitting to admire them, contemptible just in case it is fitting to have contempt for them, and so on.

The concept of the fitting is sometimes claimed not to be analyzable by reasons.[9] For example, on one famous view due to Justin D'Arms and Daniel Jacobson, what makes something admirable is that the state of mind that you are in when you admire it represents it in a way that is true.[10] But re-tweeting, of course, is not an emotion or attitude, and famously according to many people's Twitter bios, not all re-tweets represent something as true. So the D'Arms and Jacobson account appears to be too narrow to offer a general analysis of the fitting, as opposed to simply the specific conditions under which emotions are fitting.

And it turns out that the very same features that motivated Ross to claim that all-things-considered duty is a matter of the competition between reasons also arise in the case of fittingness. For example, ethical vegetarians are generally admirable for their commitment to avoiding contributing to the suffering of animals. But not *all* ethical vegetarians are admirable. Sometimes ethical vegetarians have other traits that make them *un*-admirable, no matter how great their commitment to their vegetarianism. Hitler, for example, is reputed to have been a vegetarian for ethical reasons, but it is safe to say that Hitler was not admirable. Though Hitler's commitment to ethical vegetarianism is *some* reason to admire him, it is clearly outweighed

---

[9] For an exhaustive argument that fittingness is a distinctive normative category not analyzable by reasons, see Berker [2023].

[10] D'Arms and Jacobson [2000a], D'Arms and Jacobson [2000b].

by the many other compelling reasons not to admire him. There are reasons to admire, but they admit of outweighing defeat.

We've seen in earlier chapters that reasons can also be *undercut*—failing to contribute at all to make something what you ought to do, when they otherwise would so contribute. But admirability also admits of undercutting defeat. Take, for example, persistence, which is a trait that in general tends to make someone admirable. Other things equal, people who persist in the pursuit of their goals are admirable. But sometimes persistent people fail to be admirable—indeed, they sometimes fail to be admirable *because* of their persistence. Hitler was persistent. But persistence in the pursuit of evil goals does not make you admirable. Indeed, it makes you less admirable. So though persistence *generally* make someone admirable—it is sometimes the distinguishing trait that makes one person admirable while another otherwise similar person is not—it is sometimes undercut by further facts about the goals in pursuit of which they are persistent.

But whether someone is admirable, we said, is a matter of whether it is fitting to admire them. So fittingness—at least, the fittingness of admiration—is subject to the same kinds of complications arising from outweighing and undercutting that what is *required* or what you *ought* to do are subject to. And similar considerations can be raised for the contemptible, scary, awful, annoying, loathsome, and blameworthy. Taken together, these considerations provide substantial support for the claim that it is *at least as compelling* to think that the fitting must be understood in terms of the balance of competing reasons as it is to think that requirement or *ought* must be.

However, there is a famous problem about how to analyze fittingness in terms of the balance of competing reasons. And it comes from the fact that it seems that *not all* reasons matter for which responses are fitting. Obviously if we are considering whether it is fitting to admire someone, the reasons that matter must be reasons for and against[11] *admiring* them. But it seems at least *prima facie* possible for there to be reasons to admire someone that do not contribute in any way toward making them admirable. For example, the fact that someone's mother offers you money to admire them plausibly counts in favor of admiring them, but people do not get to be more admirable in any way just because their mothers offer people money to admire them. So not all reasons for and against admiring someone can matter for whether they are admirable. Any account of fittingness in terms

---

[11] Or: for *not* admiring them, or for *alternatives* to admiring them, etc.

of the balance of reasons must therefore distinguish between the so-called *right kind* of reasons to go into the analysis and the *wrong kind* of reasons that do not. This challenge has come to be known as the *wrong kind of reasons* problem.[12]

One way that some people have explored of trying to solve the wrong kind of reasons problem is to avoid it altogether by denying that there are any wrong-kind reasons. A common form of this strategy is to say that when someone's mother offers you money to admire them, that gives you a reason to try to get yourself to admire them, or a reason to want to admire them, but it does not actually give you a reason to admire them. If this is so, and this strategy can be generalized in a principled way, then an analysis of fittingness in terms of reasons can appeal to all reasons for and against admiring after all. This strategy of responding to the wrong kind of reasons problem is known as *wrong kind of reasons skepticism*.[13]

Wrong kind of reasons skepticism is made plausible by the fact that many philosophers are independently compelled by the thought that you cannot admire someone for the reason that their mother had offered you money to do so. So in contrast to their persistence or ethical vegetarianism, this advantage of admiring them cannot obey the deliberative role of reasons, and that provides a rationale for thinking that it is not strictly speaking a reason to admire them at all. However, this rationale for wrong kind of reasons skepticism does not extend to other kinds of responses that can be expressed by the verbal roots of '-able'/'-ible'/'-y' words. For example, according to many philosophers, blaming is not just a mental state that you have toward someone, but something that you *do* to them. And of course re-tweeting is not an attitude.[14] But the fact that someone's mother gives you money to blame them or to re-tweet their tweets does not make them more blameworthy or their tweets more re-tweet-able, and yet you can easily blame (in the act sense) or re-tweet for money. So the wrong kind of reasons problem for reasons-based analyses of fittingness is more general than can be evaded by wrong kind of reasons skepticism.

---

[12] Crisp [2000], Rabinowicz and Rønnow-Rasmussen [2004].
[13] Compare Way [2012], who offers a more sophisticated argument for wrong-kind reasons skepticism than we consider here.
[14] For an argument that actions, and not just attitudes, can be fitting, see Schroeder [2007b], chapter seven]. But for a defense of the view that actions like re-tweeting can never be fitting, see McHugh and Way [2022b].

9.5 Goodness

The kinds of properties expressed by words like 'admirable', 'loathsome', and the like are sometimes called *value* properties. But the paradigmatic value property, of course, is *goodness*. So if you have gotten this far without being dissuaded by the challenges for analyzing requirement, *ought*, and fittingness in terms of reasons, then the next challenge worth thinking about is whether *good* can be analyzed in terms of reasons.

The most direct way of connecting *good* to what we have said so far is to embrace Mill's suggestion that we can equate what is *good* with what is *desirable*.[15] If being good is being desirable, as Mill suggests, and being desirable is being fitting to be desired, then whether goodness must be analyzed in terms of reasons stands or falls with whether fittingness must be analyzed in terms of reasons.

We could, of course, argue independently from the dialectic about fittingness—considering various factors that might make something good, and constructing cases in which those factors do not succeed in making something good, and so on. But in fact all of the actual leading proposals for how to analyze *good* in terms of reasons do take goodness to be a matter of certain responses being fitting or otherwise supported by reasons. Indeed, it is not puzzling why this should be so, for the kinds of things that can be said to be good do not include only actions or other things that can be expressed by verbs or for which there can be reasons. So if the goodness of a person or a ball or a state of affairs consists in the balance of reasons, there must be a recipe that gets us from the person or the ball or the state of affairs to the thing that we must compare reasons for and against. And it is natural to think that only something that is a response *to* the person, ball, or state of affairs would be sufficiently closely related to it, for reasons for that response to count as making the person, ball, or state of affairs good.

However, any attempt to analyze *good*—whether in terms of reasons or otherwise—must come to grips with the diversity of claims that we make about what is good. We can say, for example, that something is a good knife, that it is good to open letters with, that he is good to her or that he is good to have around or that he is good for her to have around, and we can say that it is good that something happened, or good for it to happen. Any systematic and promising approach to analyzing *good* is going to have to first

---

[15] Mill [1863].

systematize each of these uses of 'good', come to an understanding of what 'good' is predicated of in each case, and then proceed from there.

It turns out that there are arguably three main classes of syntactic uses of 'good' that need to be distinguished. Sometimes 'good' is used in what Geach called an *attributive* construction, as when we say that something is a good knife, a good person, a good sunset, or a good state of affairs. Plausibly very similar to attributive 'good' are cases where we say that someone is good *at skiing*, which likely means just that they are a good skier. In attributive 'good' constructions, 'good' is followed by a noun phrase, which it modifies to create a complex predicate, 'good knife', and as Geach observed, the fact that something is a good K does not entail that it is good.

A second, distinct use of 'good' belongs to the category of what are known as *experiencer adjectives*, like 'fun' and 'pleasant'. This use is sometimes called *good for*. Syntactically, experiencer adjectives take a non-finite clause like 'to hang out with Crystal' and have an external argument expressed by 'for'. So their canonical form is 'it is fun for David to hang out with Crystal', where 'David' and 'to hang out with Crystal' are the two arguments of 'fun'. Similarly: 'it is good for David to hang out with Crystal'. In these sentences 'it' is semantically void—it doesn't denote anything, but just appears to satisfy the grammatical requirement that English sentences must have a subject. But it turns out that as with other syntactic constructions that don't have proper subjects, this grammatical requirement can also be satisfied by what linguists call *movement*, as in 'Crystal is fun/good/pleasant for David to hang out with'. And different parts of this construction can also be dropped and made implicit, as in 'Crystal is fun/good for David' or 'Crystal is fun/ good to hang out with' or even simply, 'Crystal is fun/good'.

Once we understand that 'good' is an experiencer adjective, we can see that 'good' is not being predicated of Crystal at all, but rather of the relation between David and the prospect of David's hanging out with Crystal. Whereas in attributive goodness claims, being a good knife can be predicated of a particular thing, in *good for* claims, goodness is only predicated of a relationship between an experiencer subject and a prospect expressible by a non-finite clause.

Many philosophers also believe in a third, distinct, concept of goodness that is neither attributive nor relational to a particular experiencing subject. Consider the claim, "it is good for criminals to be punished". On one reading, this is plausibly true—or at least, it is what retributivists claim to be true. But it is not good *for criminals* to be punished—the whole point of punishment, according to retributivism, is for criminals to get the bad things that they deserve. In spoken language, you can get the contrast between these two readings of "it is good for criminals to be punished" by shifting whether you pause after 'good' or pause after 'criminals'. The first pause yields the reading that retributivists say is true, while the second pause yields the reading that retributivists say is false.

These two readings are distinguished by whether 'for' functions as a complementizer or a preposition. On the second reading, it is a preposition, supplying the 'for' argument that we are familiar with from *good for* claims. But on the first reading, it is a complementizer like 'that', supplying 'for criminals to be punished' as the prospect of which 'good' is being predicated—giving it a similar meaning to 'it is good that criminals are punished', but without the factive implication that criminals are actually being punished. Philippa Foot has famously maintained that even this first reading is a disguised *good for* claim, meaning that it is good *for us* for criminals to be punished, or something similar. But others hold that it expresses a third, distinct and non-relational, kind of goodness—the kind of goodness that consequentialists are interested in, when they say that what you ought to do is whatever action is such that it will be best if you do it. We can call this concept of good *impersonal good*.

The distinction between *attributive good*, *good for*, and *impersonal good* organizes and systematizes the vast range of superficially different sentences that we can construct using 'good' and identify where superficially identical sentences really should be understood as having different meanings. But it leaves us with three different notions of goodness to potentially be analyzed in terms of reasons. If 'good' means 'desirable', then presumably it is *impersonal* 'good' that means 'desirable'—the retributivist really does think that it is desirable that criminals be punished. But if attributive good and *good for* are to be understood in terms of the competition of reasons, we still don't know exactly how those are going to go.

At least two related questions remain open. First, *which responses* are the relevant ones for determining what is good for someone, or what is a good knife? If the claim that it is impersonally good for criminals to be punished means that it is fitting to desire that criminals are punished, then the claim that it is good for (in the sense of *good for*) criminals to be punished cannot be a matter of whether it is fitting to desire that criminals be punished, or else it will incorrectly come out as true. So either it must involve the fittingness of a different response, *or* it must involve the competition among a different subset of the reasons for and against desire than fittingness does. As a result, the second important remaining question is *which* reasons for this response matter for *good for*.

A similar problem arises for attributive good. If a certain knife being a good knife is a matter of some response to it being fitting, we need to know what that response is. On the face of it, it can't be that what is fitting is desiring the knife, because what makes someone a good assassin is quite different from what makes it good that they are an assassin. So again, either we need to appeal to a different response, or we need to appeal to a different subset of reasons from that appealed to for fittingness.

Chapter Summary

In this chapter we have surveyed some of the normative concepts that philosophers have aspired to use reasons to analyze. It is one of the major themes of this book that it is very *helpful* to appeal to reasons in analyzing other normative concepts, but in this chapter we have been focused primarily on the complications and challenges in doing so. We saw that even in the core cases for balance-of-reasons analyses—*required* and *ought*—complicated issues arise about which reasons get compared and whether this requires postulating further deep distinctions among reasons. We encountered puzzling features of information-dependence of *ought* that challenge whether it can be analyzed in terms of either objective or subjective reasons. We saw how analyzing fittingness requires distinguishing 'right' from 'wrong' kinds of reasons, and that the question of whether 'good' can be analyzed in terms of reasons cannot be separated from questions about the relationship between goodness and desirability.

Recommended Reading

For some of the complexities and choice points about which reasons are to be compared, see Schmidt's "How Reasons Determine Moral Requirements". Snedegar's "Reasons, Competition, and Latitude" offers an excellent comparative treatment of different ways of trying to distinguish 'ought' from 'required' in the context of reasons explanations, and Schroeder's "Getting Perspective on Objective Reasons" explores the four-envelope problem for reasons-based analyses of 'ought'. The classic sources for the wrong kind of reasons problem are Crisp's review of *Value... And What Follows* and Rabinowicz's and Rønnow-Rasmussen's "The Strike of the Demon: On Fitting Pro-Attitudes and Value", and Hieronymi's "The Wrong Kind of Reasons" is the classic source for wrong kind of reasons skepticism, also supported by further arguments in Way's "Transmission and the Wrong Kind of Reason". For a helpful treatment of *good for* as an experiencer adjective, see Shanklin's *On Good and 'Good'*, and for a reasons-based treatment of *good for*, see Darwall's *Welfare and Rational Care*.

Exercises

9.1 *Comprehension.* Explain why Otherwise Requirement can be thought of as just a special case of Options Requirement.

9.2 *Extensions.* We have said in many places throughout this book that defeated reasons can still be reasons—that there can be considerations on *both* sides of a moral question, at one and the same time. For this exercise, look for evidence to support this claim by comparing the case in which you ought to stop and help the cyclist even though you have been invited to a wedding to a case in which you ought to stop and help the cyclist but have nothing else pressing to be doing. What differences can you describe between these two cases? Which, if any, of those differences might be attributable to the fact that there is still a reason in the former case?

9.3 *Extensions.* Try to construct an "options" analogue version of the principle of Contra-Against Requirement from section 9.2. Make sure that your analogue follows Contra-Against Requirement in trying to define requirement out of reasons against. But it may require making other significant changes to the formulation of the principle. Which other changes does it require you to make?

9.4 *Extensions.* According to a plausible principle that is sometimes called the *opportunity cost principle*, a reason in favor of an alternative to φ-ing automatically counts as a reason against φ-ing. Compare the ways of thinking about reasons against that are articulated by the principles of Against Requirement (advocated by Snedegar) and Contra-Against Requirement (advocated by Greenspan). Which of these two principles fits better with the opportunity cost principle? Why?

9.5 *Extensions.* According to Gert [2004], the reasons that must be compared to determine what you are required to do are what he calls *permitting* and *requiring* reasons. According to Mill [1863], what you are required to do is a matter of what others *should require* you to do. For this exercise, show how Gert's view can be reconciled with a variation on Mill's view by treating the '-ed' in 'required' and 'permitted' as belonging to the class of '-able'/'-ible' suffixes that were argued to express the concept of the fitting in section 9.4.

9.6 *Extensions.* In the four-envelope case, Xiao, Ying, and Zach all accept contrasting views about what Xiao ought to do. Challenge the view that this requires there to be three different senses of 'ought' in two different ways: First, by constructing a 'five-envelope' case in which four different observers with different amounts of information rationally disagree about what Xiao ought to do. And second, by showing that each of these uses of 'ought' can be captured by a single meaning of 'ought' that is sensitive to the speaker's information. When you ask yourself what Xiao ought to do, which of these senses of 'ought' are *you* using? If it is not the same one as Xiao and Ying, how can you tell?

9.7 *Extensions.* Wrong-kind reasons skeptics say that putative examples of wrong-kind reasons, such as the mother's offer of money in return for you admiring her child, are not really reasons for what they appear to support (in this case, admiring her child) at all, but just reasons to *want* to do this. For this exercise, challenge the implied exclusivity between something being a reason to do something and also being a reason to want to do it, by identifying an example of a consideration that is both. What does this tell you about how to think about the dialectical burdens of wrong-kind reasons skepticism?

9.8 *Extensions.* Construct a reasons-based account of attributive goodness by writing down a formula for the conditions under which something counts as a good K that applies no matter which noun phrase we substitute for 'K'. Test your account against the examples both of 'good knife' and 'good assassin'. Can your account be paraphrased in terms of the fittingness of some response? Why or why not?

10
What Can Analyze Reasons?

10.1 Philosophical Analysis and Reasons

In Chapter 9 we surveyed both some of the power of and many of the problems with analyzing other normative properties and relations in terms of reasons. This power is illustrated by the Rossian diagnosis of many of the complexities of each normative domain and by how it allows those complexities to arise naturally from the balance of competing factors—reasons. It also builds on one of the important ideas from Chapter 7—that reasons are explanatory not because it is part of the nature of reasons to explain, but because it is part of the nature of other things to be explained by reasons. And in Chapter 12, we will encounter one more important part of the power of analyzing other normative properties in terms of reasons. But we've also seen that analyzing other things in terms of reasons is not without its problems—even in the core cases that some have believed to be the most obvious targets for analysis by reasons, there are complex issues about which reasons compete and how they compete.

Whatever the scope of normative properties that we can use reasons to analyze, however, there is a further pressing question of what, if anything, can be used to analyze reasons. If the explanatory role of reasons comes from the fact that it is part of the nature of other things to be explained by reasons, then what does that leave about the nature of reasons themselves—the things that do that explaining? In Chapters 6 through 8, we considered the possibility that the reason relation might be analyzable in terms of some of the other concepts with which reasons are closely associated: evidence, explanation, or their role in deliberation or reasoning. But this approach was piecemeal. In this chapter we will take a more general look at what might be part of the analysis of reasons, paying special attention to whether reasons must be analyzed in terms of some other normative property or relation—and if so, which one.

The reasons to pay special attention to whether any other *normative* property or relation is part of the analysis of reasons are many. For one, some proponents of the centrality of reasons in ethics have gone so far as to defend the claim that reasons are the basic normative property or relation, in parallel but contrast to Moore's claim in *Principia Ethica* that all of ethical theory is the study of the good. This thesis is sometimes called *Reasons First*, or the *fundamentality of reasons*. This thesis can be easily confused with another thesis that is often also endorsed by many of the same people—namely, that the property of being a reason is *unanalyzable* or *primitive*. This thesis is appropriately called *reasons primitivism*, though sometimes people use 'reasons fundamentalism' as a name for the conjunction of these two theses. But if the problems with analyzing other normative properties in terms of reasons outweigh the promise of the power of such analyses, then it is doubtful that reasons are fundamental in this sense.

But more importantly, the question of what normative properties or relations are part of the analysis of reasons sets important constraints on what reasons can be, in turn, used to analyze. Throughout the last four chapters, we've been making many claims about priority or analysis. And of course different philosophers will prefer different idioms for making these claims or they will place more or less emphasis on what they see to be differences between these claims. But what we take them all to have in common is that they are varying expressions of the question Socrates asks of Euthyphro: not what things are pious, but *what is piety*? They are each attempts to formulate what is at stake in the project of *philosophical analysis*.

But even though philosophers have had many theories over the centuries about what the project of philosophical analysis is really trying to do, one of the central constraints emerges early in the *Euthyphro* itself. And this constraint is that you can't have it both ways. Philosophical analyses should not go in circles, and so you can't both analyze *good* in terms of *reasons* and also analyze *reasons* in terms of *good*. More generally, nothing that we use reasons to analyze—either directly or indirectly—can be part of the analysis of reasons.

10.2 Telic Analyses of Reasons

In earlier chapters we encountered two of the most well-studied styles of analyzing reasons—desire-based (or Humean) and value-based theories. Although the idea that either value or desires can be used in some way or other to analyze reasons is a bit more general, the most common developments of each of these theories give them a *telic* structure. Each can be described as the view that what you have reason to do is what will serve or promote some *objective*, and the difference between the two theories can be located in where the objectives that give rise to reasons come from. On the desire-based theory, these objectives are set by what the agent desires (perhaps under some idealized conditions), whereas on the value-based theory, these objectives are set by what is of value. Despite other quite prominent differences—including that only the desire-based theory is compatible with the fundamentality of reasons—this common structure makes it quite natural to compare these theories side-by-side.

The following is a natural way of formulating versions of each of these theories that makes obvious their deep similarities despite the strong disagreements among their proponents:

Desire-Based Reasons A consideration is a reason for an agent to φ just when it helps explain why their φ-ing promotes some objective that the agent desires.

Value-Based Reasons A consideration is a reason for an agent to φ just when it helps explain why their φ-ing promotes some good objective.

However, despite their obvious parallels, only the desire-based view is *reductive* in the sense that it is compatible with analyzing the normative phenomenon of whether something is a reason in entirely non-normative terms. We can foreground this difference by showing how the two telic views conflict with different parts of what is sometimes called the classical argument for error theory, which holds that moral discourse is erroneous because it falsely presupposes that things can be morally good or right.

According to this argument, which we first briefly encountered in Chapter 8 as one of Mackie's [1977] central motivations for thinking that nothing is genuinely wrong, if anything is wrong, then there are reasons not to do it that are "intrinsically action-guiding" or *objectively prescriptive*. For example, having one's toe stomped on hurts. That it hurts provides a reason not to go about stomping on people's toes, which is special in two respects. First, this reason guides action; ignoring its significance when deciding what to do leaves you open to important kinds of blame and sanction. Appreciating how it feels to the trodden to be trod upon calls on you to avoid treading on their toes. The reason thus has authority over how you act; it *prescribes* how you are to act. And second, it's a reason for anyone, regardless of their perspective on the world, to avoid stomping on toes. It's a reason grounded in the worldly reality of hurt toes, not in how hurt toes figure in our perspective. This makes its prescriptivity "objective" not in the way that objective reasons contrast with subjective reasons, but by having a kind of universality or stance-independence.

But the second premise of the classical argument is that *nothing* could be objectively prescriptive. And together, these premises entail that nothing can be wrong. Even those who do not accept the error theory are frequently moved by this argument. For example, Gilbert Harman's [1975] famous defense of ethical relativism is just what we get by running this argument backwards from the assumptions that morality is prescriptive, but the error theory is false to the conclusion that morality is not objective—and so wrongness is relative in the sense that what it is wrong for each person to do depends on what she wants or is committed to. And Philippa Foot's [1972] famous proposal that morality is a system of hypothetical imperatives is just what we get by running Harman's argument backwards from the assumptions that morality is objective but the error theory is false to the conclusion that morality is not, after all, prescriptive.

A natural way to think about the large and important issues still at stake between the desire-based and value-based theories of reasons, despite their common features, is in terms of the different challenges that each faces in light of morality's apparent objective prescriptivity. Because the desire-based view holds that all reasons are, roughly, instrumental reasons, it secures the prescriptivity of morality in a particularly clear way. The reasons of morality move you because to be a reason at all, something must relate to your desires in the right way, and your desires are what move you.

Yet even totally rational agents, it seems, can have wholly divergent desires. If all reasons flow from those desires, then it seems that those agents' moral reasons will be wholly divergent also.[1] This divergence conflicts with morality's supposed objectivity. This is why the desire-based theory of reasons is often pointed to as the culprit in the classical argument for the error theory. If what gives morality its prescriptive character is a connection to what people want, then surely it cannot be objective, because the differences between what people want are deep and obvious.

By contrast, the value-based theory of reasons can easily secure the objectivity of morality's prescriptivity, so long as the values that reasons

---

[1] Schroeder [2007b] denies this.

must serve are objective values—the same values to explain everyone's reasons. And the value-based theory can offer a cheap answer to why this objectivity is genuinely prescriptive—by saying that what it means for morality to be "prescriptive" for you is just that there are reasons for you to comply. But the assumption that the values that reasons must serve are objective values carries with it its own problems, analogous to ones that we first encountered in Chapter 3 for the Meinong-Chisholm view about what reasons support.

The problem is that if each person's reasons come from the ways in which their actions can serve or promote a single, universal good, then the paradox of deontology rears its head. Recall our example from Chapter 3. It's wrong to kill, so everyone has reason not to kill. This injunction forbids Ally from killing, even if she could prevent two further killings from Hally and Sally by doing so. And likewise for Hally and Sally: they shouldn't kill even if it would prevent the other two from killing.

But the problem is that if Ally's reason not to kill comes from something bad that would happen if she kills, then in order to get the result that Ally shouldn't kill even in order to prevent Hally and Sally from killing, we have to posit that it is worse for Ally to kill than for both Hally and Sally to kill. But this would be a bizarre thing to claim because Ally is not special. And it would give the wrong results in cases in which Hally and Sally can, by both killing, prevent Ally from killing.

Let's walk through this reasoning more slowly. If Ally should not kill, then she has more reason to let Hally and Sally kill than to kill herself. And if the value-based view is right, then this implies that *it's worse* that Ally kills than that Hally and Sally kill—at least if the weight or strength of Hally's reasons for acting is proportional to the degree of value promoted by that action. Let A represent the outcome where Ally kills and let [A] represent its degree of value. The fact that Ally should let Hally and Sally kill rather than kill herself implies that $[H]+[S]>[A]$. But it follows from parallel reasoning that $[H]+[A]>[S]$ from the fact that Sally should not kill and that $[A]+[S]>[H]$ from the fact that Hally should not kill. These three claims about value are logically inconsistent if killing is always bad. So, value-based views of reasons fail to adequately prescribe action if we accept agent-relative restrictions on actions like killing.[2]

The root of this conflict is simple. Injunctions like the one against killing recommend conflicting aims to different agents, telling Ally to ensure that Sally rather than Ally kills and telling Sally to ensure that Ally rather than

---

[2] For crucial complications in this line of reasoning, see Oddie and Milne [1991] and Nair [2014].

Sally kills. But the clear-eyed pursuit of what's good can't lead to this kind of conflict because what's good doesn't vary between agents. The foregoing reasoning is essentially a kind of summary of what happens in Thomas Nagel's [1970] book *The Possibility of Altruism*, which starts out by trying to argue against the idea that reasons depend on desires and ends up arguing that agent-centered constraints are impossible.

In sum, the desire-based view creates the risk that there won't be shared reasons. Conversely, the value-based view allows for shared reasons since what's good is good to all. But common-sense morality seems to imply that my reasons to see to it that you avoid killing are weaker than your reasons to see to it that you avoid killing. That's not possible if those reasons flow from the (dis)value of your killing, which is invariant between us. So the idea that *everyone* has strongest reason to promote what's best *overshares* reasons. A priori, it is a bit surprising that it should turn out that resisting the error theory requires rejecting so much of common-sense morality. The fact that so many philosophers have felt the pull of this dilemma is suggestive of the prevalence of telic conceptions of reasons. The key to developing a value-based view is mitigating this risk. One promising way of doing so is to keep the values but give up the teleology.

10.3 Non-Telic Value-Based Approaches

As we saw in the last section, the telic value-based view seemingly fails to guide action if we accept agent-relative restrictions on actions such as killing. We can trace this failure to the telic idea that value must be promoted. If we have most reason to promote what's best, a telic approach to value forces agents to converge on promoting or pursuing that thing. But morality sometimes seems to require that agents have divergent aims, acting at cross purposes, as in the case of Ally, Hally, and Sally. We can avoid this convergence while still explaining reasons using value if we allow for *non-telic* responses to value.

For example, we can reject the presupposition that value exists to be promoted, as does the following view:

Kantian Value-Based Reasons A consideration is a reason for an agent to φ just when it helps explain why their φ-ing respects or honors some value.

The basic idea behind the view is that moral value does not call us to promote or sustain it. Rather, we can sometimes react appropriately to something's value by honoring it or by respecting it.[3] And it seems that, for example, respecting the value of human autonomy does not require us to converge on a single outcome. Proper respect for that value may call for us to act in conflicting ways. We might think that Ally would evince heinous disrespect for the value of human autonomy by *killing*, even to prevent more killings. After all, you don't evince respect for the Lincoln Memorial by vandalizing it, even if your vandalization would deter further and greater vandalization. So, it seems, the conflict between value-based views and morality's prescriptivity emerges only when we require a telic approach to value.

Alternatively, rather than renounce the connection between value and teleology, we can appeal to forms of value that allow value to precede action rather than be its aim. For example, Alex Gregory defends a view like the following:

Attributive Value-Based Reasons A consideration is a reason for an agent to φ just when it provides a good basis for φ-ing.

Motives are better or worse. For example, it would be better if Kant's shopkeeper charged the same price to all his customers out of a desire to be honest rather than out of a desire to be seen as honest. As a result, that charging the same to all is honest provides a better motivating reason to act honestly than the fact that it will be seen as honest.

It's natural to ask in what sense one motivating reason is better than another. Gregory's answer is that the first is better than the second in the same way that a sharp knife is better than a dull one or that a reliable car is better than an unreliable one. From Chapter 9, we can recognize that Gregory is talking about *attributive* good. So whereas telic value-based views are naturally interpreted as analyzing reasons in terms of impersonal goodness, Gregory proposes to analyze reasons in terms of attributive good. He is arguing that a good basis or a good motivating reason for some action is good as a motivation for doing it. *Attributive Value-Based Reasons* implies

---

[3] The idea that some actions can respect or honor a value without promoting it is particularly clearly articulated by Philip Pettit [1989], and elaborated on by Pettit in his contribution to Baron, Pettit, and Slote [1997]. See also McNaughton and Rawling [1992], and Sylvan [2020], [2021] for prominent developments and uses of this idea. This idea counts as "Kantian" insofar as it is a working out of Kant's own emphasis on the idea that persons have a distinctive kind of value that he calls dignity.

that motivating reasons like that some act is honest are better *as motivating reasons* than ones like that some act will be seen as honest.

Gregory's intriguing appeal to *attributive* value can be profitably illuminated by testing it against a very commonly held view about the conditions under which something is attributively good. According to this theory, one thing is a better *K* than another iff it better fulfills the characteristic function of *K*s.[4] This correctly predicts that sharp knives better fulfill the characteristic function of knives (i.e., helping to cut) and that reliable cars are better at fulfilling the characteristic function of cars (i.e., helping to travel). If we accept this idea about attributive good, then the defensibility of Gregory's claims about attributively good motivating reasons will depend on what the function of motivating reasons turns out to be.

As we know from Chapter 2, motivating reasons are often thought to play two roles. Some think that they are the causes of action. Others think that they *rationalize*, or help to make rational sense of, action. And some think that they play both roles. Each role provides a sense in which a motivating reason for φ-ing could, in principle, be good as a reason to φ, but it seems that only the rationalizing role offers a plausible account of normative reasons. After all, given that Kant's shopkeeper is selfish, the thought that some act would be seen as honest is more causally efficacious at getting the shopkeeper to perform that act than the thought that it is honest. But the latter reason is the more important reason!

Thus, if, for example, moral reasons are especially good as motivating reasons, it must be because they are especially good at rationalizing action. This is an idea with some pedigree. A historically influential line of thought known as *moral rationalism* runs from Aristotle and Plato through to Kant and aims to show that what's moral is the same thing as what's rational.

Not all find this thought plausible. Simon Blackburn puts the point well enough to quote in full:

> This is the permanent Chimaera, the holy grail of moral philosophy, the knock-down argument that people who are nasty and unpleasant and motivated by the wrong things are above all *unreasonable*: then they can be proved to be wrong by the pure sword of reason. They aren't just selfish

---

[4] Some will be quick to point out that this kind of goodness concerns the *telos* of a certain kind of object, so Gregory's proposal is not properly classed as a non-telic approach. However, the account is non-telic in the sense that matters to us by focusing on the antecedent motivation for an action rather than its aim, outcome, end, etc.

or thoughtless or malignant or imprudent, but are reasoning badly, or out of touch with the facts. It must be an occupational hazard of professional thinkers to want to reduce all the vices to this one.[5]

It is not at all clear whether stating that some act is honest makes clearer rational sense of the shopkeeper's action than stating that it is seen as honest, given the shopkeeper's selfish aims. Consequently, advocates of this approach require not just a plausible account of how reasons can be good *qua* motivations but one that also classifies all and only normative reasons as good motivations.

However, as we've already seen in some detail in Chapter 8, there are other ways of vindicating the thought behind Gregory's proposal that normative reasons are particularly good as motivating reasons. One way or the other, it had better turn out that reasons figure in reasoning. Episodes of reasoning can vary in quality along several dimensions. So it makes sense to think that motivating reasons are at their best, as it were, when they figure in distinguished episodes of reasoning. We return, therefore, to the enticing thought that reasons belong to good reasoning—considerations are good because they figure in a good kind of reasoning.

10.4 Defeasible Reasons and Reasoning

So far in this chapter, we've considered ways of trying to analyze reasons telicly in terms of impersonal good and how such approaches contrast with telic analyses of reasons in terms of desire. We've also seen the appeal of non-promoting responses to impersonal good, and we saw how attributive good—perhaps because it is predicated of things rather than prospects—is a particularly apt place to look for goodness that does not require promotion of anything. But we also expressed some worries about whether the standards of being a good *motivating reason* are the right standards to ground the existence of normative reasons.

In Chapter 8 we encountered a class of theories—various forms of the Reasoning View—which attempted to analyze reasons in terms of good or sound *reasoning*. In that chapter we were focused on the role of *reasoning* or *deliberation* in these analyses, but we can now see that one natural way of

---

[5] Blackburn [1984, 222].

interpreting these views is as views on which it is *good* reasoning—as we now know, *attributively* good reasoning—in which something must have the right role in order to count as a reason. So it is worth revisiting this class of views with the prospect in mind that we can think of them as a new way of following Gregory's strategy of analyzing reasons in terms of attributive goodness, but which appeal to the standards of *reasoning*, rather than the standards of *motivating reasons*.

In Chapter 8, we considered a variety of proposals connecting reasons to reasoning, and focused on how the problem of elusive reasons makes it hard to get *enough* reasons out of such views and Schmidt's problems of chains of reasoning make it hard to avoid getting *too many* reasons. For purposes of this chapter, let's grant that we have figured out how to solve both of these problems—either in the way that we suggested in Chapter 8 or in some other way. Here we want instead to think about reasoning views as falling into two different classes, on the basis of being built on top of two different pictures about what makes reasoning attributively good. We can think of each of these pictures as built on a different answer about what normative concept is doing the ultimate explanatory work of explaining what makes some reasoning good, and hence this chapter is the right place for us to consider this contrast.

On the first picture, what makes steps of reasoning good is that they *preserve* something important.[6] This picture capitalizes on the idea familiar from logic that valid inferences are those that preserve truth, but generalizes to accommodate the possibility that reasoning can start from beliefs as premises and lead to an intention or an emotional response or even an action as its conclusion. But none of these things are naturally understood as being true or false. So if we want to generalize the idea that good reasoning preserves something, the thing that it preserves cannot simply be truth. Once we have this insight, we can explore different possible ideas about what good reasoning has to preserve. According to one possible view, for example, good reasoning should never take you from a rational state of mind to an irrational state of mind. But according to a different view that is even more closely modeled on the preservation of truth, what must be preserved is *fittingness*. On the assumption that a belief

---

[6] A qualified and more sophisticated version of this idea—qualified for exactly the reasons that we go on to give here—is endorsed by McHugh and Way [2016], McHugh and Way [2022b].

is fitting just in case it is true, the fittingness-preservation view encompasses valid inferences between beliefs, but it is more general.

Fitting Reasoning   A consideration r is a reason for s to φ just when and because s's reasoning from acceptance of r to (intending) φ-ing preserves fittingness from the former attitude to the latter.

On a different picture, what makes reasoning good is not that it preserves anything *per se*, but rather simply that it satisfies certain norms about how reasoning is to go.[7]

Norms of Reasoning   A consideration r is a reason for s to φ just when and because s's reasoning from acceptance of r to (intending) φ-ing satisfies the norms of reasoning.

Each of these views provides a picture about what makes reasoning good, but they are different pictures. And each of these pictures leads to its own challenges.

Let's take the fittingness-preservation view, first. We argued in Chapter 9 that fittingness displays many of the same features that make it a strong candidate to be analyzed in terms of the balance of reasons—for example that there are default features that make it fitting to admire someone that don't do so when other conditions are present that defeat them. For example, being an ethical vegetarian normally makes you admirable, but Hitler is not admirable—it is not fitting to admire him. We suggested that this is because the fact that Hitler was an ethical vegetarian *is* a reason to admire him, but one that is outweighed by the many compelling reasons not to admire him. And if fittingness is analyzed in terms of the balance of reasons, then we cannot turn around and analyze reasons in terms of the preservation of fittingness—we must choose.

But as we have formulated it, the fittingness-preservation view imposes too strong a constraint on what is required in order for the fact that Hitler is an ethical vegetarian to be a reason to admire him. If the belief that Hitler was an ethical vegetarian is fitting, then admiring Hitler has to also be fitting. This is just the idea that reasons must preserve fittingness. But we have been assuming that a belief is fitting just in case it is true, and it *is* reputedly true

---

[7] Compare Asarnow [2017], Setiya [2012].

that Hitler was an ethical vegetarian. So we face a dilemma: either this view must deny that the fact that Hitler was an ethical vegetarian is a reason to admire him, or it must conclude that it is in fact fitting to admire Hitler.

Note that this is not a problem about Hitler per se, but just about the fact that there are reasons—*right-kind* reasons—to do things that are not in fact fitting. In this way, this problem is very closely analogous to the problem that we encountered in Chapter 7 for the idea that reasons are explanations of why you ought to do something. That problem, recall, was that there are reasons to do things that it is not the case that you should. You might think that it is okay to deny that Hitler's ethical vegetarianism is any reason to admire him, and we would sympathize with you for not getting too worked up about whether we acknowledge all of the reasons to admire him, but it seems very unpromising to adopt as a general response to this strategy that there are never right-kind reasons for unfitting responses.

Note also that this problem is just what we would expect if fittingness is explained by reasons, rather than conversely. If what is fitting is a matter of the balance of reasons, then there will be reasons that lose this balance and hence support options that are not, on balance, fitting. In Chapters 7 and 8 we noted that the reasoning view can respect the role that reasons play in explaining what we *ought* to do by holding that the explanatory role of reasons comes from the nature of *ought*, and not from the nature of reasons. But if we make the analogous move for the role of reasons in explaining what is *fitting*, then we are using reasons to analyze the fitting, rather than conversely.

This pushes us to the second horn of the dilemma. Rather than concluding that there is no reason to admire Hitler, we embrace the conclusion that it is in fact fitting to admire him. But this conclusion seems to us to be absurd! Hitler is not at all admirable! You might think that we can blunt this horn by distinguishing between *degrees* of fittingness—weakening the view to only require that a conclusion must be fitting to *some* degree. It is more defensible to think that it is to some minimal though positive degree fitting to admire Hitler than it is to think that it is fitting to admire him full stop. But this, we think, would be a grave error. This seems to imply that it is fitting to be at least a little bit ambivalent about Hitler, and we contend that there is no room for such ambivalence.

Just as bad, weakening the fittingness-preservation view in this way has catastrophic consequences for which steps of reasoning will preserve fittingness—for example, anything that is always at least a *little* bit fitting will be such that *everything* counts as a reason for it. Take, for example, going for ice cream. There is always at least *some* reason to go for ice cream—and so going for ice cream is always at least a little bit fitting. Therefore every transition from any belief whatsoever to going for ice cream will preserve at least some degree of fittingness, and hence the view would predict that everything is a reason to go for ice cream. But this is clearly too cheap.

So we can't understand good reasoning in terms of the absolute preservation of fittingness. This is why McHugh and Way [2016], in their fittingness-preservation account of good reasoning (and derivatively of reasons), say instead that steps of good reasoning are steps that that preserve fittingness "other things being equal".[8] To say that good reasoning must preserve fittingness "other things being equal" is not to say that it must preserve fittingness. It is just to say that fittingly accepting the premises of good reasoning is the *right kind of thing* to make accepting the conclusion fitting, unless something else interferes, making it unfitting. This, of course, is what *reasons* do—they support things *other things being equal*. The reason to keep your promise doesn't make it correct to keep your promise; it is only the right kind of thing to make it correct to keep it so long as nothing else—such as an emergency—makes it incorrect to keep it. Friends of the explanatory role of reasons will recognize, once more, an appeal here to the kind of work that we postulate reasons to do.[9]

Fitting Reasoning explains facts about reasons with facts about attitudes. We started off this chapter by mentioning the *Euthyphro* as a way of illustrating how, roughly, our claims were neutral between various ways of thinking about the asymmetric relation of dependence between whether something is pious and whether it is loved by the gods. One conception of that relation holds that something is pious because it is loved by the gods. Famously, the challenge for this position is to explain why the gods love something without conceding that it's because it's pious. Similarly, you might worry about how we can explain patterns in our reasons with patterns in our fitting attitudes, rather than vice versa. According to the view, the painfulness of having your toe stepped on isn't a reason not to step on your toe all by itself. Rather, it's only because reasoning from belief in the pain to the intention to avoid stepping on the toe is fittingness-preserving that the

---

[8] McHugh and Way [2016], McHugh and Way [2022b]. See also Way [2017].
[9] Inferences that are good only other things being equal are the province of *nonmonotonic logic*. Note that John Horty [2012] has argued that one of the leading approaches to nonmonotonic logic, known as *default* logic, is best interpreted as showing how premises provide *reasons* for accepting conclusions.

pain provides a reason. Just as Socrates' question to Euthyphro doesn't force him to adopt either answer, nothing forces us to go one way or the other here. But you still might think that this is getting things the wrong way around.

10.5 Norms of Reasoning

Rather than preserving some other property, we might think that what makes reasoning good is simply that it satisfies certain norms. Consequently, rather than conceiving of good or ideal reasoning as reasoning that preserves fittingness across premise and concluding attitudes, we can instead conceive of it as good or ideal when it satisfies the set of norms of practical reasoning. In a certain sense, *Fitting Reasoning* is just a special case of this view according to which there's a single norm of reasoning: preserve fittingness when reasoning from premise attitudes to concluding attitudes.

But because the norm to preserve fittingness is only one norm among many, the *Norms of Reasoning* approach to analyzing reasons is more flexible than *Fitting Reasoning*. One important reason why we might think this flexibility is important comes directly out of our reasoning in the last section. There we saw that even the proponents of fittingness-preservation views are pushed to appeal to an "other things being equal" clause, because not all reasoning guarantees the fittingness of its conclusions. Some of it only makes its conclusions *reasonable*. Such reasoning is what logicians call *nonmonotonic*, because it doesn't obey the principle that what is supported by a set of premises increases *monotonically*—i.e., only goes up or stays the same, and never goes down—as we add additional premises. So the Norms of Reasoning view is naturally motivated by the flexibility with which it can identify non-fittingness-preserving rules of inference as still norm-compliant. Nevertheless, as we'll now argue, defeated reasons still pose a challenge to *Norms of Reasoning*, though here the challenge takes a different shape.

Recall that the dilemma faced by the fittingness-preservation view was to make sense of how there could be reasons for an unfitting response. Samuel Asarnow [2017] suggests that this problem can be evaded, so long as the norms of reasoning are *defeasible*. Suppose, for example, that our reason to liberate someone is that they have been falsely imprisoned, but it is not in fact fitting to liberate them because there is a pressing public health need for them to pass a quarantine first. In this case, the norm that licenses reasoning from belief in their false incarceration to the intention to liberate them is *defeated* by new information about the pressing need to quarantine them. Though there is a defeasible rule of reasoning that allows reasoning from the belief that someone was falsely imprisoned to liberating them, this reasoning is only defeasibly good, and it is not good when you also believe that public health requires the prisoner to first clear a quarantine period.

Defeasible norms offer the advocate of *Norms of Reasoning* the shape of an answer to the challenge of defeated reasons. But, by themselves, defeasible norms do not answer the challenge. As we learned in Chapter 7 when discussing Broome's analysis of reasons, defeasibility is a structural requirement of *any* norm-based analysis of reasons. Part of what an analysis of reasons must explain is reasons' defeasibility. So *Norms of Reasoning* must do more than merely posit defeasible norms. Otherwise, its analysis depends on the very judgments about reasons that the theory aims to explain. *Norms of Reasoning* requires a theory of defeat.

Outweighed reasons suffer a kind of defeat known as *rebutting* defeat. Advocates of *Norms of Reasoning* can appropriate this phenomenon by claiming that when a reason is outweighed, that's because the initial norm of reasoning that requires intending the action on the basis of the reason suffers a rebutting defeat by some weightier norm that forbids that action given some further reason. Consequently, just as we need to accept that fittingness comes in degrees to mirror competition between reasons, we also need to accept that there are stronger and weaker norms to do so.

The trouble with using rebutting to mount a theory of defeat for norms of reasoning, once again, has roots in the *Euthyphro*. According to *Norms of Reasoning*, when a surgeon must amputate your leg to save your life, a norm that requires action because inaction is deadly outweighs a competing norm that requires inaction because action is injurious. But common sense suggests that it's the competition between harm and death that requires surgery, not the fact that intending surgery better satisfies norms of reasoning. It's a cost to the view that it must affirm this counterintuitive answer.

Moreover, even if we accept that these norms are *super* important—more relevant to how to act than whether an act is harmful or deadly—then it had better be that we have good reason to uphold them. Otherwise, we seem to be engaged in an objectionable kind of rule worship. But the idea that reasons underlie the norms conflicts with the analysis, which aims to explain *all* reasons by norms and so it cannot tolerate—much less rely on—claims about reasons that don't themselves reduce to claims about norms of reasoning.

We think that these are serious challenges, which deserve more space than we can dedicate to them. Rather than develop them, we will close by raising a different worry: to adequately characterize defeasibility, *Norms of Reasoning* needs to mirror the entire conceptual apparatus that we use to characterize the conflict of reasons. But that apparatus is well-suited to describing how we weigh considerations and ill-suited to how we weigh norms.

As we've seen, rebutting defeat isn't the only kind of defeat. Reasons for action can also be *undercut*. Other things equal, the fact that someone has been imprisoned on false charges is a reason to free them. The wrongness of false incarceration can be explained: it is confinement that stifles the autonomous pursuit of our ends. However, suppose we learn that the incarcerated—call him Jim—enthusiastically and competently consents to, indeed *endorses*, his false incarceration. After all, Jim faces the threat of murder "on the outside" and his prison actually doubles as a luxury spa where his friends and family can visit whenever. If Jim freely consents to his incarceration, your case for liberating him evaporates.

Rebutting defeat isn't up to the task of explaining Jim's case. For example, when a reason is rebutted, it leaves a trace. If you promise to show up for dinner at seven, but an injured cyclist requires your help, which will delay you, then (let's suppose) you do the right thing by helping the cyclist and breaking your promise—your reasons to help the cyclist outweigh your reasons to keep the promise. But your reasons to keep your promise still affect what you should do subsequently, even if they've been rebutted: it makes sense to apologize for the delay, to regret that you could not have both helped the cyclist *and* kept your promise, etc. If your reasons to liberate Jim were merely rebutted, then it would make sense to feel similar feelings of regret and apology. But that's absurd. Jim doesn't regret being imprisoned... why should you regret it? Should you apologize to Jim for not freeing him? No. The false charges therefore provide no reason to free Jim if they're his only ticket to another day at the spa. So we must appeal to a different kind of defeat to properly explain Jim's case: *undercutting* defeat.

Norms of Reasoning implies that reasoning from the belief that someone's incarceration is wrongful to the intention to liberate them ordinarily satisfies the norms of reasoning. But reasoning from the belief that Jim's incarceration is wrongful to the intention to liberate him does *not*. We need to explain this interaction between the norms. So we must accept that not only can norms rebut each other, they can also undercut each other. According to *Norms of Reasoning*, the explanation of why the ordinary pattern of reasoning from apprehension of wrongful incarceration to the intention to liberate fails to hold in Jim's case is that some other pattern holds, somehow undercutting the first one. But that's not *nearly* as satisfying as an explanation that appeals to the relevant considerations *qua* reasons: Jim doesn't need liberating because he's happy where he is. There may be even more exotic forms of defeat such as so-called "valence-switching" defeat, where a reason for an action becomes a reason against it, that further highlight this problem for *Norms of Reasoning*. To be clear, we're engaging in a little bit of table-thumping on behalf of reasons. But it's important to realize reasons are popular precisely because they are the natural *explanans* for this kind of phenomenon.

10.6 Conclusion

In Chapters 9 and 10 we have been trying to survey just a sampling of the issues about what we can use reasons to analyze and what we can use to analyze reasons. One of the key morals that we have been keen to emphasize is that you can't have it both ways—if we use *good* to analyze reasons, then we will not also be using reasons to analyze *good*. But more, if the philosophical evidence that, say, attributive good is to be analyzed in terms of reasons is equally good as the philosophical evidence that impersonal good is to be analyzed in terms of reasons, or if we have independent cause to think that attributive good and impersonal good are at all similar properties, then we should not be drawing the conclusion that one is used to analyze reasons but the other is analyzed by reasons. Clearly, much work remains in order to satisfactorily sort out the issues facing any of the views that we have considered.

A second moral that we have been keen to emphasize is that while the potential power of reasons as potential analyzers of other normative properties and relations is great, there are also serious problems confronting their use to analyze each of these things. Our final two chapters are dedicated to exploring one very general source of problems (in Chapter 11) and one very general source of power (in Chapter 12).

Chapter Summary

In this chapter we have turned to consider what other concepts we might use to analyze reasons. We saw that for reasons of circularity, the answer to this question must be constrained by our answer to what we want to use reasons to analyze. In earlier chapters we considered whether evidence, explanation, or reasoning might play a role in the analysis of reasons, but in this chapter we focused on which *normative* concepts might play this role, perhaps alongside concepts like evidence, explanation, or reasoning. We considered the historically prominent attempts to analyze reasons in *teleological* terms by appeal to a goal, and explored pitfalls of both desire-based and value-based versions of this idea. We then turned to non-teleological versions of value-based views. And we returned to the Reasoning Account from Chapter 8, this time focusing on which normative concept might best be used along with the concept of reasoning in order to complete an analysis.

Recommended Reading

We recommend that this chapter be read alongside Gregory's "Reasons as Good Bases", on whose account we have focused here. A classic source for summarizing the ways in which desire-based theories of reasons put pressure on moral objectivity is the opening of Foot's *Natural Goodness*, and for an illustration of the ways in which resisting desire-based views leads to endorsing the kind of agent-neutrality characteristic of classical consequentialism, see Nagel's *The Possibility of Altruism*. Geach's "Good and Evil" both introduces the concept of attributive good and endorses the relationship between attributive goodness and function that motivates our worry about Gregory's view. The classic source for the honoring/promoting distinction is Pettit's "Consequentialism and Respect for Persons". And we strongly recommend Chapter 2 of Robert Shanklin's *On Good and 'Good'* for an introduction to the syntax of experiencer adjectives and how it applies to a wide range of sentences involving 'good' whose structure is commonly misunderstood.

Exercises

10.1 *Comprehension*. Explain how the distinction between promoting and honoring values can be used by some but not other value-based views to resist the paradox of deontology.

10.2 *Extensions*. Although desire-based reasons are often thought to be threatening in metaethics because of the *necessity* condition that they place on reasons, a common way to get independent leverage to argue against desire-based theories is by arguing against the *sufficient* condition that they place on reasons. Why might someone think that the necessity and sufficiency directions of the desire-based theory must stand or fall together? Is this a good reason? Why or why not?

10.3 *Extensions.* In section 10.3 we relied on a common theory about the conditions under which something is attributively good in order to put pressure on Gregory's thesis that normative reasons are good motivating reasons. According to this theory, what makes something a good *K* depends on the function of *K*s. For this exercise, try to put pressure on this theory by considering the conditions under which something is a good sunset or someone is a good person. Do these examples require rejecting the theory wholesale, or just modifying it to say something about *K*s that lack a function?

10.4 *Extensions.* In their defense of the fittingness-preserving account of good reasoning, McHugh and Way [2022b] reject examples like our example of the reason to admire Hitler. They say, following Maguire [2018], that there is no *pro tanto* reason to admire Hitler even though he is not admirable overall; instead what is true is that it is fitting to *admire Hitler's diet*, a narrower attitude that is compatible with not admiring Hitler overall. For this exercise, consider the strategy of resisting our objection based on this kind of example by always distinguishing narrower and narrower attitudes. Is there any attitude that is so narrow that you can't think of pros and cons of having it? (Compare Ward [2022]).

10.5 *Extensions.* McHugh and Way [2022b] also have an answer to why appealing to what preserves fittingness other things being equal does not involve a covert appeal to reasons, as we worry in section 10.4. They say that for an inference to preserve fittingness other things being equal is for it to preserve fittingness in *normal* conditions. For this exercise, try to use examples of reasons that do *not* preserve fittingness in order to impose conditions on what "normal" conditions must be like. Are there any penguins in normal conditions? Does anyone play games that involve deception? Are there any wars? What, exactly, must "normal" conditions be like?

10.6 *Extensions.* As we saw, some kinds of "good reasoning" theories focus on the *preservation* of some important feature in reasoning—rationality, fittingness, or the like. Show that you can revive Schmidt's objection from Chapter 8 to such views unless they are modified in some way. How would you modify them?

10.7 *Extensions.* In what is sometimes called "valence-switching" defeat, something that would ordinarily be a reason to do one thing becomes, in some special circumstance, a reason *not* to do it. Come up with your own example of "valence-switching" defeat and identify the corresponding defeat for the relevant norms of reasoning that would be appealed to by the "norms of reasoning" account. Can we use the value-based and desire-based views to explain "valence-switching" with reasons? How can we explain the corresponding behavior in norms?

10.8 *Extensions.* Suppose that we accept the "norms of reasoning" account. These norms, as we've seen, must apply only *other things equal* in reasoning in order to allow for defeasibility of reasons. Using a particular example, try to say what would be required in order to be able to follow such an other-things-equal norm by knowing whether other things are in fact equal. Do you worry that knowing whether other things are equal requires a prior grasp of what sorts of things would be a reason for what? Why or why not? What does your answer tell you about whether this is a promising way to analyze reasons?

10.9 *Extensions.* Taking into account everything that we have covered in the last two chapters, which considerations can be thought of as providing support for the thesis of the fundamentality of reasons? Which considerations can be thought of as providing support for reasons primitivism? How if at all do these lists of considerations come apart? Which seems to you more likely to be true: that reasons are primitive but not the sole fundamental building blocks of the normative because other normative properties are also primitive and not analyzable in terms of reasons, or that reasons are the sole fundamental building blocks of the normative but are not primitive because they can be analyzed in non-normative terms?

11
Weights

11.1 The Epiphenomenal Challenge

In the last two chapters we have considered some of the power as well as some of the problems of using reasons to analyze other normative properties and relations. In every case, the power of using reasons to analyze comes from taking these other normative properties or relations to consist in facts about the balance of competing reasons. (And that is why the problems all come in the form of how to say which reasons compete, since whether an analysis is a success or failure rests on adequately characterizing that competition.) But this analytical structure makes one thing very clear: the power of reasons to analyze other normative properties and relations comes from the way that they can *compete* with one another—from the fact that some reasons are *weightier* than others. So it seems that what is really important in each of these explanations is not *what* the reason is, but which side is supported by the *weightiest* reasons. Consequently any serious attempt to come to grips with reasons and their role in normative theory must ultimately grapple with the questions of what makes reasons weighty, and how the weights of reasons combine and compete.

In this chapter we are going to be concerned with these very general questions about the weight of reasons, but our way into them is going to follow a very specific question that we face once we observe that what really matters in the competition between reasons is the relative *weights* of the totality of reasons on each side, and *not* which particular reasons compete: what role do *reasons* actually play, if their weights alone determine what to do? This observation makes salient the possibility that *even if* many or even all other normative properties and relations really are explained by the balance of competing weights of reasons, reasons themselves are *epiphenomenal* in these explanations, in the sense that they don't do any of the explanatory work themselves. Reasons end up being mere vehicles for what's *actually* foundational: the quality of weight. If reasons really are epiphenomenal in this way, then it might turn out that even the apparent power of reason-based explanations is not ultimately due to reasons.

The question of whether reasons are epiphenomenal is not just the question of whether the things that count as the *substance* of reasons—the things that count *as* reasons, such as the fact that we need milk—are epiphenomenal. These considerations might not be epiphenomenal, because it might be only because we do need milk that the totality of reasons in favor of going to the store is so weighty. But the analytic question that we were concerned with in Chapters 9 and 10 was never about whether other normative properties and relations are analyzable in terms of the fact that we need milk. It was about whether they are analyzable in terms of which things stand in the normative *reason* relation. So let us grant that the fact that we need milk explains why the totality of our reasons to go to the store is sufficiently weighty. And let us grant that the fact that we need milk is a reason for us to go to the store. If the explanation of the former doesn't appeal to the latter, then the latter fact is epiphenomenal. If the fact's reasonhood doesn't play an important role in explaining what to do, then it is irrelevant in an important way.

Daniel Fogal [2016] presses a version of this worry acutely, in a form that we will call the *individuation challenge*. If it is true that the fact that we need milk is a reason for us to go to the store, each of the following is also likely to be true:

1. The fact that the store has milk is a reason for us to go there.
2. The fact that we need milk and the store has some is a reason for us to go there.
3. The fact that the store is open and has milk is a reason for us to go there.
4. The fact that we need milk and the store is nearby is a reason for us to go there.
5. The fact that we need milk and can afford it is a reason for us to go to the store.

Each of these sentences ascribes being a reason to go to the store to different facts, and so in at least some sense it is true that there are many reasons to go to the store. But intuitively there are not many reasons to go to the store—so far as we have said, there is at least some intuitive sense in which there is only one reason to go to the store, which we are dancing around in different ways by describing different facts as the reason to go to the store. So Fogal's challenge—the *individuation* challenge—is the challenge of individuating how many reasons there actually are to go to the store, and which ones they are. Fogal himself argues that there is no principled and context-independent way of doing this.

The individuation challenge presses the epiphenomenal challenge. *Given* that we need milk and can afford it and the store is nearby and has milk and is open, so long as there is weighty reason for us to go to the store, it clearly doesn't matter *which* of these facts count as reasons to go there. So even if some or all of them do count as reasons to go to the store, the question of which things stand in the normative reason relation to the option of going to the store seems to be irrelevant to what explains why we ought to go to the store. The reason relation, and what stands in it, appear to be epiphenomenal in this explanation.

This challenge is a problem about how to distinguish reasons. But it is complemented and strengthened by a deep and general problem about how to *combine* reasons. Importantly, the power of reasons explanations requires reasons to sometimes combine. For example, even if we need milk and can afford it and the store is nearby and has it and is open, there can nevertheless be reasons not to go—for example, the weather could be unpleasant. If we need milk enough, the fact that the weather is unpleasant will not be enough to make it the case that we ought not to go. Similarly, today could be the day when the rude shop clerk is on duty, but if we need milk enough, this may not be enough to make it the case that we ought not to go. But even if neither the unpleasant weather nor the rude shopkeeper is enough by itself to make it a bad idea to go get milk today, together they both *could* be enough to make it the case that we ought not to go. So somehow these two reasons need to be able to combine to defeat the reasons to go to the store, even though neither can defeat it separately.

The question of how a combination of reasons can have greater weight together than any of the individual reasons is known as the problem of how reasons *accrue*.[1] And it turns out that the problem of accrual is quite difficult. One of the things that makes it difficult is that weighing reasons is not just a matter of counting how many reasons there are—a small number of reasons can outweigh a large number of reasons, if the smaller number are sufficiently important. But a more important part of the problem is that some reasons *don't* actually accrue. For example, the fact that we need milk and the fact that the store has milk don't combine to provide greater support for going to the store than either provides separately, even if each counts as a reason to go there.

---

[1] Nair [2016].

The kinds of cases in which reasons fail to accrue actually turn out to be intuitively quite diverse. Suppose, for example, that you need to visit your father for the holidays. You could do so either by taking a plane or by taking a train, but have not yet decided which to do. The fact that to afford a plane ticket you need cash is a reason for you to take out some cash, and the fact that to afford a train ticket you need cash is a reason for you to take out some cash. But the second fact doesn't improve the case for taking out cash beyond that fact that you need it for a train ticket. So these reasons don't accrue, either, but it is not intuitively because there is only one point of taking out cash, as in the milk example—there are two different possible points of doing so.

A natural way of thinking about the problem of accrual is that despite their superficial diversity, all of the cases in which reasons fail to accrue are actually reasons that are not fully *independent*, in some sense. On this idea, even if the fact that we need milk and the fact that the store has milk are both reasons to go to the store, they are not *independent* reasons. And similarly, even if the fact that you need cash to afford a plane ticket and the fact that you need cash to afford a train ticket are both reasons to take out cash, they are not independent reasons, because taking a plane and taking a train are both ways, ultimately, to see your dad.

This diagnosis of the non-accrual of reasons gives us a second way of sharpening the problem of the epiphenomenality of reasons—what we might call the *independence* challenge. If reasons only accrue when they are fully independent, then it can seem that it is only fully independent clumps of reasons that do the competing in determining what you ought to do—and not reasons themselves. From this perspective, it can seem epiphenomenal to this explanation which reasons actually belong to each of these independent clumps and which do not.

11.2 Two Strategies for Weight

In the last section we introduced the importance of reasons' weight and identified the epiphenomenality challenge by separating out the individuation and independence challenges. We are now equipped to appreciate what motivates two of the leading approaches to understanding the weight of reasons. Each of these approaches can be thought of as offering an answer to what *makes* reasons "clump" in the kind of non-independent ways that prevent them from accruing. But as we will show, each of these answers to what makes reasons clump actually sharpens our intuitive worry from the last section that the explanatory role of reasons themselves has been displaced.

The first leading approach to understanding the weight of reasons, due to Nair [2021], derives from the observation that there is already a well-studied area of philosophy in which we encounter a structure very much like the problem of accrual: Bayesian confirmation theory. Confirmation theory is the study in probabilistic terms of the evidential support relations that propositions bear to one another, and it turns out that it is a familiar and well-studied fact that while sometimes independent propositions can add to each other's support for some hypothesis H, it can also happen that each of two independent propositions provides evidence of H but their conjunction provides no more support than either does separately.

For example, the proposition that Bella is a black swan evidentially supports the proposition that not all swans are white, as does the proposition that Chloe is a black swan, but the conjunction that Bella *and* Chloe are black swans provides no more support for the proposition that not all swans are white than either does separately. But the proposition that David had a motive and the proposition that the murder weapon was found in David's car not only each provide evidence that David was the culprit, but they do so in a cumulative way. The fact that evidential confirmation has this structure where it is already well-studied motivates the idea that we can take the weight of reasons to be measured by a kind of confirmation measure.

Fortunately, we have already encountered the idea in Chapter 6 that what it is to be a reason is to be evidence that you ought to do something. And indeed, one of Kearns and Star's original arguments for this view is that since reasons have weights and evidence comes in degrees of confirmation, the equivalence of reasons with evidence allows for the corresponding equivalence of the weight of reasons to do something with the degree of confirmation of the proposition that you ought to do it.

Although many different measures of confirmation have been proposed in confirmation theory, it turns out that one of them—what is known as the *log likelihood* measure—has many important properties, including a variety of nice formal properties about where the zero point is of degrees of weight, and it allows us to represent accrual formally as addition, which feels simple and intuitive.[2] It also imposes structure and limits on how reasons accrue—though not exactly the limits that we were expecting, above. Because degree

---

[2] See Nair [2021].

of confirmation is sensitive to background probabilities, it is going to turn out that which reasons accrue and how they accrue is going to depend on those background probabilities. For example, if our background probability that the store is open, nearby, and has milk is near 1, then the fact that we need milk will not accrue with each of these other reasons to go to the store, but if we have a lot of background uncertainty about how close to a store we are (perhaps we are on a road trip), and whether the store is open and carries milk, then each of these propositions will separately raise the probability that we ought to go to the store.

However, though the confirmation theory approach offers an elegant way of thinking about the problem of the accrual of reasons, it does not appear to vindicate the role of reasons in explanations of what we ought to do. On the contrary, it appears to actually sharpen our worry that reasons will turn out to be epiphenomenal. One of the crucial lessons we learned in Chapter 6 is that a fact can be evidence of something without explaining it. If reasons are nothing more than evidence of what you ought to do, then what you ought to do must be itself explained by something other than reasons—namely, the thing of which reasons are ultimately evidence.

An alternative account of the accrual of reasons (compare Nair [2016]) takes a very different approach. On this approach, we take seriously the idea that reasons do not accrue when they are not independent, and try to first clump reasons together into non-independent clusters, before accruing those clusters. For example, a natural way of developing this view appeals to the idea that each reason serves some objective—either a desire or value that the reason explains, as on the telic views considered in Chapter 10, or an objective that is part of the reason itself, as on the dual-aspect theory first encountered in Chapter 2, or an extra argument of the *reason* relation as on Finlay's end-relational theory first encountered in Chapter 4. We take reasons to be independent when they serve different objectives.

Take, for example, the various reasons to go to the store, because we need milk and the store has some and is nearby and open. The point of all of these reasons, intuitively, is for us to have milk on hand. Because they all, ultimately, serve this one point, they do not accrue. In contrast, the fact that the weather is unpleasant and the fact that the rude store clerk is working today, though both reasons against going to the store (today), serve distinct objectives. One serves the objective of not suffering the rain while the other serves the objective of not suffering the rudeness. Since it is natural to think both that having milk on hand is something that we want and that it is something good, it is easy to see that this approach is ecumenical among different ways of theorizing about where the objectives associated with reasons come from.

Similar points go for our example of visiting your dad. The facts that you need to take out cash to buy each of a plane and a train ticket do not accrue, because each serves the objective of visiting your dad. In a different situation, of course, in which you separately need both a plane ticket and a train ticket for different travel occasions, they *would* accrue. And this view explains precisely why—it is because in that case these two facts would be reasons serving different objectives. So again, the objective-based picture of accrual helps to explain which reasons should accrue and which should not.

However, like the confirmation theory account of reasons' accrual, the objectives-based account does not exactly seem to vindicate the central explanatory role of reasons. On the contrary, in the end it is objectives that are being compared. We must compare the objective of having milk on hand to the objectives of avoiding the rain and of avoiding the rudeness, and we must compare the objective of visiting your dad to the objective of skipping the inconvenience of stopping by a cash machine. Whether objectives sideline reasons, of course, depends on questions of substance. If all reasons for action include objectives as parts, as the dual-aspect account holds, then appealing to objectives when explaining accrual does not risk making the reasons epiphenomenal. But this does nothing to silence the complaint that the facts that give reasons may be less important than many have assumed.

So again, looking just a little bit harder at the details of how reasons weigh together—how they accrue—seems only to sharpen the worry that ultimately reasons are epiphenomenal in the explanations of what you ought to do. Ralph Wedgwood expresses this thought particularly sharply:

> What we fundamentally need to aggregate are the different reason-providing values – not the facts that we call the "reasons", which explain how the relevant alternatives compare in terms of these reason-providing values. Statements that presuppose different backgrounds create a mere illusion of different reasons. In this case, these statements are really just different ways of talking about the same practically significant fact – the fact about how the options of going to the party and not going to the party compare with respect to the reason-providing value of Ronnie's pleasure.
>
> (Wedgwood [2022, 136])

It is worth observing in passing that questions about accrual are just one small piece of a very large and difficult space of questions about how reasons combine. We know from earlier chapters not only that reasons compete against one another but that reasons can be undercut and even plausibly have their valence switched.³ According to some philosophers, reasons can be "silenced" or "excluded", and according to others they can be modified by being attenuated or augmented in strength by additional considerations.⁴ There are also difficult questions that arise in the relationship between means and ends or between wholes and parts, when achieving an end requires different actions over time, when actions require the cooperation of others, and many, many others.⁵ This is a very rich area of philosophical research, where progress has the potential to either vindicate the role of reasons or further marginalize them as epiphenomenal.⁶

11.3 Masses of Reason

One view that we have encountered in earlier chapters has the potential to partially vindicate the idea that reason is central after all in ethical theory, even if reasons are epiphenomenal. It is the idea due to Fogal [2016] that it is *reason* in its mass noun form that is central, even if reason*s* (count noun) are more epiphenomenal than many philosophers have believed them to be. Fogal's idea is that we should focus more on the question of what there is reason to do and less on that of what there are reasons to do. In the last section, we saw that objectives could be a way of clumping reasons together, but perhaps reasons just come clumped naturally—in masses of reason that we can individuate, perhaps somewhat arbitrarily, as Fogal would argue, in different ways. This doesn't vindicate the centrality of *reasons'* explanatory role in ethics, but it does vindicate the centrality of *reason's* explanatory role in ethics—and that, you might think, is the closest that we are going to come. So it is well worth giving this important idea more time than we have given it so far.

---

[3] See especially Dancy [2004, chapters one and two].
[4] Compare McDowell [1998], Raz [1975], and Dancy [2004].
[5] On means and ends: Kolodny [2018]; on actions over time: Jackson and Pargetter [1986]; on the cooperation of others: Dietz [2016] and Nefsky [2017].
[6] For just one example, the dual-aspect view claims some of the explanatory appeal of Fogal's cluster view, discussed before and below, with respect to independence and individuation without risking epiphenomenal reasons. However, Cunningham [forthcoming] argues that the cluster view claims some of the dual-aspect account's explanatory advantages with respect to ambidextrous reasons, discussed in Chapter 9, without risking non-factive reasons. This symmetry suggests a deeper conflict between the commitment that reasons are non-epiphenomenal and the commitment that they are facts, discussed in Chapter 2.

Could Fogal be right? Should this book have been titled *The Fundamental of Reason* instead? There is lots of evidence to support Fogal's view. For one, 'reason' does admit of both mass and count noun uses in English, and typically when a word has both mass and count noun uses, the count noun seems to pick out some amount of the mass noun use. For example, 'a water' and 'a beer' pick out quantities of water and beer, respectively. We saw in Chapter 7 that it provides a candidate for what reasons in the count noun sense are—namely, that they are what explain why there is reason to do something. And it offers a deep and general picture of what we mean when we say that a reason is weighty—it is that we mean that there is a lot of reason to do that thing.

Another nice thing to like about this picture is that it fits particularly well into the standard model account of reasons that we first encountered in Chapter 3. Recall that on the standard model, we take it that what individuals have reasons to do in their particular circumstances can always be traced back to things that everyone has reason to do in any possible circumstance. The standard model explains why a particular person has a reason to do something with the more general claim that it's a way of doing what everyone has a reason to do. Consequently, the standard model explains a particular fact about reasons by *subsuming* it under a more general one. By taking these subsumptive explanations to their ultimate end, we reach things that necessarily everyone always has reason to do, no matter what—and thus the standard model is a kind of generalism par excellence.

Jonathan Dancy has argued that the general truths about reasons on which the standard model relies are elusive. It is very difficult to come up with anything that there is necessarily reason for anyone to do no matter what. But proponents of the standard model face an even sharper problem. They are committed not only to the claim that there is a list of things that there is necessarily reason to do that is long enough or general enough that everything anyone has reason to do can be derived from a way of doing something on that list, but also to the claim that *something* is the reason to do those things. But this is very hard to make out. Take, for example, the reason not to cause pain. Maybe there is a reason for anyone not to cause pain at any time, but what *is* the reason not to cause pain? It turns out to be surprisingly hard to say what this is! But the mass noun view fits in very neatly with the standard model. If the things that there is necessarily reason to do no matter what are just things that there is *reason* (mass noun) to do, the standard model could get away without having to postulate what the particular reasons are to do these things—what there is reason to do doesn't depend on the existence of any particular reasons.

So we like all of these things about Fogal's mass noun primacy view. Nevertheless, it leaves many open questions that deserve more careful investigation. To begin with, the evidential relationship between Fogal's linguistic observations and the conclusion that mass noun reason is more fundamental than count noun reasons is somewhat more vexed than we have made it out to be so far. Take, for example, the case of 'hair', which, like 'water' and 'beer', has both mass and count uses. One's head of hair, in the mass sense, is composed of the countable hairs on one's head; what's fundamental are the hairs. So it's not a general truth that count nouns are to be understood in terms of their counterpart mass nouns. So we need substantive philosophical argument to establish that 'reason' is like 'water' and not like 'hair'.

The mass noun view also raises deep and puzzling questions about where it leaves the central explanatory and deliberative roles of reasons that we have been exploring throughout this book. It's hard to think about questions of substance with respect to masses of reason. While we have competing answers to the question of what substance composes reasons, canvassed in Chapter 2, it is much less clear what kind of substance composes a mass of reason. Indeed, because they chop off the count noun, mass noun uses of 'reason' seemingly have no *substance* in our sense from Chapter 2—nothing that does the counting in favor. Instead of looking like:

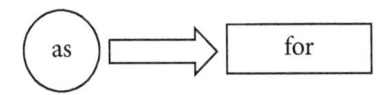

$$\left(\text{as}\right) \Longrightarrow \boxed{\text{for}}$$

They instead look simply like:

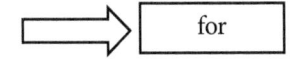

$$\Longrightarrow \boxed{\text{for}}$$

But it turns out that the substance of reasons was very important both for their explanatory and for their deliberative roles!

Let's take the explanatory role, first. Because reasons provide a link between what does the supporting and what is supported, one way of thinking about reasons is as providing the explanatory glue that explains why certain normative facts are true at some world ultimately in virtue of *non*-normative facts about that world—the facts that count as the ultimate reasons for and against different outcomes at that world. The same thing goes for subjective reasons as for objective reasons; in Chapter 5 we introduced the idea that both objective reasons and subjective reasons are reflections of what we called *core* reasons, which consist in an abstract support relationship between propositions and whatever reasons support that is independent of whether those propositions are either believed or true. On this view, objective reasons are just true core reasons, and subjective reasons are just core reasons that satisfy the appropriate mind-to-world and world-to-mind perspective conditions.

It's the law that if you're in North America, you drive on the right. The core reason expressed by 'you're in North America', objectively supports driving on the right when true and subjectively supports it when believed. So core reasons are, in a way, an expression of the *laws* (*pro tanto* laws, of course) that dictate how the way that the world is normatively supervenes on the way that the world is non-normatively. On this picture, reasons have the right structure to explain the relationship between the normative and the non-normative because reasons (both objective and subjective) *consist* partly in the laws that make the way the normative features of the world consequent upon its non-normative features. From this perspective, dropping the substance out of reasons is like replacing laws that *connect* the non-normative to the normative simply with wholly normative claims.

Obscuring this relationship obscures some natural answers to pressing questions about differences between normative kinds. What you prudentially ought to do differs from what you morally ought to do, which differs from what you rationally ought to do and so on. What's the difference between them? An appealing answer lies in the nature of the considerations that give moral or prudential reasons: an *ought* is moral when it is (suppose) explained by considerations involving others' pain and our promises. Likewise, an *ought* is prudential when it is (suppose) explained by considerations involving our pleasure or what's good for us. According to this account, an *ought* expresses one kind of prescription rather than another when it depends on one class of reasons rather than another. Of course, we need to explain how classes of reasons differ to account for the moral class, the prudential class, the rational class, and so on. But classes are uniquely identified by the elements that constitute them. So it's natural to think that a class of reasons is moral rather than prudential precisely *because* it encompasses considerations involving others' pain and our promises rather than considerations involving our pleasure or what's good for us.

Yet this appealing account of the difference between morality and prudence is lost if we make what we ought to do consequent on what there is most reason for us to do but deny that what there is most reason to do depends on the reasons for us to do it. The denial severs the connection between the *ought* facts and the countable reasons that accounts for differences in what ought to be done, morally or prudentially speaking. It is also unclear what alternative explanation can be offered in its place. And whatever it is, that explanation constrains our account of the substance of mass reason: that substance must be the kind of thing that explains how moral prescriptions differ from prudential ones.

Removing the substance from reasons also obscures their deliberative role. It makes great sense to be thinking about things like whether we are out of milk and whether the weather is unpleasant in the process of trying to decide whether to go to the store today. But when it comes to mass noun reason, there aren't individuals doing the supporting, only a *mass* doing the supporting. And it is very obscure what this mass is, or what it would be to think about it![7] It is not enough just to think about what the mass supports—good thinking requires thinking about what counts on each side.

Recall that we originally glossed the deliberative role of reasons by saying that reasons are what you are thinking about when you are reasoning well. But even if reasons in the count noun sense have this role, it is hard to see how they could get it from anything special about the nature of reason in the mass noun sense, unless it was true that reasoning well requires thinking about what you have most reason to do *as such*. But it is highly controversial in moral philosophy whether good reasoning should ever involve thinking about what you have most reason to do as such. Michael Smith and Nomy Arpaly have argued that thinking very much like this constitutes an important and objectionable kind of moral fetish.[8]

An additional puzzle about mass noun reason is also perplexing. In the case of count noun reasons, we found cause to distinguish between objective and subjective reasons, with objective reasons counting in favor of what is correct and subjective reasons counting in favor of what is rational. Fogal seems to think of mass noun reason as objective, but it is not obvious why this should be so. If objective count noun reasons are explanations of what there is reason to do, then we need to figure out whether subjective count noun reasons are derivative from objective count noun reasons, a possibility

---

[7] For example, as Laskowski [forthcoming] notes, it's unclear where mass-noun reason figures in the distinction between natural and non-natural entities.

[8] Smith [1994, chapter three], Arpaly [2002].

that we raised some problems for in Chapter 5, or whether they are explanations of what there is *subjective* mass noun reason to do instead. An additional consideration favoring the latter view is that subjective reasons, like objective reasons, must also have *weight*. So if the weight of objective reasons is how much objective reason there is to do that thing, then only a parallel account of subjective reasons that derives them from subjective mass noun reason can offer a parallel account of weight.

But once we postulate both objective and subjective mass noun reason, we need an answer to the question of how they are related to one another. It would be premature to speculate about how this dialectic will turn out, but an adequate answer needs to avoid conditional fallacy problems that might arise from subjunctively analyzing either in terms of the other. Yet the solution that we have favored for count noun reasons—that they have a common core, *core* reasons—seems to work only because we can distinguish objective, subjective, and core reasons in terms of properties of what counts as their substance. Obviously many more details of this kind of view remain to be worked out.

11.4 The Mosaic of Reasons

At this point in the book, it's natural to expect a proposal for calculating a reason's weight and how it accrues with the weights of other reasons, subject to defeaters and modifiers. Others have proposed such algorithms.[9] We won't, partly because it is self-defeating to raise concerns about the epiphenomenality of reasons, then turn around and seemingly make reasons epiphenomenal ourselves as we focus on their weights. We'll instead show how to discuss weight without eclipsing reasons.

Weights seem to eclipse reasons because reasons only contingently indicate what to do. The fact that an action is hurtful sometimes co-occurs with the fact that you shouldn't do it, but sometimes it doesn't. These two facts thus trace a complex normative pattern across modal space, leaving us with the question of why those two facts co-occur at some worlds and not others—the questions of why *that* pattern holds rather than another. If we can't explain this pattern, then it seems that we've left something important unexplained. So it seems that we must posit a third entity to do the

---

[9] See, for example, Horty [2012] and Bader [2016].

explaining. This third entity risks displacing reasons by usurping their explanatory role. After all, if the balance of reasons determines what to do, that balance is determined by the *weight* of competing reasons, not their number or identity. So questions about *which* reasons figure in the analysis ultimately seem irrelevant to what to do. And if weights directly determine what to do, what use are reasons?[10]

Whether we need weights to explain normative patterns is part of a more general debate. Modal patterns *in general* have long interested philosophers. Patterns of cause and effect attract particular interest. Just as reasons tend to indicate what to do but generally don't necessitate it, certain events, regarded as *causes*, tend to indicate that certain effects will follow, but do not generally necessitate those effects. Consequently, structurally similar questions often apply across the two domains and a domain-specific answer to one of these questions often has a counterpart answer in the other domain.

One influential account of causal patterns mirrors the account of normative patterns that centers weight. According to this account, *causal powers* explain patterns of cause and effect.[11] For example, a sphere rolls when influenced by gravity or by another inertial force, absent interference. What explains this behavior is that the ball is disposed to or has the *causal power* to roll under these circumstances. Naturally, this explanation raises its own questions: if causal powers explain causal patterns, what explains the causal powers themselves? As some put it, what *grounds* the sphere's power to roll when properly influenced? According to this account, causal powers are themselves explained by non-dispositional or categorical properties. For example, the sphere's power to roll is explained by or grounded in its spherical shape.

Hume was famously skeptical about causal powers. He found no sensory evidence of causal powers. Rather, he simply observed patterns where events of one type were regularly followed by (sometimes "constantly conjoined" with) events of a second type. But he never directly observed a causal power that glues an effect to its cause. All we observe is, for example, a correlation between the sphere's shape and the fact that it rolls when properly

---

[10] A version of this line of argument appears in Fogal and Risberg [2023b], which proposes to analyze reasons as sources of normative support, a precisification of the idea of normative weight. See also Fogal and Risberg [2023a]. Scanlon's [2014] focus on the reason relation, rather than on reasons, can also be read in this vein. Chris Tucker, as we saw in Chapter 10, draws distinctions in kinds of weight rather than in kinds of reasons.

[11] See Cartwright [1989] for an influential articulation of this view; see Mumford and Anjum [2010] for a nice discussion of powers that structurally mirrors the role that weights play according to some.

influenced—more generally, all we observe is a correlation between certain effects and the categorical properties thought by some to ground a causal power.

David Lewis coined an evocative phrase for the metaphysics underlying this approach to modal patterns: the *Humean Mosaic*. The term evokes the idea that a modal pattern, such as a causal pattern, is constituted by nothing more than a distribution of discrete elements across worlds. Consider an analogy. We find all kinds of patterns in the stars: crabs and fish and bears great and small; we can find mythical creatures and kitchen tools. These shapes cluster individual stars in groups. But the presence of that shape isn't explained by some law governing the distribution of stars or a "power" of stars to trace the shape of fish or crabs or spoons. The distribution of stars is random, at least from the point of view of familiar shapes.

Similarly, just as constellations are shapes projected on outer space, Humean causation is a kind of constellation projected on the space of possible events. At bottom, there is nothing more to causation than this mosaic of events just as, at bottom, there is nothing more to Pisces than a mosaic of stars. Rather, the lawless scattering of antecedent and subsequent events across modal space *constitutes* the mosaic of causation. We can identify theoretically interesting clusters of events in the causal mosaic by using generalities or "laws", but the laws do not govern the distribution of events across the mosaic any more than Pisces governs the locations of its constituent stars.

Talk of "laws of nature" or "causal powers" is, for the Humean, merely a kind of shorthand or heuristic for thinking about the mosaic. We know that an object's being spherical correlates in a particular way with its rolling in certain circumstances. The Humean might say that the shape causes the rolling, but they mean only that the shape is correlated with rolling. They might ask what more we gain, by way of explanation, with the further claim that the object's being spherical *grounds* a further property, the causal power of rolling, which explains why the object rolls in certain circumstances. Little, it seems.

Claims about normative weight and about causal power are clearly similar. Each aims to explain some modal pattern; indeed, they each aim to explain how one fact (about an effect or what to do) can be "conjoined" with a prior fact (such as that the match was struck or that the action hurts someone). Moreover, both weight and causal power come in degrees; both conflict with countervailing forces. And neither weight nor power is brute; each is explained by some feature of the attendant reason or cause.

Given this resemblance, a Humean skepticism about causal powers outlines a similar skepticism about normative weight. According to such an approach, there is, for lack of a better term, a *normative mosaic* composed of answers to the question of what to do (or think or feel) and facts like that an action is hurtful to someone or helpful to others or respectful to all or beautiful. In many worlds, when an action is hurtful, we shouldn't do it. However, in some rare worlds, we should do what's hurtful. These worlds contain complicating factors like that the act is more helpful than hurtful or that it expresses an important kind of respect. We can describe how an action's being hurtful patterns with what to do across these worlds by saying that it provides a weighty but not conclusive reason against performing the action. But the invocation of 'weight' here (and similar terms such as 'balance of reasons' and 'competition between reasons' and so on) is derivative of the mosaic in the same way that a Humean's talk of cause is.

Chapter Summary

In this chapter we have considered a sampling of some of the interesting questions that come up when we start to pay attention to the significant role of reasons' *weights*, continuing our discussions in sections 4.2 and 9.2. Rather than focusing on what it means for reasons to have weight, we have focused on whether the weight of reasons obviates the need to appeal to facts about what is or is not a reason at all in the kinds of balancing explanations that were supposed to be characteristic of the explanatory role of reasons. And we brought out this challenge by exploring what things look like through the lens of a focus on the weight of mass noun *reason*, as opposed to the weight of *reasons*. We closed by sketching the form of one possible answer to this challenge.

Recommended Reading

We recommend reading this chapter alongside the primary source for the centrality of mass noun reason, Fogal's "Reasons, Reason, and Context". The other papers collected in Lord and Maguire's *Weighing Reasons*, including Nair's "How Do Reasons Accrue?", provide a rich and still accurate sense of many of the issues about the weight of reasons. Wedgwood's "The Reasons Aggregation Theorem" offers a forceful version of the epiphenomenality challenge for reasons in favor of his preferred value-based view, Horty's *Reasons as Defaults* develops the most powerful general view about how reasons compete, and Nair's "'Adding Up' Reasons: Lessons for

Reductive and Nonreductive Approaches" is the most sophisticated contemporary treatment of the accrual of reasons.

Exercises

11.1 *Comprehension.* Construct your own example to illustrate the individuation and independence challenges. In what ways does your example resemble the examples from the text? In what ways is it different?

11.2 *Extensions.* In the chapter, we noted that telic accounts of reasons can address the independence challenge by clumping reasons together in terms of which objective they serve. For this exercise, assume some telic account of reasons to be true, and try to give your own account of what it means for one reason to be weightier than another.

11.3 *Extensions.* Suppose that you need to buy both a plane ticket *and* a train ticket in order to visit your dad. What does the telic answer to the independence challenge from this chapter say about whether your two reasons to take out cash (namely, to buy a plane ticket and to buy a train ticket) accrue? Is this the correct answer? Why or why not?

11.4 *Extensions.* According to Hurka [2014], H.A. Prichard tried to persuade Ross to identify duty proper with the strongest *prima facie* duty. Show how to use the problem of accrual as an objection to Prichard's suggestion. How do you recommend that Prichard fixes this problem?

11.5 *Extensions.* In Chapter 9 we encountered ambidextrous reasons, considerations that seem to be a reason that has two different flavors. For this exercise, try to use an example of an ambidextrous reason in order to push the epiphenomenality challenge even further, by comparing how the ambidextrous reason weighs in the answer to each of two different normative questions.

11.6 *Extensions.* At several places in this book we have worried about views that struggle with making sense of reasons that are defeated. For this exercise, try to assess whether or not a version of this problem can be raised for the 'Humean Mosaic' view of the weights of reasons introduced in section 11.4, given that this view identifies the weights of reasons with a *pattern* across possible worlds of being associated with what you ought to do. Why or why not?

12
The Fundamentality of Reasons

12.1 The Priority of Reasons

In this book we have set out to introduce some of the fundamentals of reasons in at least a relatively nondogmatic way. We have tried to show how different philosophers can make very different assumptions about what reasons are and how they work, and that these different assumptions sometimes hang together in tidy packages that can make it difficult, if you are in the grips of one package, to appreciate how things look different to someone who is attracted to another. Yet at the same time we have not been shy about indicating where some of the chief difficulties seem so far to lie with respect to defending each of these packages of views, especially where we think that some of these difficulties have so far been underappreciated. And throughout we have called attention to some views whose strengths and resources we think have yet to be adequately appreciated. We hope you have found something to learn from or think harder about in our coverage of these ideas, no matter your level of background in this topic.

We began, in Part 1, *Parts*, by investigating different possible views that we might take as philosophers about the semantics and ontology of reason ascriptions. There we saw that different philosophers have taken different views about the *substance* of reasons, different views about what reasons count in favor of, and different views about what the other relata are of the reason relation. They have also taken different views, or can be interpreted as taking different views, about the relative priority of different closely associated relations, each of which we might successfully ascribe by using the word 'reason' in English.

Then, in Part 2, *Province*, we moved our attention outward to focus on the connection between reasons and some of the things with which reasons are most closely associated: evidence, explanation, and deliberation, and also the intimate relationship, whatever it might be, between objective and subjective reasons. There again we saw that many views are possible, and that many of these relationships have been exploited, because of their intimacy, to provide possible *analyses* of what it is to be a reason—that it is, for example, to be evidence for a certain kind of thing, to be the explanation or part of the explanation of some other kind of thing, to be connected to some particular kind of deliberation in the appropriate kind of way, or to be related to some other kind of reason in the right kind of way. And these answers, as we saw, are not independent of the many questions introduced in Part 1; on the contrary, they lend themselves to greater or lesser degrees to different combinations of these views.

And finally, in Part 3, *Place*, we have turned to consider some of the more traditional questions about reasons that have occupied the more explicit attention of philosophers for longer—questions like whether reasons are prior to and explanatory of value, or conversely. It is worth closing in this chapter by considering whether the place of reasons earns them the prominence that we noted in the opening paragraph of this book:

> Answering these other questions has seemed, to many philosophers at least, to require first answering or at least defending answers to related questions about reasons. Hiding behind these other issues has therefore given reasons a kind of derivative prominence in contemporary philosophy. It is the kind of prominence peculiar to philosophers—that is, among thinkers who are particularly interested in getting to the bottom of things and in seeing the spaces in between.[1]

Reasons are prominent in philosophy, we suggested at the opening of this book, not because reasons are the first things that we become interested in when we theorize as philosophers about different topics, but because reasons are "hiding behind" these other issues. On our gloss, philosophers have come to be interested in reasons because they are interested in "getting to the bottom" of things.

Now, there are a variety of ways in which it could turn out that reasons are "behind" many other issues in philosophy. It could turn out, for example, that because there are plausible bridge premises linking claims about reasons with claims about many other things, it is fruitful to think about reasons in order to think about these many other things, regardless of whether reasons are "behind" or "at the bottom" of them, in any stronger sense. But there is a prominent view in moral philosophy

---

[1] *Fundamentals of Reasons*, Chapter 1.

according to which reasons are at the bottom of these other issues because reasons are *more fundamental* than many of the other things that we want to theorize about in normative philosophy. On this view, the other things that reasons lurk "behind" or "under" are things that are properly analyzed in terms of reasons, or systematically grounded in facts about reasons. This is the view that the prominence of reasons is due to their (analytic or grounding) *priority*.

According to a sweeping generalization of this idea about the priority of reasons, the reason relation is the *most* fundamental normative property or relation, and every other normative property or relation is analyzed in terms of reasons or systematically grounded in facts about reasons. This thesis is sometimes called the thesis of *Reasons First*, or referred to as the *fundamentality of reasons*. So understood, the thesis of Reasons First is a claim of the *relative* priority of reasons. It does not claim that reasons cannot themselves be further analyzed—it just entails that if they can be, then the analysis of reasons must itself be non-normative, on pain of circularity. This makes it the *global* version of the thesis that reasons have relative priority, and much stronger than we need, in order to endorse the thought from the previous paragraph that we often find reasons lurking "behind" topics in philosophy because reasons have *local* relative priority—they are part of the analysis of the thing that we are interested in in that area of philosophy. Those who say that reasons are fundamental sometimes go even further than this, and claim that the fundamentality of reasons is *absolute*. Whereas the thesis of Reasons First is a claim about what reasons help to analyze—namely, everything normative—the thesis that reasons are absolutely fundamental is a claim about what can help to analyze reasons—namely, nothing.

Whether or not reasons are absolutely fundamental, the idea that they are globally prior in normative theory has many attractive features for theorists with ambitious explanatory aims. If reasons *do* come first, then that offers us an answer to what is *special* or *distinctive* about normativity—it is a domain whose subject matter is *reasons*. If reasons do come first, then all it takes to determine whether normativity itself is reducible in non-normative terms is to determine whether *reasons* are reducible in non-normative terms. And if reasons do come first, then all it takes to determine whether an expressivist treatment of normative discourse is correct is to determine whether an expressivist treatment of *reasons* is correct. Of course, similar consequences would follow even if Reasons First were false, so long as some other normative property or relation turned out to be first in the same way. But the hypothesis that reasons play this central role in normative theory has been particularly prominent over the last twenty-five or more years of normative theory, and this book is about reasons. So it is the priority thesis about reasons that interests us here.

If the thesis of Reasons First were true, then that would also be a resounding validation of the idea that reasons are often lurking "behind" or "at the bottom" of many other issues in philosophy, particularly where normative questions are at stake. But we do not know how to evaluate in any straightforward way whether this ambitious hypothesis is true. Indeed, we do not know of anyone else who knows how to argue for it directly, either. The ambitious global generalization of Reasons First is better understood, we suggest, as a kind of generalization from a much more compelling thesis that we *do* know how to argue for: namely, that reasons have local *relative* priority, relative to *many* of the normative concepts that concern us in ordinary life. And even this more restricted claim would amount to a very strong validation of the idea with which we started—that we are *right* to find reasons lurking "behind" so many other topics—wherever we are concerned with something that needs to be explained or analyzed in terms of reasons.

12.2 The Classical Argument

In Chapter 1 we encountered the main reason why many other things have been thought to be analyzable in terms of reasons. It is that explanations in terms of reasons can explain the variable and complex texture of *when* something is, for example, what someone ought to do, wrong to do, admirable, fearsome, courageous, or appropriate. Explaining what you ought to do in terms of reasons can explain why normally when you promise to meet someone for tennis you ought to meet them for tennis but also why circumstances can arise in which you ought not, and it offers testable predictions about which kinds of circumstances these will be. In general, they will be circumstances in which there are reasons to do things that compete with meeting them for tennis, and where the reasons to do these other things are individually or collectively more important than the reason provided by your promise to meet them. This, in turn, can explain why it takes a bigger emergency to justify not showing up for your wedding than to justify not showing up for tennis. And similar points can be raised about what it is wrong for you to do, what or who is admirable, what conduct or response is appropriate in some situation, and many more. This is the *Classical Argument* for the relative priority of reasons.

The Classical Argument tries to establish that reasons are prior to (for example) *ought* by arguing that the best explanation of what we ought to do will always appeal, ultimately, to the balance of competing reasons. To settle whether the Classical Argument works, we must do three things. First, we must establish that explanations of what you ought to do are at least *sometimes* the best explanations—better than the explanations that we would get by appeal to, for example, Kant's categorical imperative, or Benthamite utilitarianism. Second, we must establish that *all* facts about what you ought to do are explained in terms of the balance of reasons. And third, we must establish that it is *because they are reasons* that reasons explain what you ought to do, rather than that they count as reasons because they help to explain. None of these steps are trivial, and so whatever its attractions (and we are both attracted to it), the Classical Argument for the relative priority of reasons is far from trivial.

P1   The best explanation of what we ought to do requires the assumption that *ought* is grounded in *reasons*.

P2   If the best explanation of what we ought to do requires the assumption that *ought* is grounded in *reasons*, then *ought* is grounded in *reasons*.

C   *Ought* is grounded in *reasons*.

Taking the first case first, although Ross has given us a template for arguing that what we ought to do is often explained by the balance of reasons, and his template provides arguably compelling (to us, at any rate) diagnoses of why it seems like we can construct counterexamples to Kant's ethical theory by imagining cases in which lying will have very bad consequences, and why we can construct counterexamples to Bentham's ethical theory by imagining cases in which small improvements in overall happiness come at the cost of violating someone's rights. We get both such classes of counterexamples, Ross argued, because each of these views describes at best *one* class of moral reason, and what you morally ought to do is determined by the balance of *all* of the moral reasons.

But even though Ross can argue in this way, things are more complicated. Not only do Kant and Bentham have well-worn strategies to combat these classes of putative counterexamples, but there are other, non-reasons-based, views that can give similar but distinct diagnoses of the counterexamples to Kant and to Bentham. According to pluralistic consequentialist views, just to take a particularly prominent and important example, the susceptibility of Benthamite utilitarianism to counterexamples arises not because there are competing reasons that it ignores, but because it depends on an incomplete conception of the *good*. Several books could be (and have been) written about which of these explanations is better—the *reasons* explanation or the *goodness* explanation—and more could be written about yet other alternative explanatory strategies.

It is also worth noting that we have encountered, in Chapters 7 and 9, the ingredients for a powerful debunking story about why it might *seem* that what you ought to do is explained by reasons even though pluralistic consequentialism is true. The debunking story is given by *value-based* accounts of reasons, according to the most natural formulation of which reasons are explanations of why your doing something promotes or respects something *good*. If a value-based account of reasons is true, and all reasons concern the promotion of value, then reasons will be explanatorily linked to what you ought to do even though consequentialism is true and what you ought to do is most directly explained in terms of value. But if what you ought to do is explained by pluralist consequentialism and each of the plural values is associated with corresponding reasons, then that could explain why it might seem so easy to give reasons-based explanations of what you ought to do even though consequentialism is true.

But even once we agree that what you ought to do is *sometimes* explained by the balance of reasons, that leaves open whether it is *always* so explained. And if what you ought to do is not *always* explained by reasons, then it does not look very likely that reasons could be part of the analysis of *ought*—for surely whatever is in the analysis of *ought* must *always* be present in order for *ought*-facts to obtain. But this is again non-trivial. Although there are many parts of life where the question of what you ought to do appears to allow for tradeoffs, it has been argued by some that there are at least some absolute *side-constraints* on what you ought to do—things that you always ought not to do, no matter what, such as torturing babies.

Outside of moral philosophy, the idea that there are some things that you ought to do no matter what, or some attitudes that are inappropriate no matter what, is even more prevalent. Many people think that you always ought to believe the truth, for example, and that nothing can make it the case that you ought to believe something false. And many people believe that it is always irrational to believe contradictions, or that it is always inappropriate to have contradictory intentions. Cases like these are not an *obvious* home for reasons explanations, because we don't need to appeal to the balancing of reasons in order to explain them. So nothing about these cases, by themselves, requires us to explain them in terms of reasons.

But all of these cases *could* be determined by the balance of reasons, even though they don't have to be—so long as it turns out that there is always some guarantee that the reasons work out in the right sort of way. For example, if the reason not to torture babies is simply so weighty that nothing else could outweigh it, then the fact that you necessarily ought not to torture babies could be explained perfectly well. But whether we should think this is the right explanation or not is surely going to turn on how powerful we think the reasons explanations of other things that we ought to do are, and how important we think it is that our explanations of what we ought to do are unified (and similarly for explanations of what is rational, correct, obligatory, laudatory, and the like).

But again suppose that we agree that everything that you ought to do is explained by reasons. Still, we must rule out another possibility, first discussed all of the way back in Chapter 1 and returning in Chapter 7. John Broome, as we saw, thinks that what we ought to do is always explained by reasons, but does not think that this tells us that reasons are analytically prior to *ought*. On the contrary, Broome's view is that reasons explain what you ought to do because it is in the nature of *reasons* that they are the things that explain what you ought to do, rather than because it is in the nature of *ought* that it is explained by reasons. We found some reason to cast doubt on Broome's view in Chapter 7, and there we explored the idea that the reason why intuitive counterexamples to the thesis of Reasons as Evidence work is that it is in the nature of *ought* to be explained by reasons, rather than because it is in the nature of reasons to be explainers of something. This move, or one like it, is needed to complete the abductive argument that the best explanation of what we ought to do appeals to an analysis of *ought* in terms of reasons that forms the backbone of the Classical Argument for the relative priority of reasons. We are both sympathetic to the view that this argument can in fact be completed, but this is very far from being obvious or settled ground.

Finally, even if the Classical Argument convinces us that *reason* is more fundamental than *ought*, its work is still cut out for it to convince us that *reason* is more fundamental than *must, good, wrong, fitting*, and many other normative properties. Some philosophers who are attracted to the Classical Argument believe that similar reasoning can be extended to many of these other relative priority questions, while others are happy to accept the conclusion of the Classical Argument for the relative priority of *reason* over *ought*, while rejecting its extension to many of these other cases.

12.3 The Fundamental Argument

The Classical Argument, as we've just seen, is attractively simple, and yet it takes a great deal of work to chase down the details. Its simplicity lies in the ease with which we can construct counterexamples to sweeping general theories of what we ought to do, what is rational, appropriate, or called for, or the like, and is grounded in a simple diagnosis of the working strategy for constructing such counterexamples: find a case in which the reasons codified by this sweeping general theory come into conflict with reasons of a different sort. And the work in chasing down the details is required because there are so many alternative hypotheses that can also be at least intelligibly argued to be consistent with this phenomenon.

But in a key respect the Classical Argument for the relative priority of reasons is hamstrung by the fact that it relies only on the explanatory role of reasons. As we have discussed throughout this book, reasons have complementary explanatory and deliberative roles. And so there is leverage that the Classical Argument leaves on the table. An alternative, complementary motivation for thinking that reasons are analytically prior to many other normative properties and relations derives from what we call the *Fundamental Argument* for the relative priority of reasons. Unlike the Classical Argument, the Fundamental Argument draws on both the explanatory and deliberative roles of reasons. That is why we call it the "Fundamental" Argument, by analogy to the practice in mathematics of dubbing central theorems in each as the "fundamental" theorem of that domain.

Like the Classical Argument, the central idea of the Fundamental Argument for the explanatory role of reasons is best illustrated by focusing on the relative priority of reasons and one other normative property at a time, before generalizing to other cases. This time we'll focus on the property of the *rational*. Some acts are rational things for you to do at a time, and others are not. But there is an important difference between doing what it is rational for you to do, and acting *rationally*. If you are acting rationally, then you do something that it is rational for you to do. But more—in order to be acting rationally, the process that leads you to do this thing must also be the right sort of process. Acting rationally entails doing what is rational, but it is more demanding—it imposes constraints on *how* as well as *what*.

The core idea of the Fundamental Argument can be put as saying that we have to accept that *reasons* are prior to *rational* in order to account for the distinctive nature of *rationally*.

P1 The best explanation of the relationship between *rational* and *rationally* requires the assumption that *rational* is grounded in *reasons*.

P2 If the best explanation of the relationship between *rational* and *rationally* requires the assumption that *rational* is grounded in *reasons*, then *rational* is grounded in *reasons*.

C   *Rational* is grounded in *reasons*.

So why is it, then, that we should think that premise P1 is true?

We can see the appeal of this idea by considering cases in which someone does what it is rational for her to do but does *not* act rationally. Suppose, for example, that she is offered a job at the firm where she wants to work, for a higher salary than she thought she would ever make, doing what she enjoys doing most. It is natural to think that in paradigmatic cases like this one, it is rational for her to take the job. And suppose that she does take it. But suppose that she takes it only after rolling dice and getting an odd number. Getting an odd number when you roll dice has nothing to do with whether it is rational for her to take a job. So when she takes the job only after rolling dice and getting an odd number, it seems that she is not acting rationally, even though she is doing the rational thing.

What, then, is missing in this case? A natural answer, which philosophers have returned to again and again when confronted with similar questions, is that she is taking the job for the wrong reasons. The reason for which she takes the job has nothing to do with the reasons that make it rational for her to take it. In contrast, in typical cases in which someone does act rationally, and doesn't just do the rational thing, the reasons for which he does it *are* among the reasons why it is rational for him to do so. This observation generalizes into the hypothesis that the reason *why* there is such a thing as acting rationally that entails but is stronger than doing what it is rational to do, is that what it is to act rationally is to do what it is rational to do for the reasons that make it rational. And this hypothesis seems to require that what it is rational to do is itself explained by reasons, as postulated by the Classical Argument.

Like the Classical Argument, the Fundamental Argument can be resisted in a variety of ways. One common way of resisting the Fundamental Argument is to argue that instead of understanding *rationally* as adding some further condition to what is involved in doing the rational thing, we must instead understand what is rational in terms of what someone who is acting rationally does. So, for example, epistemologists make an analogous distinction between propositional and doxastic justification, where being doxastically justified in your belief entails having a propositional justification for the belief and imposes further a constraint on *how* you believe it.[2] Probably the most common view about the relationship between propositional and doxastic justification is that doxastic justification is something like a matter of believing what you are justified in believing on the basis of the propositional justification that you have to believe it—which sounds a great deal like believing it for the reasons that make it justified. But some epistemologists argue that doxastic justification is prior, and propositional justification is just what the doxastically justified believer believes.[3]

Another way of resisting the Fundamental Argument is to agree that *rational* is prior to *rationally*, but reject this style of analysis of *rationally* in terms of *rational*. This strategy of resistance is particularly familiar not from the particular case of *rational* and *rationally*, but in the context of the topic of *moral worth*. On a traditional distinction, acting with moral worth entails doing the morally right thing just like acting rationally entails doing the rational thing, but acting with moral worth also requires more—it requires doing the right thing non-coincidentally, or in the right *way*. Much of the recent literature about moral worth takes for granted that we must understand moral worth in terms of rightness rather than conversely,[4] and *one* of the prominent standard views about moral worth is that acting with moral worth is doing what is right for the reasons that make it right.[5] And this view is the one that corresponds to embracing the Fundamental Argument.

But one of the prominent families of theories about moral worth amounts to a significant way of resisting the Fundamental Argument. It says that acting with moral worth is doing what is right *because you know it is right*.[6] This view analyzes moral worth in terms of rightness but without placing any constraints on the nature of rightness. And since it places no constraints on the nature of rightness, it cannot motivate the conclusion that *reason* is prior to *right*. But this style of theory of moral worth is extremely limited. Acting rationally is much less plausibly understood as acting out of knowledge that what you are doing is rational than acting with moral worth is understood as acting out of knowledge that what you are doing is morally right. A promising way for proponents of the Fundamental Argument to

---

[2] Firth [1978], Conee [1980].   [3] Compare Turri [2010].
[4] Arpaly [2002], Markovits [2010], Markovits [2012], Sliwa [2015], Johnson King [2020].
[5] Markovits [2010].
[6] Sliwa [2015]; compare Johnson King [2020] for a different but similar view.

push back against this style of explanatory strategy is by challenging its generality.

Of course, one more way that the Fundamental Argument can be resisted is by accepting the conclusion that acting rationally is a matter of doing what it is rational to do for the reasons that make it rational, but denying, analogously to Broome's model, that *reason* must be prior to *rational* in order for what it is rational for you to do to be explained by reasons. On this view, as we have seen it before, what it is rational for you to do gets explained by certain things, and those things count as reasons for you to do it, but they count as reasons for you to do it because they explain why it is rational, rather than explaining why it is rational for you to do it because they are reasons for you to do it.

All of the same reasons to reject this order of explanation apply as before, but in the context of the Fundamental Argument we get a further form of leverage against this Broomean idea. And that is that while explanation is transitive, the motivations of people who are acting rationally are less indiscriminate.[7] Return for example to the case of the woman who is offered her dream job. It's rational for her to take the job because it is her dream job, and it's her dream job because she likes working with people, and she likes working with people because she grew up as an only child, and she grew up as an only child because her parents struggled with fertility issues, and her parents struggled with fertility issues because they grew up near an industrial waste dump. So now suppose that she takes the job, motivated by the consideration that her parents grew up near an industrial waste dump. She is not acting rationally in doing so. It may explain why it is a rational thing for her to do, but it is neither necessary nor sufficient for her to act for that reason in order to act rationally. By contrast, if reasons explain rationality in virtue of being reasons, then the things that themselves explain reasons will not *ipso facto* count as explaining rationality.

The Fundamental Argument that we have just surveyed only aims to establish the relative priority of *reason* over *rational* and *rationally*. But once we see how it goes, we can see that it provides a similar structure by which to argue for the relative priority of *reason* over *ought, morally right, justified*, and many other normative properties. And that is because many other normative properties have stronger cousins that stand to them in the same way that *rationally* stands to *rational*. If the relative priority of *reason* over

---

[7] Daniel Star [2011], [2015] uses this same observation to draw a very different conclusion—that the explanatory and deliberative roles of reasons are played by two different things.

rational is what explains the relationship between *rationally* and *rational*, the proponent of the Fundamental Argument conjectures, then the relative priority of *reason* over each of these other normative properties must be what explains each of these other analogous relationships. Again, we are both reasonably sympathetic to the suspicion that this line of argument is ultimately promising, but as we have seen, there are many ways to resist, and many details still to be worked out.

12.4 The Prominence of Reasons

Throughout this book we have been examining the Parts, Province, and Place of reasons, and even, in this chapter, their Priority. But the fact that you picked up this book in the first place suggests that you are well aware of their Prominence. As we have noted, talk about reasons is used as a common vocabulary in which to carve out key theoretical distinctions in many different areas of philosophy, and so reasons talk has become a kind of vernacular that is needed in order to contribute to all of these topics. If the Classical and Fundamental Arguments are on the right track, then it could very well be that much of this distinction-making really does promise to be joint-carving, because reasons really are in some sense at the bottom of what we are talking about.

There is a real and obvious risk involved in becoming too committed to the vernacular of reasons. If the considerations adduced in this chapter are mistaken, and reasons are not in fact as central to the normative as they are to what has become such commonplace ideology for discussing the normative, then it is very likely that framing so many of our central philosophical questions in the vernacular of reasons poses risks for distorting our answers to those questions in objectionable ways.[8] It therefore makes sense for skeptics about the significance or centrality of reasons to be anxious about whether we are making progress or hindering it when we settle on new ways of framing central questions in reason-theoretic terms. We hope that this book makes some small progress toward helping to advance our collective understanding of whether this risk is realized.

But we have written this book in the conviction that there is a different and less obvious risk that comes with the pervasive vernacular of reasons.

---

[8] For example, compare Wedgwood [2017] on the relationship between reasons and rationality, and Maguire [2018] on the relationship between reasons and attitudes.

The risk that we have been concerned with is that even where people agree that reasons are important, they can be operating with different hidden and often taken-for-granted assumptions about how reasons work. As we have endeavored to demonstrate, there are *many* such assumptions that we must make in order to think seriously about reasons, and in our experience, theorists often do not realize that their opponents understand these things differently from how they do. Having a common vernacular can only go so far, if we interpret the significance of this vernacular in such different ways. It is our especial hope that this book is a small aid in crystallizing some subset of these important issues and helping to show why it is worth continuing to think hard about them.

Chapter Summary

In this chapter we have closed out the book by introducing the Fundamental Argument for the explanatory priority of reasons and contrasting it with the Classical Argument considered throughout this book. Whereas the Classical Argument utilizes normative reasons' explanatory role but does not rely on the fact that reasons also have a deliberative role, the Fundamental Argument draws on both the explanatory and deliberative roles of reasons, and provides some evidence that wherever there are normative concepts that pair as *rational* and *rationally* do, we have concepts that must be analyzed in terms of reasons. We observed that there are a number of ways of challenging the Fundamental Argument, but that these also face challenges of their own, and that if none of them are successful, then it provides powerful evidence of the importance of reasons in normative theory—the kind of evidence that might validate the time that you have spent reading this book.

Recommended Reading

In this chapter we have drawn on and tried to bring together the complementary expositions of the Fundamental Argument in Mark Schroeder's paper 'The Fundamental Reason for Reasons Fundamentalism' and in chapters 10-11 of his *Reasons First*. The Fundamental Argument is developed further in both places. John Turri's paper 'On the Relationship between Propositional and Doxastic Justification' is one of the clearest statements of the idea that doxastic justification is prior to propositional justification. We recommend reading this chapter alongside Keshav Singh's article 'Moral Worth, Credit, and Non-Accidentality'.

Exercises

12.1 *Comprehension.* For this exercise you will show how pluralist consequentialists can coopt the Rossian diagnosis of why there are both intuitive counterexamples to the categorical imperative and to utilitarianism without appealing to reasons. Do so by describing one apparent counterexample to the categorical imperative and one apparent counterexample to utilitarianism. For each apparent counterexample, introduce a hypothesis about what good a pluralist consequentialist can appeal to, in order to capture that case.

12.2 *Extensions.* Test the limits of the pluralist strategy for coopting Ross by considering cases in which someone has a choice between murdering and allowing two others to murder, or between stealing and allowing two other thefts. What obstacles do you face in trying to explain these cases by appeal to the badness of the outcomes of each possible choice?

12.3 *Extensions.* Consequentialists say that necessarily, you ought to do something if and only if and because doing it would produce more good than taking any alternative action. The value-based theory of reasons says that something is a reason for someone to do something if and only if and because it explains why their doing it would produce some good. How might you reconcile these two theses with the thesis that necessarily you ought to do something if and only if and because the reasons for you to do it outweigh the reasons for any alternative action?

12.4 *Comprehension.* Explain why the Fundamental Argument has more resources to draw on in order to explain reasons' central place in normative theory than the Classical Argument.

12.5 *Extensions.* In section 12.3 we encountered the idea that *rationality* might be prior to *rational*, and the analogous idea that *doxastic* justification is prior to *propositional* justification. For this exercise, answer whether *knowledge* stands in an analogous relation to *correct belief*. What similarities can you point to? What differences can you point to? In what ways is the contemporary idea that knowledge is prior to and explanatory of belief analogous to the idea that doxastic justification is prior to and explanatory of propositional justification?

12.6 *Extensions.* In the main text we treated the Fundamental Argument like it proceeds piecemeal, first establishing that *reason* is prior to *rational* and *rationally*, and then establishing that *reason* is prior to *morally right* and *moral worth*, and so on. But because the Fundamental Argument is at bottom an inference to the best explanation, it can actually gain additional leverage by looking for theoretical unity between the explanations of each of these cases. For this exercise, leverage this explanatory generality by considering cases involving card games. In many situations in many card games, there is a right move to make, but it is possible to make the right move without playing well. First establish whether the *right move/ playing well* distinction is in your view relevantly analogous to the distinction between *rational* and *rationally*. Then answer whether something counts as the right move because it is what someone who is playing well does, or whether instead you count as playing well because you both make the right moves and also satisfy some further condition. Do your answers to these questions help you to gain leverage on which of *rational* and *rationally* is prior?

12.7 *Extensions*. According to one prominent view of moral worth, an action counts as morally worthy if and because it is performed out of knowledge that it is the morally right thing to do and a desire to do the morally right thing. Apply this strategy to the relationship between *rational* and *rationally* and that between *propositional* and *doxastic* justification. Which of these two extensions of the strategy causes you more difficulty? Why? What should we learn from this about the prospects of the Fundamental Argument?

12.8 *Extensions*. For this exercise, consider how you might develop an alternative strategy for arguing that *reason* is prior to both *rational* and *rationally*. First, assume that *rational* is prior to *rationally*. Now compare the right reasons account of *rationally* to the alternative account explored in exercise 12.7. Which of these two accounts can be applied recursively, so that there is something else that stands to acting rationally as acting rationally stands to doing what is rational? *Is* the relationship between *rational* and *rationally* recursive? Why or why not?

12.9 *Extensions*. In the final paragraphs of section 12.3 we posed a challenge to combining Broome's picture with the right reasons analysis of moral worth. How would you go about answering this challenge?

Works Cited

Anscombe, Elizabeth. 1957. *Intention*. Harvard University Press.
Aristotle. 2009. *Nicomachean Ethics*. Translated by W.D. Ross and revised by Leslie Brown. Oxford University Press.
Arpaly, Nomy. 2002. *Unprincipled Virtue: An Inquiry into Moral Agency*. Oxford University Press.
Asarnow, Samuel. 2016. 'Rational Internalism'. *Ethics* 127(1): 147–178.
Asarnow, Samuel. 2017. 'The Reasoning View and Defeasible Practical Reasoning'. *Philosophy and Phenomenological Research* 95(3): 614–636.
Bader, Ralph. 2016. 'Conditions, Modifiers and Holism'. In Errol Lord and Barry Maguire (eds.), *Weighing Reasons*. Oxford University Press, 27–55.
Baron, Marcia, Philip Pettit, and Michael Slote. 1997. *Three Methods of Ethics: A Debate*. Blackwell.
Berker, Selim. 2023. 'The Deontic, the Evaluative, and the Fitting'. In Chris Howard and R.A. Rowland (eds.), *Fittingness: Essays in the Philosophy of Normativity*. Oxford University Press, 23–57.
Bhatt, Rajesh. 2006. *Covert Modality in Non-Finite Contexts*. De Gruyter.
Blackburn, Simon. 1984. *Spreading the Word*. Clarendon Press.
Broome, John. 2004. 'Reasons'. In R. Jay Wallace (ed.), *Reason and Value: Themes from the Moral Philosophy of Joseph Raz*. Oxford University Press, 56–90.
Broome, John. 2013. *Rationality Through Reasoning*. Oxford University Press.
Brunero, John. 2009. 'Reasons and Evidence One Ought'. *Ethics* 119(3): 538–545.
Brunero, John. 2018. 'Reasons, Evidence, and Explanations'. In Daniel Star (ed.), *The Oxford Handbook of Reasons and Normativity*. Oxford University Press, 321–341.
Cartwright, Nancy. 1989. *Nature's Capacities and their Measurement*. Oxford University Press.
Chisholm, Roderick. 1964. 'The Ethics of Requirement'. *American Philosophical Quarterly* 1: 147–153.
Clarke, Samuel. 1706. *A Discourse Concerning the Unchangeable Obligations of Natural Religion and the Truth and Certainty of the Christian Revelation. Being Eight Sermons Preach'd at the Cathedral-Church of St. Paul, in the Year 1705, at the Lecture Founded by the Honourable Robert Boyle*. W. Botham.
Comesaña, Juan, and Matthew McGrath. 2014. 'Having False Reasons'. In Clayton Littlejohn and John Turri (eds.), *Epistemic Norms*. Oxford University Press, 59–79.
Conee, Earl. 1980. 'Propositional Justification'. *Philosophical Studies* 38(1): 65–68.
Crisp, Roger. 2000. 'Review of *Value...And What Follows*'. *Philosophy* 75(3): 452–462.
Cudworth, Ralph. 1731. *A Treatise Concerning Eternal and Immutable Morality*. Edited by Sarah Hutton. Cambridge University Press.

Cunningham, J.J. Forthcoming. 'Factivism Defended: A Reply to Howard'. *Journal of Philosophy*.
D'Arms, Justin, and Daniel Jacobson. 2000a. 'The Moralistic Fallacy'. *Philosophy and Phenomenological Research* 61(1): 65–90.
D'Arms, Justin, and Daniel Jacobson. 2000b. 'Sentiment and Value'. *Ethics* 110(4): 722–748.
Dancy, Jonathan. 1993. *Moral Reasons*. Blackwell.
Dancy, Jonathan. 2000. *Practical Reality*. Oxford University Press.
Dancy, Jonathan. 2004. *Ethics Without Principles*. Oxford University Press.
Darwall, Stephen. 2002. *Welfare and Rational Care*. Princeton University Press.
Davidson, Donald. 1963. 'Actions, Reasons, and Causes'. *Journal of Philosophy* 60(23): 685–700.
Dietz, Alex. 2016. 'What We Together Ought to Do'. *Ethics* 126(4): 955–982.
Finlay, Stephen. 2014. *A Confusion of Tongues*. Oxford University Press.
Firth, Roderick. 1978. 'Are Epistemic Concepts Reducible to Ethical Concepts?' In Alvin Goldman and Jaegwon Kim (eds.), *Values and Morals*. Kluwer, 215–229.
Fogal, Daniel. 2016. 'Reasons, Reason, and Context'. In Errol Lord and Barry Maguire (eds.), *Weighing Reasons*. Oxford University Press, 74–103.
Fogal, Daniel, and Olle Risberg. 2023a. 'Explaining Normative Reasons'. *Noûs* 57(1): 51–80.
Fogal, Daniel, and Olle Risberg. 2023b. 'The Weight of Reasons'. *Philosophical Studies* 180(9): 2573–2596.
Foot, Philippa. 1972. 'Morality as a System of Hypothetical Imperatives'. *Philosophical Review* 81(3): 305–316.
Foot, Philippa. 2001. *Natural Goodness*. Oxford: Oxford University Press.
Franklin, Benjamin. 1772. Letter to Joseph Priestly. Reprinted in Frank Mott and Chester Jorgensen (eds.), *Benjamin Franklin: Representative Selections*. American Book Company, 1936, 348–349.
Geach, Peter. 1956. 'Good and Evil'. *Analysis* 17(2): 33–42.
Gert, Joshua. 2004. *Brute Rationality: Normativity and Human Action*. Cambridge University Press.
Gert, Joshua. 2007. 'Normative Strength and the Balance of Reasons'. *Philosophical Review* 116(4): 533–562.
Gibson, J.J. 1979. *The Ecological Approach to Visual Perception*. Houghton Mifflin.
Greenspan, Patricia. 2005. 'Asymmetrical Practical Reasons'. In J.C. Marek and M.E. Reicher (eds.), *Experience and Analysis: Proceedings of the 27th International Wittgenstein Symposium*. Obv and Hpt, 115–122.
Greenspan, Patricia. 2007. 'Practical Reasons and Moral "Ought"'. In Russ Shafer-Landau (ed.), *Oxford Studies in Metaethics 2*. Oxford University Press, 172–199.
Gregory, Alex. 2016. 'Reasons as Good Bases'. *Philosophical Studies* 173(9): 2291–2310.
Grice, H. Paul. 2001. *Aspects of Reason*. Oxford University Press.
Harman, Gilbert. 1975. 'Moral Relativism Defended'. *Philosophical Review* 84(1): 3–22.
Hawthorne, John, and Ofra Magidor. 2018. 'Reflections on the Ideology of Reasons'. In Daniel Star (ed.), *The Oxford Handbook of Reasons and Normativity*. Oxford University Press, 113–140.

Hieronymi, Pamela. 2005. 'The Wrong Kind of Reasons'. *Journal of Philosophy* 102(9): 437–457.
Hieronymi, Pamela. 2006. 'Controlling Attitudes'. *Pacific Philosophical Quarterly* 87(1): 45–71.
Hitchcock, Christopher. 1996. 'The Role of Contrast in Causal and Explanatory Claims'. *Synthese* 107(3): 395–419.
Hornsby, Jennifer. 2008. 'A Disjunctivist Conception of Acting for Reasons'. In Adrian Haddock and Fiona Macpherson (eds.), *Disjunctivism: Perception, Action, Knowledge*. Oxford University Press, 244–261.
Horty, John F. 2012. *Reasons as Defaults*. Oxford University Press.
Howard, Nathan Robert. 2021a. 'Ambidextrous Reasons'. *Philosophers' Imprint* 21(3): 1–16.
Howard, Nathan Robert. 2021b. 'Primary Reasons as Normative Reasons'. *Journal of Philosophy* 118(2): 97–111.
Howard, Nathan Robert, and Nicholas Laskowski. Forthcoming. 'Robust vs. Formal Normativity II: No Gods, No Masters, No Authoritative Normativity'. In David Copp and Connie Rosati (eds.), *The Oxford Handbook of Metaethics*. Oxford University Press.
Hurka, Thomas. 2014. *British Ethical Theorists from Sidgwick to Ewing*. Oxford University Press.
Hutcheson, Francis. 1728. *An Essay on the Nature and Conduct of the Passions*. London. Page references from Aaron Garrett (ed.). Liberty Fund.
Jackson, Frank, and Robert Pargetter. 1986. 'Ought, Options, and Actualism'. *Philosophical Review* 95(2): 233–255.
Johnson King, Zoë. 2020. 'Accidentally Doing the Right Thing'. *Philosophy and Phenomenological Research* 100(1): 186–206.
Joyce, James, and Alan Hayek. 2008. 'Confirmation'. In S. Psillos and M. Curd (eds.), *The Routledge Companion to Philosophy of Science*. Routledge, 146–159.
Kagan, Shelly. 1989. *The Limits of Morality*. Oxford University Press.
Kant, Immanuel. 1993. *Grounding for the Metaphysics of Morals*. Translated by James W. Ellington. Hackett Publishing.
Kearns, Stephen, and Daniel Star. 2008. 'Reasons: Explanations or Evidence?' *Ethics* 119(1): 31–56.
Kearns, Stephen, and Daniel Star. 2009. 'Reasons as Evidence'. In Russ Shafer-Landau (ed.), *Oxford Studies in Metaethics* 4. Oxford University Press, 215–242.
Keeling, Sophie. 2022. 'Believing for a Reason is (at Least) Nearly Self-Intimating'. *Erkenntnis*. Online First.
Kiesewetter, Benjamin. 2017. *The Normativity of Rationality*. Oxford University Press.
Kolodny, Niko. 2018. 'Instrumental Reasons'. In Daniel Star (ed.), *The Oxford Handbook of Reasons and Normativity*. Oxford University Press, 731–763.
Kolodny, Niko, and John MacFarlane. 2010. 'Ifs and Oughts'. *The Journal of Philosophy* 107(3): 115–143.
Korsgaard, Christine. 1986. 'Skepticism About Practical Reason'. *Journal of Philosophy* 83(1): 5–25.
Kratzer, Angelika. 1977. 'What "Must" and "Can" Must and Can Mean'. *Linguistics and Philosophy* 1(3): 337–355.

Kratzer, Angelika. 1981. 'The Notional Category of Modality'. In H.-J. Eikmeyer and H. Rieser (eds.), *Words, Worlds, and Contexts: New Approaches in Word Semantics*. De Gruyter, 38–74.
Laskowski, Nicholas. Forthcoming. 'The Stuff That Matters'. In Russ Shafer-Landau (ed.), *Oxford Studies in Metaethics* 19. Oxford University Press.
Logins, Artūrs. 2022. *Normative Reasons: Between Reasoning and Explanation*. Cambridge University Press.
Lord, Errol. 2010. 'Having Reasons and the Factoring Account'. *Philosophical Studies* 149(3): 283–296.
Lord, Errol. 2018. *The Importance of Being Rational*. Oxford University Press.
Lord, Errol, and Barry Maguire (eds.). 2016. *Weighing Reasons*. Oxford University Press.
McDowell, John. 1995. 'Might There Be External Reasons?' In J.E.J. Altham and Ross Harrison (eds.), *World, Mind, and Ethics: Essays on the Ethical Philosophy of Bernard Williams*. Cambridge University Press, 68–85.
McDowell, John. 1998. 'Virtue and Reason'. In *Mind, Value, and Reality*. Harvard University Press, 50–76.
McGee, Vann. 1985. 'A Counterexample to *Modus Ponens*'. *Journal of Philosophy* 82(9): 462–471.
McHugh, Conor, and Jonathan Way. 2016. 'Fittingness First'. *Ethics* 126(3): 575–606.
McHugh, Conor, and Jonathan Way. 2018. 'What is Good Reasoning?' *Philosophy and Phenomenological Research* 96(1): 153–174.
McHugh, Conor, and Jonathan Way. 2022a. 'All Reasons are Fundamentally for Attitudes'. *Journal of Ethics and Social Philosophy* 21(2): 151–174.
McHugh, Conor, and Jonathan Way. 2022b. *Getting Things Right*. Oxford University Press.
McKeever, Sean, and Mike Ridge. 2012. 'Elusive Reasons'. In Russ Shafer-Landau (ed.), *Oxford Studies in Metaethics* 7. Oxford University Press, 110–137.
Mackie, J.L. 1977. *Ethics: Inventing Right and Wrong*. Penguin Books.
McMahon, Christopher. 1991. 'The Paradox of Deontology'. *Philosophy and Public Affairs* 20(4): 350–377.
McNaughton, David, and Piers Rawling. 1992. 'Honoring and Promoting Values'. *Ethics* 102(4): 835–843.
McNaughton, David, and Piers Rawling. 2011. 'The Making/Evidential Reason Distinction'. *Analysis* 71(1): 100–102.
Maguire, Barry. 2018. 'There Are No Reasons for Affective Attitudes'. *Mind* 127(507): 779–805.
Mantel, Susanne. 2018. *Determined by Reasons: A Competence Account of Acting for a Normative Reason*. Routledge.
Markovits, Julia. 2010. 'Acting for the Right Reasons'. *Philosophical Review* 119(2): 201–242.
Markovits, Julia. 2012. 'Saints, Heroes, Sages, and Villains'. *Philosophical Studies* 158(2): 289–311.
Mill, John Stuart. 1863. *Utilitarianism*. Parker, son, and Bourn. https://www.loc.gov/item/11015966/.

Milona, Michael. 2017. 'Intellect vs Affect: New Leverage in an Old Debate'. *Philosophical Studies* 174(9): 2251–2276.
Moore, G.E. 1903. *Principia Ethica*. Cambridge University Press.
Mumford, Stephen, and Rani Anjum. 2010. 'A Powerful Theory of Causation'. In Anna Marmodoro (ed.), *The Metaphysics of Powers: Their Grounding and their Manifestations*. Routledge, 143–159.
Nagel, Thomas. 1970. *The Possibility of Altruism*. Clarendon Press.
Nair, Shyam. 2014. 'A Fault Line in Ethical Theory'. *Philosophical Perspectives* 28(1): 173–200.
Nair, Shyam. 2016. 'How Do Reasons Accrue?' In Errol Lord and Barry Maguire (eds.), *Weighing Reasons*. Oxford University Press, 56–73.
Nair, Shyam. 2021. '"Adding Up" Reasons: Lessons for Reductive and Nonreductive Approaches'. *Ethics* 132(1): 38–88.
Nebel, Jacob. 2019. 'Normative Reasons as Reasons Why We Ought'. *Mind* 128(510): 459–489.
Nefsky, Julia. 2017. 'How You Can Help, Without Making a Difference'. *Philosophical Studies* 174: 2743–2767.
Oddie, Graham, and Peter Milne. 1991. 'Act and Value'. *Theoria* 57(1–2): 42–76.
Paakkunainen, Hille. 2017. 'Can There Be Government House Reasons for Action?' *Journal of Ethics and Social Philosophy* 12(1): 56–93.
Parfit, Derek. 2011. *On What Matters*. Oxford University Press.
Pettit, Philip. 1989. 'Consequentialism and Respect for Persons.' *Ethics* 100(1): 116–126.
Price, Richard. 1748. *A Review of the Principal Questions in Morals*. T. Cadell.
Rabinowicz, Wlodek, and Toni Rønnow-Rasmussen. 2004. 'The Strike of the Demon: On Fitting Pro-Attitudes and Value'. *Ethics* 114: 391–423.
Raz, Joseph. 1975. *Practical Reason and Norms*. Oxford University Press.
Raz, Joseph. 1999. *Engaging Reasons: On the Theory of Value and Action*. Oxford University Press.
Ross, Jacob. 2010. 'The Irreducibility of Personal Obligation'. *Journal of Philosophical Logic* 39(3): 307–323.
Ross, W.D. 1930. *The Right and the Good*. Oxford University Press.
Rossi, Benjamin. 2021. 'Elusive Reasons and the Motivational Constraint'. *Journal of Ethics and Social Philosophy* 20(1): 82–110.
Scanlon, T.M. 1998. *What We Owe to Each Other*. Harvard University Press.
Scanlon, T.M. 2003. 'Metaphysics and Morals'. *Proceedings and Addresses of the American Philosophical Association* 77(2): 7–22.
Scanlon, T.M. 2014. *Being Realistic About Reasons*. Oxford University Press.
Schaffer, Jonathan. 2004. 'From Contextualism to Contrastivism'. *Philosophical Studies* 119(1–2): 73–104.
Schmidt, Eva. 2017. 'New Trouble for "Reasons as Evidence": Means That Don't Justify the Ends'. *Ethics* 127(3): 708–718.
Schmidt, Eva. 2021. 'Where Reasons and Reasoning Come Apart'. *Noûs* 55: 762–781.
Schmidt, Thomas. 2023. 'How Reasons Determine Moral Requirements'. *Oxford Studies in Metaethics* 18. Oxford University Press.

Schroeder, Mark. 2007a. 'Reasons and Agent Neutrality'. *Philosophical Studies* 135(2): 279–306.
Schroeder, Mark. 2007b. *Slaves of the Passions*. Oxford University Press.
Schroeder, Mark. 2008. 'Having Reasons'. *Philosophical Studies* 139(1): 57–71.
Schroeder, Mark. 2009. 'Buck-passers' Negative Thesis'. *Philosophical Explorations* 12(3): 341–346.
Schroeder, Mark. 2018. 'Getting Perspective on Objective Reasons'. *Ethics* 128(2): 289–319.
Schroeder, Mark. 2021a. 'The Fundamental Reason for Reasons Fundamentalism'. *Philosophical Studies* 178(10): 3107–3127.
Schroeder, Mark. 2021b. *Reasons First*. Oxford University Press.
Schroeder, Mark. 2023. *Noncognitivism in Ethics*, 2nd edition. Routledge.
Setiya, Kieran. 2012. 'What is a Reason to Act?' *Philosophical Studies* 167(2): 221–235.
Shaftesbury, Anthony Ashley-Cooper, Third Earl of. 1999. *Characteristics of Men, Manners, Opinions, Times*. Edited by Lawrance E. Klein. Cambridge University Press.
Shanklin, Robert. 2011. *On Good and 'Good'*. PhD dissertation, University of Southern California.
Shope, Robert K. 1978. 'The Conditional Fallacy for Contemporary Philosophy'. *Journal of Philosophy* 75(8): 397–413.
Sidgwick, Henry. 1907. *The Methods of Ethics*, 7th edition. Macmillan.
Silverstein, Matthew. 2016. 'Reducing Reasons'. *Journal of Ethics and Social Philosophy* 10(1): 1–22.
Silverstein, Matthew. 2017. 'Ethics and Practical Reasoning'. *Ethics* 127(2): 353–382.
Sinclair, Neil. 2016. 'On the Connection between Normative Reasons and the Possibility of Acting for Those Reasons'. *Ethical Theory and Moral Practice* 19: 1211–1223.
Singh, Keshav. 2020. 'Moral Worth, Credit, and Non-Accidentality'. In Mark Timmons (ed.), *Oxford Studies in Normative Ethics* 10. Oxford University Press, 156–181.
Sinnott-Armstrong, Walter. 2008. 'A Contrastivist Manifesto'. *Social Epistemology* 22(3): 257–270.
Skorupski, John. 2010. *The Domain of Reasons*. Oxford University Press.
Sliwa, Paulina. 2015. 'Moral Worth and Moral Knowledge'. *Philosophy and Phenomenological Research* 93(2): 393–418.
Smith, Michael. 1994. *The Moral Problem*. Blackwell.
Snedegar, Justin. 2013. 'Reason Claims and Contrastivism About Reasons'. *Philosophical Studies* 166(2): 231–242.
Snedegar, Justin. 2014. 'Contrastive Reasons and Promotion'. *Ethics* 125(1): 39–63.
Snedegar, Justin. 2016. 'Reasons, Ought, and Requirements'. *Oxford Studies in Metaethics* 11: 155–181.
Snedegar, Justin. 2017. *Contrastive Reasons*. Oxford University Press.
Snedegar, Justin. 2021. 'Reasons, Competition, and Latitude'. In Russ Shafer-Landau (ed.), *Oxford Studies in Metaethics 16*. Oxford University Press, 134–156.

Star, Daniel. 2011. 'Two Levels of Moral Thinking'. *Oxford Studies in Normative Ethics* 1: 75–96.
Star, Daniel. 2015. *Knowing Better*. Oxford University Press.
Stratton-Lake, Philip. 2000. *Kant, Duty, and Moral Worth*. Oxford University Press.
Sylvan, Kurt. 2020. 'An Epistemic Nonconsequentialism'. *Philosophical Review* 129(1): 1–51.
Sylvan, Kurt. 2021. 'Respect and the Reality of Apparent Reasons'. *Philosophical Studies* 178(10): 3129–3156.
Tappolet, Christine. 2016. *Emotions, Value, and Agency*. Oxford University Press.
Thomson, Judith Jarvis. 2008. *Normativity*. Open Court.
Titelbaum, Michael. 2019. 'Reason without Reasons For'. In Russ Shafer-Landau (ed.), *Oxford Studies in Metaethics* 14. Oxford University Press, 189–215.
Tucker, Chris. 2021. 'The Dual-Scale Model of Weighing Reasons'. *Noûs* 56(2): 366–392.
Tucker, Chris. 2022. 'Parity, Moral Options, and the Weight of Reasons'. *Noûs* 57(2): 454–480.
Turri, John. 2010. 'On the Relationship between Propositional and Doxastic Justification'. *Philosophy and Phenomenological Research* 80(2): 312–326.
von Fintel, Kai, and Sabine Iatridou. 2008. 'How to Say *Ought* in Foreign: The Composition of Weak Necessity Modals'. In J. Guéron and J. Lecarme (eds.), *Time and Modality*. Springer, 115–141.
Ward, Shane. 2022. 'We Have Reason to Think that There are Reasons for Affective Attitudes.' *Inquiry*. Published Online.
Way, Jonathan. 2012. 'Transmission and the Wrong Kind of Reason'. *Ethics* 122(3): 489–515.
Way, Jonathan. 2017. 'Reasons as Premises of Good Reasoning'. *Pacific Philosophical Quarterly* 98(2): 251–270.
Wedgwood, Ralph. 2006. 'The Meaning of "Ought"'. In Russ Shafer-Landau (ed.), *Oxford Studies in Metaethics* 1. Oxford University Press, 127–160.
Wedgwood, Ralph. 2017. *The Value of Rationality*. Oxford University Press.
Wedgwood, Ralph. 2022. 'The Reasons Aggregation Theorem'. In Mark Timmons (ed.), *Oxford Studies in Normative Ethics* 12. Oxford University Press, 127–148.
Whiting, Daniel. 2014. 'Keep Things in Perspective'. *Journal of Ethics and Social Philosophy* 8(1): 1–22.
Whiting, Daniel. 2018. 'Right in Some Respects: Reasons as Evidence'. *Philosophical Studies* 175(9): 2191–2208.
Williams, Bernard. 1979. 'Internal and External Reasons'. In Ross Harrison (ed.), *Rational Action*. Cambridge University Press, 101–113.
Wodak, Daniel. 2019. 'An Objectivist's Guide to Subjective Reasons'. *Res Philosophica* 96(2): 229–244.

Index

For the benefit of digital users, indexed terms that span two pages (e.g., 52–53) may, on occasion, appear on only one of those pages.

Accrual of reasons 194–8
Agent-relative deontic morality 47
Agent-relative reason 49
All-things-considered duty 7, 121, 157–8, 163
Anscombe, G.E.M. 83–4
Aristotle 11, 179
Asarnow, Samuel 134, 137, 146, 182, 185

Broome, John 8, 9, 14, 19, 32–3, 49, 122–4, 129–31, 186, 215, 219, 223
Brunero, John 108–11, 117–18

Classical argument for Reasons First 151, 174–5, 212, 212–15
Competition among reasons 7–8, 48–9, 63, 66, 104, 113, 129–30, 154, 157, 163, 168, 186, 192, 207
Conditional fallacy 94–7, 104, 132
Confirmation theory 115, 196–8
Contrastivism 69, 70, 76, 77, 155
Core reasons 97–101, 114–18, 127–8, 145, 169, 172, 202–4

Dancy, Jonathan 19, 26–7, 36–7, 41–2, 68, 70–1, 74–8, 117–19, 123, 200
Davidson, Donald 37–43, 74
Deliberative role of reasons 9–12, 17–19, 23–4, 34–6, 40–1, 112, 116, 127, 133–6, 141–2, 165, 201–3, 216, 219, 221
Desire 26–30, 30, 37–43, 57–8, 70–4, 83–4, 88–90, 101, 125, 128–132, 135, 139, 166, 168, 173–8, 180, 189–91, 197, 223
Desire-based theory of reasons 130–1, 173–77, 189–91
Direction of fit 84
Domain view vs. Subset view 157–8
Dual-aspect account of reasons 37, 39–43, 57–8, 74–6, 78, 90, 101, 197–99

Elusive reasons 140–3, 181, 200
End-relational theory of reasons 71–3, 78, 197
Envelope case 161, 169, 171
Epiphenomenal challenge 192–99, 204, 207–8
Evidence as reasons 113–16, 130, 146
Exclusivity 68–71, 74–5, 77–8, 109–110, 119, 171
Explanatory role of reasons 8, 9 12, 14, 17–24, 31–6, 40–1, 66, 70, 111, 113, 116, 120, 124, 130, 133–4, 146, 172, 181–3, 192, 196–99, 201, 207, 211, 216, 219, 221

Factivity 15, 20, 32–4, 84, 95, 121–3, 126, 126, 168, 199
Factoring account 92–3
Finlay, Stephen 32, 71–6, 78, 122, 130, 197
Fittingess 90, 137, 163–71, 181–6, 190, 215
Fogal, Daniel 18–19, 57, 59, 125, 131, 193–4, 199–203, 205, 207
Fundamental argument for Reasons First 216–220

Goals (ends; objectives) 15, 39, 71–6, 78, 83, 89, 142, 164, 174, 187, 197–9, 199
Goodness 166–9

Hieronymi, Pamela 46, 67, 70, 76–7, 169
Howard, Nathan Robert 41, 76, 157
Humean theory of motivation 10, 19, 30, 135–6
Humean theory of reasons (*see also* Desire-Based theory of Reasons) 83, 89–90, 100–1, 105, 124, 135, 173
Humean mosaic of reasons 206–8
Hutcheson, Francis 13, 19, 86

Internalism about rationality 85–86

Kant, Immanuel 6, 11, 135, 177–9, 213, 227
Kearns, Stephen 104–8, 111–17, 143–4, 196
Korsgaard, Christine 136–7, 146
Kratzer, Angelika 99–100

Lewis, David 206

Maguire, Barry 50, 76, 190, 207, 220
McHugh, Conor 50, 137, 143, 145, 165, 181, 184, 190
Meinong-Chisholm reduction 50, 137, 143–5, 165, 181, 184, 190
Mill, John Stuart 6, 57, 67, 114–15, 118, 166, 170–1
Moral rationalism 179
Moral worth 11, 12, 20, 151, 210, 214, 218, 221–3
Motivating reasons 10–31, 36, 37–43, 57, 74, 178–81, 190

Nagel, Thomas 45–9, 57, 68, 177, 189
Nair, Shyam 176, 194–7, 207
Nature of reasons 3, 18–21, 29, 32, 44, 77, 120, 124–34, 154, 172, 183, 202–3, 206, 215–16
Norms of reasoning 137, 182, 185–88, 191

Objective reasons 15–28, 33–4, 37, 39–44, 51, 57–8, 81–3, 87–98, 100–1, 103–4, 114–15, 117–18, 125–9, 131–2, 145, 147, 158–9, 169, 175–6, 202–4, 209

Paradox of Deontology 47–9, 51–2, 59, 176, 189
Particularism, Ethical 52–3

Raz, Joseph 168, 199
'Reason' as count noun or mass noun 18–20, 57, 59, 63, 101, 125, 128–131, 199–201, 203–4, 207
Reason relation 5, 21–5, 36, 42, 44–9, 51–78, 82, 158, 173, 193–4, 197, 205, 210–11

Reasoning 5, 9, 10–12, 17, 28, 47–8, 53–5, 88, 103, 118, 127, 133–47, 172, 176–77, 180–91, 203
Reasons as evidence 103–113
Requiring reasons 156–7, 159, 161, 170
Ross, W.D. 5–9, 19–20, 46, 62, 113, 122, 130, 137, 151–4, 160, 163, 172, 208, 213, 222

Scanlon, T.M. 13, 16–17, 50, 60–1, 64, 91, 123, 205
Schmidt, Eva 138, 140, 143–7, 156, 169, 181, 190
Schroeder, Mark 19, 36, 54, 59, 76, 92, 100, 110, 113, 124–5, 130, 140, 146, 161, 165, 169, 175, 221
Sentimentalism 88–90
Setiya, Kieran 137, 146, 182
Sidgwick, Henry 5, 6, 19, 53
Silverstein, Matthew 137–8, 142–3, 146
Smith, Michael 19, 36, 41, 51–3, 55, 59–60, 64, 137, 203
Snedegar, Justin 68–70, 75–77, 155, 169–70
Star, Daniel 104–8, 111–17, 143–4, 196, 219
Subjective reasons 15–23, 33–4, 40–2, 58, 73, 81–104, 114–18, 125–32, 145, 158–9, 169, 175, 202–4
Substance of reasons 21–43, 56–7, 73–5, 81, 84–6, 125–6, 137, 193, 201–4, 209

Value-based theory of reasons 124–131, 173–8, 189, 191, 207, 214, 222

Way, Jonathan 50, 137, 143, 145, 165, 170, 181, 184, 190
Wedgwood, Ralph 9, 49, 128, 198, 207, 220
Weighing explanation 77, 122–5, 129, 152–4, 194
Weight of reasons 62–6, 76–7, 93, 123, 125, 154, 156, 158–9, 176, 186, 192–6, 200, 204–8, 215
Williams, Bernard 10, 19, 134–6, 146–7
Wrong-kind reasons 164–5